Stealth Reconstruction

Stealth Reconstruction

An Untold Story of Racial Politics in Recent Southern History

GLEN BROWDER

JACKSONVILLE STATE UNIVERSITY

IN COLLABORATION WITH
ARTEMESIA STANBERRY
NORTH CAROLINA CENTRAL UNIVERSITY

NewSouth Books
Montgomery | Louisville

NewSouth Books
105 S. Court Street
Montgomery, AL 36104

Library of Congress Cataloging-in-Publication Data

Browder, Glen.
Stealth reconstruction : an untold story of racial politics in recent Southern history /
Glen Browder in collaboration with Artemesia Stanberry.
p. cm.
Includes bibliographical references and index.
ISBN-13: 978-1-58838-239-9
ISBN-10: 1-58838-239-7
1. Southern States—Politics and government—1951– 2. Southern States—Race relations—
Political aspects. 3. Political leadership—Southern States—History—20th century.
I. Stanberry, Artemesia. II. Title.
F216.2.B763 2010
976'.044—dc22

2009049608

Design by Randall Williams

Printed in the United States of America
by Rose Printing Company

GLEN BROWDER: TO BECKY AND JENNY

ARTEMESIA STANBERRY: TO MY MOTHER, KATHLEEN B. THOMAS

CONTENTS

PREFACE

This book concentrates on quiet, racially progressive actions by white elected officials in the South during the particularly interesting post-civil rights movement period of 1970–2000. As will be explained in the Introduction and then developed through the chapters of this book, we have coined the terms "stealthness," "stealth leadership," and "stealth politics" to describe this style of campaigning and serving by white politicians.

Essentially, we contend that some white officials worked with some black activists to mitigate the often unsavory role of race and move politics forward in the post-movement South. Our thesis is that, together, these biracial leaders helped reconstruct southern politics in the 1970s, 1980s, and 1990s.

OF COURSE, BLACK political leaders likewise have attempted to minimize racial factors in order to bridge the racial divide in this region and throughout the nation. Barack Obama represents the latest and most prominent incarnation of "deracialized" politics, but such efforts have been fairly common in the past few decades, as evidenced by David Dinkins in New York, Douglas Wilder in Virginia, and Tom Bradley in Los Angeles. This variance from insurgent black politics obviously poses an unsettling dilemma for many interested in the more aggressive agenda of black progress. African American scholars in particular have struggled with the idea of race-neutral elections and service. (For further discussion on these points, consult the works of authors like Charles V. Hamilton, Georgia A. Persons, Huey L. Perry, and others as detailed in the bibliography.)

Much of the "deracialization" literature resonates in our project, as the stealth proposition, issues, and activities reported in our research among white leaders sometimes reflect, in ironic ways, the experiences of biracial black politicians.

So, a logical question is how our notion of "stealthness" relates to "deracialization." The simplest generalization is that our stealth concept focuses on white leaders courting and serving black voters, while deracialization research addresses black officials and their relationship with white voters. Of course, the single, dominant practicality is that all these politicians— both stealthy whites and deracializing blacks—wanted to get elected and stay elected. The most accurate assessment is that such "crossover" efforts sometimes worked and sometimes failed, depending to a great degree on context. However, there are important differences between stealthness and deracialization besides simple terminological preference.

These other differences relate to both theoretical definition and normative ramification. The definitional differences are: (a) our thesis limits the time period for stealth politics to 1970–2000, while deracialization is a practice of continuing interest; (b) stealth was a phenomenon of peculiarly regional and cultural pertinence, while deracialization has been observed and studied in varied locales throughout the country; and (c) the political nature of stealthness was low-profile, sometimes secretive, and especially risky considering the attitudes of white Southern voters, while deracialization is more obvious and acceptable, although certainly problematic in terms of contemporary public mores.

Additionally, there is the critical matter of context. Stealth politics began and took place in a one-party, semi-segregated system of elections and governance, while deracial endeavors have been attempted in varied, less "peculiar" environments. According to coauthor and ex-politician Browder, regional contextual factors placed tremendous pressures on Southern white officials:

> I can only imagine the problems that black leaders have had to deal with in various situations, but I know from personal experience that it was virtually impossible for me to eliminate race from politics back then.

Of course, I tried to keep both whites and blacks from "racializing" public issues in an already race-sensitive arena; I also had to "deracialize" myself by talking in communitarian language. At the same time, ironically, I often had to quietly but surely "bi-racialize" certain aspects of my campaign and service—in the sense of informal, dual operations—because of the legacies of white supremacy and racial segregation. Furthermore, I sometimes just sneaked things of racial consequence through the political thicket and hoped no one would notice or call my hand on it. The situation changed over time, but you had to be very careful; racial mistakes, especially during the early years, could kill you politically in my part of the country.

Perhaps of equal interest to our readers are the normative connotations of stealthness and deracialization. Stealth strategy clearly involved racial sentiments and challenged Southern political tradition; but our estimation is that quiet, practical, biracial leadership reflected, most centrally, the realities of routine, progressive politics in the South. Stealthy white politicians probably did what they did as their situations allowed or required, quite often but not always with race-principled intent; in that process they collectively helped reconstruct and "normalize" a perverted, contorted, regional system of historically institutionalized white supremacy and racial segregation. Our concern in this project thus is to theorize and evidence those actions as a historical development—a matter of race-sensitive politics and progress, not a moral crusade—that mainly helps us understand the past. Deracialization, on the other hand, usually articulates a more defined, structured, race-based strategy of black leaders for advancing black interests in reasonably normalized locales nevertheless beset with racism and racial tensions. Understandably, prescriptive analysis of this practice figures prominently into debate about the present and future course of black politics.

In summary, our stealthy Southern pioneers charted a course that sets them apart from both the "heroes" and "villains" of the past and the more recent "deracializing leaders." Stealth leaders fundamentally challenged their own society and cultural traditions in those volatile times; yet their discrete and discreet actions, by design, would limit their careers and shade their role in history. We thus acknowledge the deracialization literature but declare that stealth politics is a very different, interesting, unexplored phenomenon that deserves scholarly attention.

READERS SHOULD ALSO take note that in this unusual, exploratory project, the authors' collaborative endeavor results in a mixed writing style. Generally, we present our analysis in plural, first-person manner ("we" and "our"). However, the Case Study in chapters four, five and six is narrated in first person ("I" and "my") by coauthor Glen Browder), from the perspective of his own political experience in Alabama and Washington; and the Biracial Roundtable discussion in chapter eight is moderated in similar first-person style by Artemesia Stanberry. We debated about employing this stylistic shift, but in the end we felt that the personalization would add richness and clarity to those four chapters of the manuscript.

Also, since much of the material presented in this manuscript is based on our experience as participant-observers, analysis and comments deriving from these twin perspectives are enmeshed in the text. Therefore, many such statements (including factual observations and personal remarks, whether directly or indirectly quoted) are not endnoted; this book serves as the original source of the material. Otherwise, standard endnoting procedures have been used.

WE RELY EXTENSIVELY in this manuscript on material from the Browder Collection, consisting of several hundred boxes of documents that have been processed for public access at Jacksonville State University (see *Analytic Guidebook for the Browder Collection*). This material can be accessed within broader context in the Browder Collection at JSU.

Besides the original and endnoted material mentioned in the preceding paragraphs, this manuscript shares limited excerptions, slight revisions, factual presentations, and political observations with three other sources. First, some background material, particularly in the Browder case study, derives from Browder's *The Future of American Democracy* (University Press of America, 2003). Secondly, some sections draw from Browder's *The South's New Racial Politics* (NewSouth Books, 2009) and *Professor-Politician* by Geni Certain with Glen Browder (forthcoming from NewSouth Books, 2010).

All three of these books share certain material through mutual permissions. We are grateful to Ms. Certain, NewSouth Books, and University Press of America for the use of this material.

NUMEROUS INDIVIDUALS CONTRIBUTED to this project, some in personal interviews, but most through telephone, email, and/or written communications. In some situations, their remarks have been edited for concision and clarity without affecting their substance. Among those interviewed and cited are the following:

Bill Alexander	Michael Andrews
Richard Arrington	Jess Brown
Kelvin Cunningham	Artur Davis
Butler Derrick	Marti Thomas Doneghy
James A. Dunn	Jim Folsom Jr.
Martin Frost	Fred Gray
Jerome Gray	Mike House
Paul Hubbert	Gerald Johnson
Martin Lancaster	L.F. Payne
Pete Peterson	Owen Pickett
Steve Raby	Joe Reed
Roy Rowland	Robin Tallon
Lindsay Thomas	George C. Wallace Jr.
Carol Zippert	

WE ARE VERY grateful to countless people who have assisted us in this project, including families, friends, and colleagues. Also, this work could not have been done without the kind support of Jacksonville State University, North Carolina Central University, and Prairie View A&M University. NewSouth Books is truly a Southern treasure, producing "regional books of national interest"—thanks Suzanne La Rosa, Randall Williams, Brian Seidman and all the staff. And, finally, thanks to many others too numerous to cite individually. Of course, any deficiencies or flaws in this book are our own; and we welcome comments and suggestions for future research.

INTRODUCTION

A merica today speaks in clear, strong voice and reverent tone about Dr. Martin Luther King Jr., Rosa Parks, the Freedom Riders, and other heroes of the civil rights revolution that rocked the South a half-century ago. Most citizens, when reflecting on the turbulent 1950s and 1960s, proudly cite *Brown v. Board of Education* as the legal and moral death knell for segregated schools. Some emotionally quote the 1964 Civil Rights Act and 1965 Voting Rights Act promoting equality in Southern society and elections. A few have actually read "Letter from Birmingham Jail" or have sung "We Shall Overcome."

Also seared into contemporary America's collective conscience and consciousness is the memory of the South's massive resistance to that revolution. Images of Southern white racism are still vivid and often brutal: George Wallace standing in the schoolhouse door, Bull Connor and his police dogs, ugly crowds at Little Rock, the Birmingham bombings, the Orangeburg Massacre, and Bloody Sunday.

However, America seems to have little sense of how that public struggle among heroes and villains during the 1950s and 1960s actually played into Southern politics during the 1970s, 1980s, and 1990s. The trauma of the mid-century civil rights movement has so dominated American public thinking and discourse that subsequent developments pale in comparison with emotional, time-frozen, black-and-white images from the earlier period. Furthermore and ironically, as recent presidential politics has demonstrated, historical sensitivities still constrict our ability to address the continuing racial dilemma in twenty-first century America.

Thus, few people understand that some leaders and activists quietly and biracially translated dramatic confrontation into the relative normalcy of a new political order in the post-movement South. There's little evidence in the public record attesting to this phenomenon, and knowledgeable participants have held their silence since those early days. In this book, we document this untold story of Southern politics and history.

The Movement: A Common Vision of Heroic Racial Drama

Over the past half century, our national news institutions, journalists, academicians, activists, and other chroniclers have developed a vibrant history of the civil rights movement as a heroic drama. Hollywood, Madison Avenue, and media merchants of all stripes celebrate, popularly and profitably, the moral challenges and courageous actions of that era. The common vision of the movement is a universal morality tale of good and evil, a raw, monolithic struggle, a clash of righteous souls and racial ogres, depicted literally and figuratively in black and white.[1]

George Wallace articulated the dark side of this struggle in a defiant pledge at his Alabama gubernatorial inauguration in 1963:

> In the name of the greatest people that have ever trod this earth, I draw the line in the dust and toss the gauntlet before the feet of tyranny . . . and I say . . . segregation today . . . segregation tomorrow . . . segregation forever.[2]

Alternatively, perhaps no speech in American history stirred our national emotion more so than Dr. King's visionary remarks at the Lincoln Memorial a few months later:

> I have a dream that one day the state of Alabama, with its vicious racists, with its governor having his lips dripping with the words of interposition and nullification, will be transformed into a situation where little black boys and black girls will be able to join hands with little white boys and white girls and walk together as sisters and brothers.[3]

Ever since, this stark vision of good-versus-evil has been ingrained in our minds as a psychic national monument. It also has served as permanent pressure on the South to conform to the "Great Experiment" of American democracy.

Now, fast-forwarding to the twenty-first century, we find an interesting situation. Almost half a century after Wallace's "segregation forever" declaration and the massive resistance of the old days, social scientists increasingly portray a new and different South that reflects real racial progress. Although such claims tend toward overstatement, demographic analysis shows the region diversifying; economic research shows blacks and whites sharing in regional growth; cultural studies show Southerners converging with the rest of the country; and opinion surveys, voting returns, and policy analyses demonstrate the coming of a more normalized, moderated political system.[4]

Most strikingly, of course, substantial biracial support in the South for Barack Obama in 2008 attests to fundamental, systemic change in this region. Race and racism are still vital matters, and much remains to be done, but the South has transformed dramatically over the past half-century.

An Intriguing Issue of Incongruent Political History

Arrival of a new racial order is a time of great interest and speculation; fortunately, too, it presents an opportunity for serious retrospection on the nature and meaning of regional transformation. Such matters are of more than casual consequence for the future of Southern and national democracy.

Our aim in this book, for example, is to pursue an intriguing, consequential question about the past half-century: How did we get from the brutally contentious civil rights movement to the substantial progress of the contemporary South? This would seem an easy task. However, it does not take much time at the library or on the computer to discover that there has been little work on the causes of racial progress of the last few decades. What we can ascertain is piecemeal, oblique, and perplexing.

We find, as has been noted, flourishing statistical depictions of many aspects of the emerging new South, such as shifting social and economic patterns, moderating cultural parameters, the expanding role of African Americans, and rising Republicanism in Southern public life. We find interesting historical and legal narratives—flush with names, dates, and places. There are fascinating anecdotes touching on changed racial interactions. And, frankly, interspersed throughout are periodic reports qualifying our notion of progress, reports that testify to the continuing problem of white-versus-black in this part of the nation. But something important—a general accounting of inside, real-world operations and systemic change—is missing from the conventional story line on racial politics of the last few decades. In particular, nothing in the literature addresses—theoretically, comprehensively, and coherently—the "what" and "how" and "why" of the broad political progress that has occurred since the contested days of the heroic drama.

Obviously, the movement's heroes deserve full credit for their moral suasion, personal sacrifices, and righteous triumphs in fighting for equal rights and racial justice during the 1950 and 1960s. However, it is highly unlikely that the movement by itself hammered the Old South into progressive submission. In many ways, the days of protest, violence, and forced desegregation were somewhat like the Civil War experience, leaving white Southerners whipped and resentful, and unleashing bad memories and fresh grievances among black Southerners. Furthermore, the ordeal afflicted all with an uncertain, distrustful future. Progressive politicians and civil rights leaders faced formidable obstacles in nurturing biracial relations and racial progress in that environment; their antagonists (including white segregationists and black separatists) were disinterested in partnerships for progress. Consequently, the triumphant heroes constantly struggled against recalcitrant villains, resistant populations, and traditional practices in the Southern states. The Second Reconstruction waned considerably during the late 1960s and early 1970s, again just as had happened with Civil War Reconstruction a century earlier. But, somehow, inexplicably, the monolithic struggle of good-versus-evil morphed into a relatively normalized political system by 2000.

In short, the stark Old South defied rational reconciliation—simply through the heroic drama—into racial progress in the contemporary period. Southern society gradually moderated, and persistent litigation kept pressure on stubborn individuals and institutions. But otherwise there has been little accounting for political developments leading to the new and different

South. Thus the nagging retrospective assignment is to square this important incongruity of Southern political history over the past half-century. Or, to slightly restate our intriguing question: "What really happened between then and now?"

We suspect that a variety of theoretical, methodological, and normative factors has underlain the failure to address this aspect of Southern change. Early on, natural fixation on the movement focused scholarly eyes too subjectively and narrowly on that mystic vision of good versus evil, heroes versus villains, and blacks versus whites to consider such mundane possibilities. In ensuing years, research was probably limited to phenomena that could be readily observed, empirically measured, and graphically presented.

Whatever the reasons, we see little in the way of causal analysis for broad racial progress, and we think that we have found and can document an important missing piece of this puzzle of Southern political history.

The Historic Role of Quiet, Practical, Biracial Politics . . .

While the civil rights movement in the 1950s and 1960s is a celebrated heroic drama, we believe there is an intriguing subplot of hushed, yet positive political endeavor in the South's history of the 1970s, 1980s, and 1990s.

We contend that Southern politics was significantly moderated during the closing decades of the twentieth century, and that it happened through the relatively progressive but quiet, somewhat secretive, sometimes uncomfortable, oftentimes less than noble, biracial service of practical politicians and activists. We believe that this moderating trend can be discerned in the raw racial conflicts, trade-offs, alliances, and transactions of "real politics"— both out front and behind the scenes—that has underlain the Southern race game for the past half-century.

By the 1970s, as the dramatic struggle cooled, some Southern leaders— doing what politicians do best—began accommodating new racial realities into routine campaigning and governing. These leaders were not much different from other politicians in their social origins and general orientations; in most ways they reflected traditional Southern politics. They were mainly interested in national defense, agriculture, the economy, building schools, and paving roads—and their own careers. In fact, their moderation coincided rather conveniently with the pressures of black voters, civil rights activists, and court litigation.

Nevertheless, relatively free from constraints of personally heroic or personally villainous history, these officials and their new allies went about the business of incorporating black and white voters, activists, and organizations into their election campaigns, and they worked together to articulate moderate policies and provide more equitable public services to both black and white constituencies. At first slowly and cautiously, with measured success, then increasingly as the situation allowed, they quietly helped move things forward without the drama and trauma of the preceding two decades.

A significant key to Southern change, then, was "stealthness," the quiet, practical, biracial politics practiced by many Southern white public officials and black allies during the 1970s, 1980s, and 1990s. The essence of their varied service is that they deftly attempted racial progress in a society wrought with racial tension. Or, to put it in political terms, they purposely and positively addressed black issues, without unduly antagonizing the white majority, while pursuing normal missions and careers as Southern public officials.

Most of these white politicos never considered themselves civil rights leaders, and their quiet endeavor has never been considered part of the civil rights movement; but, in individualistic practice and in alliance with key black activists, they helped implement important elements of the evolving movement's spirit and agenda in everyday Southern life.

. . . And the Untold Story of "Stealth Reconstruction"

The civil rights movement of the 1950s–'60s challenged and crippled institutions of the Old South. However, the movement, by itself, was unable to overcome the intransigence of the "Southern way of life" during the following decades. That aspect of the assignment inevitably fell to more functional operatives and their service inside "real Southern politics."

Thus, the heretofore untold truth is that these politicians and their friends—effectively supplementing the movement's assault on Old South ways—helped accomplish a Southern version of systemic reconstruction with their low-profile yet constructive service from the 1970s to the 1990s. There were no ballyhooed regional summits of white elected officials and black activists, nor any public pronouncements, nor any coordinated agenda, nor any media attention, nor any subsequent documentation by academic scholars. However, the record shows that things changed significantly in those decades; substantial progress was evidenced in local schools, in city halls, in county courthouses, and in state legislatures throughout the South, and even in Washington, D.C.

Of course, this stealthy reconstruction was often under duress, and stubborn racial problems persisted. Moreover, that service proved to be a temporary transition between traditional ways and a different order of the new century. But during those few decades, these leaders comprised a racial evolution that fundamentally and positively helped to reconstruct regional elections and governance.

We do not employ serious theoretical language—terms such as "thesis," "systemic," and "reconstruction"—frivolously, and we acknowledge that there has always existed a smattering of isolated mavericks who pricked the traditional culture of their communities with varying styles of surreptitiousness and/or boldness. But we "theorize" that there developed in the 1970s, 1980s, and 1990s a special sense among many mainstream Southerners of both races that, like it or not, things had to change. Some leaders—white and black—belatedly came up with a better way of dealing with civil rights, the federal government, and their own past.

We posit that these leaders collectively and significantly contributed to the evolution of the civil rights struggle and the reconstruction of Southern politics.

A Timely and Critical Mission

Our project may strike some as a simplistic and needless exercise, particularly at this point in history. However, we think that our "Stealth Reconstruction" project is a timely and critical mission on several counts.

First, we want to recognize a reality of recent Southern political history that has escaped the attention of professional scholars and that now is disappearing into an abyss of ignorance and irrelevancy. This reality needs to be documented before aging participants and witnesses of the 1970s, 1980s, and 1990s cease their earthly existence.

Our focus on white Southern public officials and their practical biracial leadership during that period is an unusual approach to the study of civil rights in the South, but it will supply new information and perspective about that era. As we have noted, conventional fixation on heroic figures and dramatic aspects of the movement has ignored a significant segment of major players and political developments of the past half-century, and this avoidance has produced an incomplete picture of the fundamentally changing South. As Jason Sokol recently remarked, "The literature on the South during this era privileges the dramatic demonstrations and famous battles of the civil rights movement, often at the expense of analyzing the very realm that those struggles sought to change—Southern life, black as well as white."[5]

Second, we want to encourage our academic associates to pursue this matter with an open, balanced, inquisitive approach. It may be time, as historian Charles Eagles argued in a survey of the literature, for exploring "new histories" of the civil rights movement, for challenging the established story, and for extending the debate in more balanced, even iconoclastic directions.[6] Historian Glenn Feldman has suggested, furthermore, that his discipline should constrain personal sentiments in future research on Southern history; "Those convictions may make good politics and good social policy, but they do not always make good history."[7]

Third, we also agree with Richard K. Scher that our discipline—political science—needs to contribute more substantively to the literature on racial politics. In a recent review, Scher recommended that we grapple with race and assess how it impacts on Southern politics in real-world terms instead of as a cold, independent variable for statistical models; "Race is a fundamental element in American politics in exactly the same way V. O. Key saw it as fundamental to Southern politics more than fifty years ago."[8]

Fourth, perhaps today's political leaders and journalists might learn something from the biracial functionaries of that era. As our colleagues Lucius J. Barker, Mack Jones, and Katherine Tate observed in their analysis of contemporary racial politics:

. . . we need to know more about the behavior and responsiveness of elected white officials from districts where there are very large and discrete black and minority populations. Conversely, we need to know how black members of Congress deal with the matter of representing white populations in their districts. Given the historical and contemporary context of racial politics and race relations in this country, along with the thorny conceptual issues surrounding political representation more generally, answering this question could prove difficult for any representative, regardless of race or ethnicity. But we suggest that precisely those representatives who are able to overcome such difficulties will do much to improve both race relations and the overall quality of life in this country.[9]

Finally, as democratic citizens, we hope that our work will help America understand Southern history and think seriously about its own challenges of the future. We believe that narrow focus on the noble vision keeps us from addressing persistent aspects of regional and national race problems. The civil rights movement was indeed a noble venture, but time-warped fixation has hindered our understanding of subsequent history and has made us so supersensitive as to impede constructive discussion about race and American democracy.

Recent presidential campaign politics, for example, demonstrates our reverent but dysfunctional temperament about the civil rights movement. The 2008 election suggests that America yearns for transformational dialogue, yet we still experience festering tension and clumsy sensitivities when dealing with the civil rights era within politics.[10] Democrat Barack Obama—the first African American presidential nominee of a major political party—struggled to explain to white voters how black liberation theology conformed to Dr. King's articulation of a vision deeply rooted in the American dream. There also were testy moments, as when Republican John McCain—who once opposed the Martin Luther King Holiday—glowingly invoked Dr. King's memory in his pursuit of African American votes. But no incident created a firestorm as volatile as Hillary Clinton's implication that it took a white politician, Lyndon Johnson, to achieve King's civil rights agenda. To be precise, candidate Clinton—liberally credentialed spouse of the so-called "first black president"—told a reporter that "it took a president to get it done."[11] Whatever her intent, the impolitic remark inflamed deep and conflicted emotions about the heroic drama.

Obviously, many white and black Americans are happy to celebrate the civil rights movement in a comfortable context and with fuzzy images from a half-century ago. However, they seem reluctant to scrutinize the conventional story for important realities of those times and lessons for contemporary democracy. Absent such information and insights, strained emotions will continue to disrupt meaningful discourse and racial progress. It is time to accord the heroic drama its proper place in history, time to accurately assess subsequent, realistic, biracial developments, and perhaps then we can advance toward implementation of Dr. King's dream.

Therefore, in this book, we hope to take a critical step forward in historical interpretation, documentation, and sophisticated awareness of biracial aspects of America's evolving Great Experiment.

The Stealth Project and Its Thesis

This book is part of a political science project conceived as a biracial approach to our own nagging questions about what really happened racially and practically inside politics in the South after the civil rights movement. In brief, our thesis is one of "Stealth Reconstruction." While the conventional version of the twentieth century civil rights movement is a compelling heroic drama, we believe that the Southern political system was subsequently reconstructed through the quiet leadership and biracial politics of practical politicians and activists during the 1970s, 1980s, and 1990s.

Obviously, both white and black elected public officials practiced biracial leadership—i.e., a leader of one race effectively representing constituents of another race—during those decades. Also, it is clear that some African American activists in our stealth relationships were powerful elected officials themselves; many were seasoned veterans of the movement. However, because of the exploratory nature of our thesis (and our own experiences and data resources), this book looks mainly at white elected officials and their special relationships with black activists and the black community in majority white areas. We will incorporate black veterans of the stealth era into a roundtable discussion of our thesis toward the end of the book.

Methodology

As has already been noted, the stealth thesis relies considerably on the authors' experience, and this book represents an unusual mixture of personal observation, original research, and existing literature.

Our methodology involves creatively thinking about, identifying, and assessing the phenomenon of quiet, practical, biracial politics. The central ideas—"stealth" and "reconstruction"—are used here in a somewhat new and specialized manner. Thus, we will define the terms and explain our planned implementation in a preliminary discussion of regional history and racial representation. Other challenges of our project—especially dealing with sensitive orientations and behaviors of the past—will be addressed as encountered throughout the book. We also must admit, frankly, that some stubborn quandaries of conceptualization and operationalization await resolution in future theory and research.

Our procedural methodology, on the other hand, is simple and direct. We set out to tap otherwise unavailable sources—people and documents—in pursuit of the relatively unexplored phenomenon of stealth leadership and representational politics. We elaborated a thesis and conceptual model based on our own experience, then we constructed a historical overview to place this idea within relevant research and literature. We began to demonstrate the thesis with a case study of Browder's campaigns and service for evidence about the nature, activities, and impact of his "stealth politics." We then explored the broader stealth proposition through an unscientific survey among other Southern political leaders of that time. Next we convened an eclectic group of individuals—both black and white—from that era for a virtual roundtable discussion about stealth leadership, politics, and reconstruction. Finally, we related our conclusions to the past, present, and future of Southern politics.

Clearly, some aspects of our thesis, methodology, and results merit refinement; future scholarship should expand the focus of biracial leadership and politics. For example, we have concentrated on white Southern elected officials during this particularly interesting period; much more needs to be addressed in the broader area of biracial politics and American democracy. However, to the best of our knowledge, the stealth project is a groundbreaking endeavor in understanding Southern history.

In the rest of this manuscript, we will (a) elaborate our stealth thesis, (b) present a case study, congressional survey, and roundtable discussion of stealthy leadership, politics, and reconstruction, and (c) consider the ramifications of our findings for the history and future of the South and America.

PART ONE

Stealth Theory

1

A New Perspective on
Southern Politics and History

As will be elaborated in a review of research and literature, conventional coverage of Southern politics and history has been dominated by the heroic drama and subsequent related developments during the latter half of the past century. There has been scant attention to white Southern politicians and their biracial activities among many sweeping generalizations about change in the South.

Of course, our subjects are not the only whites who attempted biracial politics in this region; other scholars have documented such service throughout Southern history. But most of the earlier research has depicted isolated, individualized struggle among heroes and villains; there has been little theorizing or documentation of widespread routine endeavor among white politicians that might be characterized as a positive movement of societal consequence.[1]

Therefore, we will examine these unheralded politicos and their hushed role within the peculiar politics of Southern history. We think that understanding their role in Southern history will help us chart a positive course for the present and future. We also hope that figuring out how these leaders promoted racial progress in their racially divided society can prove constructive for the broader American system which is beset with similar challenges.

First, however, we want to define our unconventional theoretical construct—"Stealth Reconstruction"—and note the controversial nature of our project.

"Stealth Reconstruction"

We chose the title—"Stealth Reconstruction"—because it seems an intriguing and logical approach for studying these overlooked leaders and their service in Southern and national history. Also, our main concept—"stealth politics"—is simply apt, evocative wording for the "quiet, practical, biracial politics" that challenged and changed the traditional ways of Southern political life during the 1970s, 1980s, and 1990s. We will elaborate pertinent style and substance in later sections, but we want to specify upfront what we're talking about when we say "stealth" and "reconstruction."

We are aware that the use of "stealth" terminology may strike some as a strange characterization of "quiet, practical, biracial politics." However, the term and the associated language of stealthness, stealthful, stealthy, stealthily, etc., accurately conveys our new theoretical proposition.

The reader can get a quick handle on our central concept by running a computerized search of cyberspace, which specifically defines "stealth" as "a U.S. Air Force project involving a range of technologies, with the purpose of developing aircraft that are difficult to detect by sight, sound, radar, and infrared energy."[2] More general definitions include: "not openly acknowledged"; "secret, clandestine, or surreptitious procedure"; and "marked by acting with quiet, caution, and ways intended to avoid notice." All these expressions are appropriate analogies or references to certain aspects of stealthness.

For our purposes, we pitch stealth leadership and politics as a calculated, constructive mixture of quietness and endeavor regarding racial challenges and changes of that period. Of course, we like to think of stealth in positive terms; however, it often involved actions of less-inspired politicking.

We define our version of "reconstruction" as addressing traditional challenges and fundamentally changing Southern politics into a normalized system without legalized white supremacy and racial segregation. Race and racism are still problematic in the region, but there's no longer a systemic "peculiarity" for perversity and contortion.

Those familiar with American history will understand that our idea is a fitting follow-up to earlier, more dramatic attempts of outsiders to reconstruct Southern regional culture. The "Southern way of life" had developed as a massive, hardened, resistant system of totalitarian white supremacy and separation of the races (except for limited interactions of necessity and personal inclination) enduring several centuries, civil war, and the civil rights revolution.

Quick review of the post-Civil War experience provides valuable background for our concept. In the federal government's experience in the defeated South can be found instructive lessons about the difficulties of attempting fundamental change in a resistant, alien society. After more than a decade of "reconstructed" public institutions—enforced through military occupation—the federal government cut a deal with insurgent resistors and withdrew.

In much the same manner as over a century ago, the Second Reconstruction[3] of the 1950s and 1960s—combining forces of the federal government and civil rights legions—assailed regionally entrenched white supremacy and segregation with great fanfare and significant success. However, the movement seemed to stagnate in the late 1960s, reflecting the reality that transformational reconstruction required more than legal pressure and celebrated heroism. We contend that further evolution required new-style leadership within the resistant establishment of the native society.

Therefore, we consider "stealth reconstruction" an interesting and appropriate analogy for studying and explaining the South of the 1970s, 1980s, and 1990s.

An Unconventional and Controversial Thesis

We acknowledge that our idea of "stealth reconstruction" is both different and controversial; it clearly challenges the focus, method, and substance of mainstream political science and historical analysis.

Our challenge is best illustrated by examining one of the most celebrated and comprehensive analyses of reconstructive politics during the past few decades—Richard M. Valelly's *The Two Reconstructions: The Struggle for Black Enfranchisement* . Valelly's book—which earned the Ralph J. Bunche award (American Political Science Association) and the V. O. Key Jr., award (Southern Political Science Association)—is a prime case of outstanding scholarship which nevertheless might benefit from our research.

In a unique historical/institutional/political analysis, Valelly compared the two reconstructive endeavors in America's experience. He showed that the "relative success" of the Second Reconstruction was due to a timely combination of national institutions and local political pressure. Valelly concluded that New Deal Democrats, federal judges, and black Southerners of the twentieth century forced the South into a more normal political environment, fostered black inclusion, and helped rebuild the Southern Democrats as a biracial party. Furthermore, he said, expansion and extension of the Voting Rights Act stabilized those gains in the latter decades of the century.

> By the year 2001, the states of Mississippi and Alabama combined had more African American elected officials, 1,628, than the entire United States had had in 1970. Black office-holding was indeed widespread in the South. Black voting, too, was routine. Southern governments' fiscal allocations for such things as hospitals, libraries, roads, and jobs, responded to the renewal of black suffrage and office-holding.
>
> Glaring problems have emerged, to be sure . . . . Still, as the twenty-first century began the second reconstruction was a thriving concern. It had produced a well-developed, biracial public sphere that was now a fairly normal part of U.S. political life.[4]

Valelly's book is a broad, powerful, valid, and persuasive analysis. With due respect, however, we fault his research for excluding critical people and actions—our quiet, practical politicians and their biracial politics—in the story of Southern change during the post-movement era. He employed a limited set of institutions/dynamics as change agents; he fixed on black voting/black office-holding as the narrow, singular definition of biracial progress; and apparently he didn't talk—or didn't talk candidly—with many Southern white politicians and black activists. He thus missed a developing indigenous phenomenon of biracial politics during the 1970s, 1980s, and 1990s. He failed to recognize or report that during those difficult times some elected officials of one race began to represent constituents of another race. While it was often a strained relationship, these white politicians and black activists helped significantly in "reconstructing" the South.

Valelly may or may not have been aware of such politicking, but if he was it is clear that he did not consider these relationships of any theoretical or constructive consequence. We can find no serious discussion of positive white-black transaction in his chapters on post-movement developments. The only pertinent reference is disparaging speculation about the possibility of "an unhealthy relationship between black voters and paternalistic white politicians doling out crumbs of public largesse to their clients."[5] This dismissive, offhand remark fails to convey the important role of biracial political relationships during this critical period, leaving us with an incomplete story of Southern reconstruction in the past half-century. Just as importantly, it leaves us to begin the twenty-first century with a flawed comprehension of our racial legacy.

Unfortunately, this tonal deficiency is standard practice in the conventional literature, a situation which we consider unacceptable at this stage of our academic disciplines. It is time to heed the advice of Sokol, Eagles, Feldman, Scher, and Barker/Jones/Tate about the focus, method, and substantive analysis of Southern politics and history. Thus we offer our unconventional, controversial analysis. We argue that our stealth leaders forsook the region's historic race-game for a variety of personal and political reasons. They tried to address minority black interests, without antagonizing the white majority, in their electoral campaigns and public service. It took a risktaking yet disciplined and committed politician and cooperative allies to attempt the personal and political venture of bridging the Southern racial divide. In an almost impossible time and environment, our reconstruction crew provided such leadership, working pretty much alone, with necessarily quiet purpose, helping their areas deal with historic problems and working to build a new, viable democratic politics. In doing so, they helped end racist vestiges of Old South Democracy, they helped moderate the tone of regional public discourse, and they collectively and substantially contributed to the normalization of Southern politics.

Of course, the very idea of stealth reconstruction, along with certain expressions and references, may offend some readers. Some likely will object to our focus on white politicians; some may complain that stealth politics was no more than unprincipled compromise; and some could assert that the South has not attained their broad, bold vision of progressive society. However, our conception of stealth leadership, politics, and reconstruction is a realistic, constructive amendment to Southern history. We do not claim that we have found *the* single most important or best agent and course of change; but we think that our stealth alliances represent much more than flaccid, irrelevant, opportunistic accommodation.

To generalize about our new perspective, then, we envision "stealth reconstruction" to incorporate quiet, practical, biracial leaders, their individualized practice of new-Southern political ways, and fundamental change during a particularly interesting period in this region of the country. Stealth reconstruction was a transitional adjustment to an evolving civil rights struggle, and it assisted in the riddance of stubborn racial legacies and the relative moderation and normalization of the Southern political system during the 1970s, 1980s, and 1990s.

We, the authors, have personally practiced stealth politics in our political careers; now we are exploring the nature of this phenomenon and its ramifications for Southern politics of that period. At the least, we are confident that our new perspective and study will provide a useful supplement to the conventional version of heroic history. More importantly, we hope that our work will encourage positive debate about the future of democratic representation in the South and America.

Our Theoretical Proposition about Stealth Leadership

We believe that amid all the heroic history of that time, there is a fascinating and useful story of "stealth leadership," "stealth politics," and "stealth reconstruction"—a story generally untold and unknown except among the reconstructing participants themselves.

Our proposition is that some leaders quietly broke with Old South ways during the 1970s, 1980s, and 1990s; we contend that these white officials, in concert with black activists, helped moderate and restructure the Southern political system in quiet biracial practicality. This stealthy white-black coalition's distinctive working style, skills, and relationships contributed to changing the nature, players, rules, issues, and outcomes of the traditional political game. They calmed Southern political discourse; and they assisted greatly in moving campaigns and governance in positive directions.

In developing our theoretical proposition for use throughout this manuscript, we conceptualized stealth leadership and politics according to the following model.

A Conceptual Model of Stealth Leadership and Politics

Our model defines stealthness—in purely analytical terms—to include Southern white elected officials who traversed five steps, or checkpoints, of stealth service during that period. These stealth leaders: (1) served in white majority areas with significant numbers of black constituents, (2) demonstrated personal orientations toward quiet, practical, biracial politics, (3) successfully waged quiet, practical, biracial electoral campaigns, (4) effectively provided quiet, practical, biracial public service, and (5) substantially helped change the Southern system of elections and governance in moderate-to-progressive direction.

Table 1 (see next page) illustrates our conceptual model by comparing stealth leaders and traditional Southern politicians. It includes the characteristic elements of stealthness, presents each element as a cumulative step in the stealth process, and generally conveys the systemic nature and function of stealth leadership, politics, and reconstruction.

Obviously, this chart is an oversimplified depiction. By design, the model states polar examples of traditionalism and stealthness, whereas actual service was of varied mixtures and degrees. It is difficult to assess real leadership precisely in such terms. Nevertheless, the conceptual model is valuable as a theoretical construct because it neatly portrays our notion that some leaders pursued that new course of politics. Also, the model provides a framework for original research exploring the validity and broader applicability of the stealth thesis. Accordingly, we will study various politicians from that era—through structured examination of settings, orientations, campaigns, service, and impact—and the results will be presented in the second half of this book.

Before starting those examinations, however, we must further define these special leaders and take a look at the "race game" in which they performed their specialized service.

TABLE I

Conceptual Model of Stealthness
Versus Traditional Southern Politics

Traditional Politician		Stealth Leader
	1. POLITICAL SETTING	
Served in a variety of white-black constituencies.		Served in majority white areas with significant black populations.
	2. PERSONAL ORIENTATIONS	
Evidenced acceptance of the historical system of white supremacy and racial segregation in southern politics.		Evidenced sentiment and/or plans for quiet, practical, biracial change in southern politics.
	3. ELECTORAL CAMPAIGNS	
Emphasized conservative messages and openly segregated campaigns to maximize white support while ignoring or manipulating blacks.		Emphasized communitarian messages and discreet dual campaigns to sustain sufficient white support while cautiously addressing black interests
	4. PUBLIC SERVICE	
Promoted conservative policies, segregated oper-, ations and racialized services that substantially reflected discriminatory governance.		Promoted moderate policies, biracialized operations and, deracialized services that reflected substantially fairer and more equitable governance.
	5. SYSTEMIC IMPACT	
Individually continued the traditional practice of Old South politics.		Incrementally helped change the nature of southern politics.

The Historical Necessity for Practical Political Action

Again, a major plank of our thesis is the premise that progress beyond the heroic drama required practical leaders who might attempt a new biracial Southern politics. As we have already noted, the dramatic struggle between heroes and villains had so divided and traumatized Southern politics that our hypothesized reconstruction could come only when those heroes and villains yielded the historical stage to less confrontational types and times.

In fact, the broader environment for sweeping transformation of the South altered substantially and adversely. Radical ideas and actions of black unrest had spread nationally, leading many Americans and the federal government to temper their feelings about the civil rights movement.

President Lyndon Johnson and Congress felt that legal victories—such as the Civil Rights Act of 1964—had effectively addressed the situation and that further aggressive actions from the federal government or from blacks themselves might be counterproductive. As King biographer David J. Garrow noted in *Bearing the Cross: Martin Luther King, Jr., and the Southern Christian Leadership Conference*:

> The president used the signing ceremony not only to congratulate those who had contributed to the passage of one of the legislative milestones in modern American history, but also to caution the black leaders about how they should greet this new achievement. After the public ceremony, the president spoke in private with King, Wilkins, Whitney Young, and other black representatives. He told them that there had to be "an understanding of the fact that the rights Negroes possessed could now be secured by law, making demonstrations unnecessary and possibly even self-defeating." Johnson suggested they would be self-defeating for the movement, but most of those in attendance, King included, knew that the president's real fear was that protests would play into the hands of Republican candidates seeking to convince fearful whites that someone other than Lyndon Johnson should be in the White House to preserve public order throughout America.[6]

In *When the Marching Stopped: The Politics of Civil Rights Regulatory*

Agencies, Hanes Walton Jr. studied regulatory implementation of the Civil Rights Act of 1964 and found that subsequent enforcement slowed considerably in the Nixon, Ford, Carter, and Reagan administrations. Walton found that the federal government spent only 15 percent of its civil rights budget on investigating complaints of discrimination and enforcing the law regarding the nondiscriminatory use of federal funds.[7]

As the heroic drama began to experience these adversities and other tensions, Dr. King realized that the movement had to revitalize and refocus itself in a more pragmatic manner. In 1967, he spoke of the necessity for practical political action both in his final presidential address to the Southern Christian Leadership Conference[8] and in his last book before being assassinated in Memphis.[9]

In the SCLC speech on August 17, 1967, Dr. King attempted to reorient his followers from moral and legal concerns to the political task of integrating blacks into American life. First, King proudly hailed the inspiring accomplishments of the heroic drama:

> . . . when our organization was formed ten years ago, racial segregation was still a structured part of the architecture of Southern society . . . all too many Negroes were still harried by day and haunted by night by a corroding sense of fear and a nagging sense of nobody-ness.
>
> But things are different now. In assault after assault, we caused the sagging walls of segregation to come tumbling down. This is an accomplishment whose consequences are deeply felt by every Southern Negro in his daily life . . .
>
> But in spite of a decade of significant progress, the problem is far from solved. The deep rumbling of discontent in our cities is indicative of the fact that the plant of freedom has grown only a bud and not yet a flower.[10]

King then called for a strategic shift toward the everyday realities of political power and action:

> Now a lot of us are preachers, and all of us have our moral convictions

and concerns, and so often we have problems with power. But there is nothing wrong with power if power is used correctly.

You see, what happened is that some of our philosophers got off base. And one of the great problems of history is that the concepts of love and power have usually been contrasted as opposites, polar opposites, so that love is identified with a resignation of power, and power with a denial of love . . .

Now, we got to get this thing right. What is needed is a realization that power without love is reckless and abusive, and that love without power is sentimental and anemic . . .

This is no time for romantic illusions and empty philosophical debates about freedom. This is a time for action. What is needed is a strategy for change, a tactical program that will bring the Negro into the mainstream of American life as quickly as possible.[11]

In his final book, expanding that discussion, Dr. King talked about new strategies and tactics for real political power. In addition to promoting the election of black officials, he advocated alliances with responsive white politicians, and he spoke specifically about the changing nature of such relationships and Southern politics in those days:

A primary Negro political goal in the South is the elimination of racism as an electoral issue. No objective observer can fail to see that even with a half-finished campaign to enfranchise Negroes some profound changes have already occurred. For a number of years there were de facto alliances in some states in which Negroes voted for the same candidate as whites because he had shifted from a racist to a moderate position, even though he did not articulate an appeal for Negro votes. In recent years, the transformation has accelerated, and many white candidates have entered alliances publicly. As they perceived that the Negro vote was becoming a substantial and permanent factor, they could not remain aloof from it. More and more, competition will develop among white political forces for such a significant bloc of votes, and a monolithic white unity based on racism will no longer be possible.[12]

As King said, the purpose of his new political plan was not simply to increase African American electoral influence, but to develop "a strong voice that is heard in the smoke-filled back rooms where party debating and bargaining proceed."[13] Furthermore, he warned, the civil rights community would have to deal with established white power structures without petty outbursts about selling-out:

> Too often a genuine achievement has been falsely condemned as spurious and useless, and a victory has been turned into disheartening defeat for the less informed. Our enemies will adequately deflate our accomplishments; we need not serve them as eager volunteers.[14]

King's emphasis on practical alliances was echoed and elaborated, with an emphasis on biracial cooperation, by sociologist Chandler Davidson in *Biracial Politics: Conflict and Coalition in the Metropolitan South*. Davidson, one of the most engaged and prolific patrons of black voting rights over the past half century, proposed a new "Southern Strategy" of black-white coalition as an alternative to both conventional politics and the black separatism being preached by some in the 1960s.

Davidson dismissed normal political action as the old Southern strategy, and he said the ultimate costs of black separatism outweighed the benefits. Davidson attempted to show that blacks and whites had similar societal aspirations, that such an approach would not compromise the interests of blacks, and that there was considerable foundation for a biracial, working-class movement. "If one accepts our earlier thesis, therefore, that justice for blacks remains ahead of us in the indefinite future, then the option of class-based coalition politics in the South and in the rest of the nation is the one most likely to achieve success."[15]

While a South-wide movement may have been impractical, Davidson noted, there were examples and clear prospects for localized success in coming years.

> Blacks, most of whom still favor working through "the system," have cooperated with whites in many different situations—formal electoral

politics, union organizing activities, public demonstrations, community action groups, and within educational settings. Usually only a minority of whites have been willing to cooperate. But in many situations, a minority of whites combined with a majority of blacks is sufficient to provide a decisive force for change. While there are very few political units in the South where blacks constitute a majority (102 counties out of of more than a thousand in 1970), for example), there are numerous units where a unified black population combined with 30 percent of the whites constitute an effective majority.[16]

Davidson insightfully foresaw the developing, historical necessity for biracial politics, but his recommendations, reflecting research during the late 1960s and political developments of the early 1970s, relied on questionable strategies, tactics, and agents of change. He insisted that the coalition would have to be a movement of class-based radicalism, significantly departing from elitist liberalism. He incorporated into his plan a combination of strikes, political rallies, disruption, and harassment of corporate and governmental routine, and above all, grassroots education and propaganda.[17] He included lower-income whites and organized labor as key class partners, and he specifically targeted middle and upper-class progressives—"university people, 'whistle blowers' within the white-collar institutions, the traditional racial liberals, the growing middle-income supporters of tenants unions, the largely middle-class feminists, and the equally middle-class peace groups, environmentalists, and other liberal-radical reformers."[18]

What Davidson failed to envision (and what King never lived to see) was the elusive, limited, but requisite capacity of real-world politics in the aftermath of the civil rights movement. Direct, radical, coalitional action in a thousand different places—even when buttressed with voting rights laws and court decrees and all the other allies of progressive change—would likely fall short unless the movement engaged a special breed of political leaders/activists with stylistic skills and substantive agendas throughout the Southern region.

In effect, King's inspirational ideas and Davidson's empirical notions sorely needed "practical men of action" as described—gender-insensitively—

by Eric Hoffer in *The True Believer: Thoughts on the Nature of Mass Movements*. We don't want to digress needlessly, but Hoffer's classic essay adds solid theoretical foundation for our proposition about stealth politics.

> What the classification attempts to suggest is that the readying of the ground for a mass movement is done best by men whose chief claim to excellence is their skill in the use of the spoken or written word; that the hatching of an actual movement requires the temperament and the talents of the fanatic; and that the final consolidation of the movement is largely the work of practical men of action. . .[19]
>
> It is usually an advantage to a movement, and perhaps a prerequisite for its endurance, that these roles should be played by different men succeeding each other as conditions require.[20]

We'll skip through Hoffer's polemic against fanaticism and focus on the language pertinent to our thesis. The part of the essay that interests us is his assertion about the role of "practical men of action," whose appearance represents the end of the dynamic phase and the beginning of a working new order. In fact, Hoffer claimed, "only the entrance of a practical man of action can save the achievements of the movement."[21] Men of thought, he continued, don't work well together, but camaraderie is an easy, indispensable, unifying agent for men of action. Among their many practical motivations, according to Hoffer, these operatives are interested in furthering their own careers as well as institutionalizing the movement; their tactics, while less than revolutionary, are often functionally successful.[22] It is difficult to draw from King's call to action, Davidson's insistence on biracial coalitions, and Hoffer's provocative essay any specific directives for stealth politics. However, we think that their discussions about "strategy for change," "cooperative majorities," and "practical men of action" provide a particularly appropriate foundation for our thesis about stealth leaders, politics, and reconstruction. Practical men and women of both races would assume critical importance in strategically and cooperatively consolidating Southern change during the 1970s, 1980s, and 1990s.

A huge, vibrant body of literature attests to the more heroic actions of celebrated persons in the movement. However, we are interested in those quiet, practical, biracial leaders who collectively played a timely and similarly vital role. Unfortunately, history records virtually nothing about their backgrounds, their attitudes, and their activities. Therefore they are our focus, and in this project we will define and document their stealthy role in the transformation of Southern politics in the latter part of the twentieth century.

Preliminary Testimony to the Reality of Stealthness

Stealthness can be viewed as having positively addressed black issues and concerns, most commonly without pronounced intent or obvious plan, and in a way that avoided unduly antagonizing the white majority. Certainly, it would be easy to deny stealthness or to label this element of Southern politics as opportunistic pandering or ideological deception or cowardly hiding from the electorate. Stealth leaders, as a group, clearly avoided exposure. They were more progressive than conservative politicians in their region, and they were less progressive than liberal politicians from other parts of the country. They have been criticized from the right and from the left as "closet this" or "closet that." In truth, they can most accurately be described as practical, moderate leaders politicking in a society still burdened with vestiges of segregation.

As preliminary testimony to this phenomenon, coauthor and former public official Glen Browder describes his stealth politics in simple, retrospective terms:

> I got into politics because I was concerned about American democracy. I knew that in order to pursue my personal democratic interests I had to be an effective, responsive, and responsible public official in terms of broad concerns of importance to my base white constituency and to those of the black minority. So, over the course of my career, I publicly concentrated on political reform, fiscal responsibility, and national security issues. At the same time, I diligently but less-publicly focused on race and racism. I worked very hard and quietly to secure enough black support to get elected in majority-white areas; I sincerely tried to be fair,

moderate, and progressive in my politics; and I didn't talk much publicly about any of this stuff.

More direct are the remarks of Dr. Joe L. Reed, one of the most important black leaders in Alabama during the past half-century. Reed has provided leadership during the post-heroic period as a Montgomery city councilman, executive chairman of the Alabama Democratic Conference, vice chair of the Alabama State Democratic Executive Committee, and associate executive secretary of the Alabama Education Association. More pertinently, he has been a premier architect of what we have labeled stealth politics; when necessary, he has worked quietly and practically with Browder, U.S. Senator Howell Heflin, and countless other white political leaders over the past several decades. Reed passionately stated the history, reality, and logic of stealthness in an in-depth discussion in Montgomery.

> We absolutely did play stealth politics! Throughout history, and especially in the days following the civil rights movement, we worked quietly with white friends. That quiet politics of accommodation was the only way we could accomplish anything during those times. You sure couldn't go to the top of the mountain and tell everything you knew and what you were doing with white politicians. There were some of them that we wanted to give awards to but we never could because it would have killed them if it got out about what they were doing for blacks.[23]

Equally corroborative are the words of Dr. Richard Arrington Jr., who, along with Reed, has played a dominant role in Alabama political history of the past half-century. Arrington was the first African American mayor of Birmingham, where he presided from 1979 to 1999. He is generally credited with founding the powerful Jefferson County Citizens Coalition and he played a lead role in creating the Alabama New South Coalition, which now rivals the Alabama Democratic Conference in state politics. Arrington said that stealth politics worked hand-in-hand with the civil rights movement.

I find the characterization of "Stealth Reconstruction" provocative, informative, and realistic. And I agree that quiet, effective, biracial cooperation was a cornerstone of much of the heralded and hard-won racial transitions in Southern attitudes and politics. Without it, the courageous and well-recorded acts of the modern civil rights movement would have had a much more difficult course. In fact, my own political participation was grounded in stealth politics as much as in the movement. I can think of numerous important people—white and black working together—who quietly laid foundations for my career and changes in our area. I doubt that they knew at the time just how productive and far-reaching their stealthy actions were for biracial progress in the South.[24]

Without doubt, the most compelling witness to the stealth concept is storied civil rights attorney Fred Gray of Tuskegee, Alabama. Gray's role in the civil rights movement stretches beyond Alabama, to broader Southern politics, and even to the core of American democracy. He represented Mrs. Rosa Parks in integrating Montgomery City buses; he was the first civil rights lawyer for Dr. Martin Luther King Jr.; he litigated representational discrimination through *Gomillion v. Lightfoot*; he successfully challenged Alabama governors John Patterson and George Wallace and various state agencies on important civil rights issues; he fought the United States government for justice for the victims of the Tuskegee Syphilis Study; he was one of the first African American legislators in Alabama since Reconstruction; and he was the moving force in establishing the Tuskegee Human and Civil Rights Multicultural Center. A mild-talking but determined civil rights champion who is still active, Gray adds unimpeachable testimony to the stealth thesis:

Yes, the thesis is valid and any research that can be presented will do a good service for our understanding of Southern politics and history. The civil rights movement began long before the 1950s and extended beyond the 1960s, and a lot of people don't realize that it took many forms—not just big legal cases and dramatic protests against segregated buses, schools, and facilities. Most white politicians and black leaders didn't even talk to each other during the 1970s, so those of us who could work together did some things quietly and in back rooms. I fought in the courts for most of my life, but a lot of good things happened, legislatively and otherwise, through this kind of politicking among practical politicians.[25]

We will hear much more "stealth talk" from other politicians and activists throughout this book.

The Practitioners of Stealth Leadership

We contend that the 1970s, 1980s, and 1990s produced practical political leaders and activist allies like Browder, Reed, Arrington, and Gray who—working quietly, independently, at various levels throughout the region—sometimes changed the nature, rules, players, issues, and outcomes of the Southern political game.

More specifically, we propose that many Southern white leaders successfully combined objective and subjective elements of stealth politics in public service. In the first place, they got elected in majority-white districts with significant black constituencies. Secondly, they personally engaged in biracial politics and demonstrated substantial support for minority interests in their public service. Finally, throughout these processes, they functionally juggled the racial realities of Southern society. In sum, we envision leaders who possessed valuable perspectives and skills, who quietly and effectively worked with community activists, partisans, and miscellaneous operatives of all persuasions, and, who, collectively, helped reconstruct campaigns and governance in the South.

Of course, there are problems in generalizing about all public officials of that era and in that area. Clearly, Southern politicians did not decide in mass to practice a new, more progressive version of Southern politics. Many simply continued as traditional politicians, or switched parties.

Even among reconstructive leaders, there was tremendous diversity. Although virtually all were Democrats, they ranged ideologically from very conservative to moderate to relatively liberal; and they displayed varying degrees of caution or brashness in their racial politics. Some went about their business without outward, obvious design; others purposefully practiced a carefully calculated biracialism. Actually, a few seemed to preach and practice their racial progressivism so openly that it is impossible to label them "stealth politicians."

So it is hard to articulate a perfect model or draw hard lines among different individuals and representational styles. Nevertheless, we believe that our thesis is an accurate generalization of important developments during that period; and we are confident that stealth politics will prove to be a useful framework for understanding biracial relations in a reconstructing regional system.

For thematic reasons, we exclude from our thesis more prominent historical figures such as President Lyndon Johnson (a Texan whose bold leadership and earthy populism were vital to important civil rights changes in the South), the wave of "New South" officials such as Georgian Jimmy Carter and Arkansan Bill Clinton (who, along with numerous state executives openly championed social change against the conservative current of their white constituents), and confrontational activists such as South Carolinian Jesse Jackson (and many others who took to the streets in their fight against racial discrimination). These leaders generally played on the stage of big issues, to a national audience, and with substantial media celebrity; their service is inappropriate for consideration because it is impossible to dissect their public/private lives in a manner meaningful to our analysis.

Finally, we exclude those Southern politicians who have famously wandered a political maze of racist politics, convenient conversions, and electoral success. Their careers are interesting and sometimes sympathetic and sincere (take the latter years of George Wallace, for example), but we are interested in leaders who fairly consistently pursued the positive politics and philosophy of stealthy biracial leadership.

The ranks of leaders within the scope of our stealth thesis include some prominent players, but we are interested mainly in their private leadership and political style away from the glare of the media, beyond the gilding reach of their public relations machinations. More specifically, we think that reconstructive action likely took place inside their political campaigns and behind closed doors of their public offices, where they employed their personalities, skills, and resources on behalf of their careers and public service, where self-interest, noble principle, and raucous exchange translated into practical politics and moderate/progressive governance.

The Tricky Essence Of Stealth Politics

Earlier, we pitched stealth leadership and politics, simply and briefly, as a calculated, constructive mixture of quietness and endeavor regarding racial challenges and changes of that period. The essence of that mixture was a representational style in which the public official projected a broadly popular and effective public image on conventional, communitarian issues, thus allowing flexibility in dealing constructively with contentious racial issues in a society historically beset with racial problems. Stealth leaders, working with allies in the new black constituency, were able to move Southern politics in relatively progressive directions of responsive service and moderate policy.

The complex and difficult work of these leaders required that they balance their progressive inclinations with the practicalities of Southern political life. Besides struggling with their own personal angst, these key officials and activists often had to deal with the demands of a stubbornly conservative white majority and an increasingly active and liberal black minority in a bitterly polarized or potentially polarizing environment.

Consequently, most of these politicians charted a centrist policy course, diverse relationships, and carefully selected activities in order to deal with their racial problems.

It is also worth noting the varying approaches among our stealth leaders. Some conducted "stealth by design," i.e., discreet, separate activities structured so as to solicit minority support without fanning fires of resentment among the majority. For example, they sometimes invited and accompanied national black leaders to local black events; but they didn't put out press releases or hold news conferences about these activities. Others engaged in biracial pursuits without such deftly calculated motives and plans, perhaps inadvertently, unintentionally, simply by chance—or what might be called "stealth by coincidence." They proceeded on a quiet, practical course with moderated message; and they treated black and white in a sincere manner that mitigated their biracial politicking.

It does not make much sense, of course, to make too big a deal out of the difference between "designed stealth" and "coincidental stealth." These are simply specific constructs that help us comprehend the broader, theoretical concept of stealth politics; it may be that this distinction is more a matter of personal self-definition than real-world consequence. Every stealth politician was an individualized combination of purposefulness and inadvertence, even without conceptualizing such stylistic considerations. The important thing is that all of these leaders were breaking with the central tradition of Southern history, and they must have understood the value of "quiet" and "practical" politics as they traveled their forward course in "de facto stealthness," without outward pandering to either of their conflicted racial constituencies. For example, adept stealth politicians—without a lot of articulated theorizing—went to black churches on Sunday and white civic clubs throughout the week, keeping their conversations appropriate for each place; in their public demeanor, they dealt with both majority and minority issues in acceptable, communitarian manner.

As we make clear throughout, the purpose here is not to sanctify stealth leaders; they were politicians of mixed personalities, motives, and actions. Our purpose is to emphasize the difficult essence of stealth politics and the challenge of stealth leadership. Stealthy practitioners were aware that they had to craft a biracial majority for electoral victory. Then, after getting elected, they had to attempt an equally daunting assignment, pursuing moderate to progressive public service, being responsive to all citizens, without unraveling their tenuous and volatile constituency. It was a tricky assignment; that is what politics is about, whether in Selma or San Francisco. The difference back then was that Southern politicking labored under a heavy and perverse hand of black-white history.

Obviously, stealth politics defied moral posturing and dramatic public coordination, and it failed then and now to elicit interest among national media and professional scholars. But this different politicking helped incorporate and implement the usually cited forces of Southern change during the past half-century.

The Mixed Civic Nature of Stealth Reconstruction

As has been noted, this is not a thesis of public magnificence like the heroic civil rights movement.

For the most part, the new breed of Southern political leadership was interested in conventional issues such as national defense, education, agriculture, and their own careers; their stealth politics has to be understood as a civic endeavor within the primacy of broader concerns.

It would be quite a stretch to champion these leaders and their work as heroic or revolutionary—they were, after all, practical political people. There was no common soul or grand collective purpose among our politicians, just their individual political personalities and everyday operations based on a mixture of selfish and unselfish character. Few had been on the front lines or in the march for equality in their areas and states; many nurtured sentiment, but no burning passion, for the heroic drama; most did not enter public life until the 1970s, and when they did, it was not for reasons of racial justice. We'll not claim for them a place among the icons of the civil rights movement. Instead, we characterize them simply as "stealth politicians" who, variously motivated, helped reconstruct Southern politics.

However, we do view stealthy biracial leadership and politics as a broad civic phenomenon that went beyond the personalized motives and actions of crass politicians. While some leaders contributed to this movement in individualized pursuit of individualized objectives, many others did so for philosophical and purposive reasons related to American democracy. They were as a group relatively progressive Southerners; so we prefer to envision stealth politics as an incremental, conflicted mixture—a purposeful/inadvertent, public/private, personal/interpersonal dynamic—and as an overall positive process whereby some leaders and activists really made things better in everyday life for most Southerners, who were caught in the black-white crossfire of their region's historical dilemma.

The Inevitable Demise of Stealth Leadership

Ironically, the racial progress of the past several decades wrought the inevitable demise of stealth leadership in the South. These leaders were transformational but transient; in a way, they may have fallen victims of their own success in helping change Southern politics.

In the 1970s, stealth politicians proceeded quietly and practically. The key challenge back then was to deal tactically and tactfully with the mainstream conservative constituency of white voters in the Democratic Party primary—coalitional blacks were just coming of age in the normal political process, and Republicans were no more than a vocal nuisance. Then, in the 1980s, it became possible for stealth leaders to pursue moderate politics more aggressively and successfully. However, these positive, evolving developments simultaneously sowed the seeds of decline for such leadership in the 1990s. As time passed, the large, conservative, white constituency began splitting off and casting its votes elsewhere; blacks became more politically mature, independent, and assertive; and Republicans became more powerful in exposing and defeating stealthy leaders in the general election. Certainly, too, enhanced media coverage and advances in campaigning injected powerful new elements of transparency and volatility into the process, making quiet biracial maneuvering less feasible and effective.

Browder notes, for example, that things changed dramatically between his entry into the political arena in 1982 and his exit in 1996:

> When I first ran for office and served in the Alabama legislature, it was relatively easy to please my majority-white constituents, keep my black friends satisfied, and hold the Republicans at bay. But in my last campaign, for the U.S. Senate, nobody was very happy. I know that I changed some over the course of my career, and there's a big difference between the Alabama House and the U.S. Senate. But much of this was due to the new racial order that made "stealthy" politicking impossible.

The shift from old-style Southern politics to new-order Southern politics undermined a fundamental quality and asset—stealthness—of biracial politics. Thereafter, stealth leaders found their course more demanding and conflicted, and they became increasingly irrelevant in Southern politics. They had helped achieve substantial transformation stealthily, and much more remained to be done; but most of them realized, in appropriate quietness and practicality, that the future belonged to new leaders with different visions and styles in an altered environment of Southern democracy. Stealth leadership and politics were essentially over, in unremarked dissipation, as a new Southern political order signaled the end of stealth reconstruction.

To summarize this part of the theoretical discussion, we believe that the consequence of collective stealth efforts represents an important, distinct, supplementary movement of reconstructive and progressive evolution. Arguably, stealth leaders accomplished Southern change in a way and to an extent that was beyond the reach of federal officials, laws, and troops. While righteous souls and racial ogres dominate the pages of history books, the stealthy reconstructionists helped bring black voters into Southern elections, helped end racist control of the Southern political establishment, helped moderate Southern governance, and, in a roundabout way, helped nudge the South toward a real two-party system.

In offering our proposition, we realize that this thesis asks the reader to reconsider decades of unquestioned truisms about Southern politics and history. Frankly, any honest depiction of the South's racial past—as we will attempt in the next few pages—poses formidable, legitimate questions regarding our high notions of stealth service.

Stealth Leaders and the Race Game of Southern History

In some ways, the South can claim to be the original, intellectual heart of the "Great Experiment" of American democracy. Even today, many Southerners pride themselves as America's real and true patriots. However, from the beginning the South steered its own regional course, a distinct culture of white supremacy in an America that at least preached idealistic principles of equality. Historically, the white leaders and people of this region have engaged in a race game of perverse politics designed to provide themselves the blessings of democracy while oppressing, exploiting, and discriminating against their fellow human beings of African origin and heritage. Gaming the system for racial advantage was not the singular, continuous, consuming passion for most Southerners, but slavery warped the Southern political system from the start and race forever lurked in the background and foreground of Southern political life.

The unsavory realities of Southern politics derive from that accursed aspect of the American story. In embracing slavery, this part of the New World launched long-term, systemic developments that would confound its better nature and democratic destiny. The South pursued its dark regional interests in fateful arrangements—and perhaps implicit collusion—with national politicians eager to promote their nationalistic dreams. During the Constitutional period, there was contentious debate over slavery, but the Southern states convinced the founding fathers to accommodate the regional slave economy as part of their entry into the new nation. Slavery endured through decades of fitful argument—adamantly and morally defended on the floor of Congress by John C. Calhoun as "the peculiar institution of the South."[26] Then, after the Civil War and Reconstruction, white Southerners negotiated an opportunistic new deal with national Democrats that excluded freed blacks from the political process as long as the South delivered total electoral support to the national party in Washington. Even after the Civil War and Reconstruction, states throughout the region continued Old South ways by legally disenfranchising blacks. As Alabama's constitutional convention president said in 1901, "It is within the limits imposed by the Federal Constitution, to establish white supremacy in this state."[27] Regional white rule continued until the civil rights era, when the national government finally eliminated official sanction of discrimination.

Unfortunately then, throughout most of its history, the South's leadership and "peculiar" political system have revolved around the unsavory realities of white supremacy and racial segregation. While Southern leaders historically pursued broad issues of national and local import, race usually lurked in the background and routinely intruded into conventional politics.

Within this racial context, we employ the terms "stealth leadership" and "stealth politics" to refer to individual leaders quietly performing biracial political roles for generally positive purposes, and "stealth reconstruction" is an incremental, collective, fundamental victory of civic progress over cynical politics in the broader race game of Southern history.

However, the stealth thesis and terminology can conjure mixed images of politicians and black-white relations; indeed, the very word that we use—"stealth"—evokes shadowy connotations from Southern politics, past and present. Our hypothetical version of stealth leadership is positive, but our designated stealth leaders were practical politicians who politicked in the real world. And in the real world of Southern politics, misdirected stealthness could just as well entail deception, fraud, and abuse of the public trust. And quiet, practical politics, when pursued for unvirtuous purposes, when exacerbated with financial considerations, and when enveloped in an environment of heated, ingrained societal division, could powerfully warp the electoral process and corrode responsive, responsible government.

So there's no denying that our stealth leaders were ungracefully mired— either in deed or through association or by appearance—in the racial politics of Southern history. We generalize that most Southern leaders—white and black—have played the game of racial politics in some manner and to some degree. Our stealth leaders, awkwardly mired in that game, had to navigate a difficult, politically conflicted course during the era under study. Few ever talked about it, and it's still not a popular subject of conversation. But the routine pursuit of power, policies, and other political goodies in this region during those times often involved racial considerations. We presume that most of the practitioners did some specific things that they would prefer history not record; that they allied with some people who did unseemly things as a matter of general practice; and that they hung around a political house of ill-repute.

The crucial difference between traditional Southern officials and our designated stealth leaders is that, routine pursuits and career interests aside, (a) traditional politicians readily and openly played the game for racial advantage within a historical environment of white supremacy and segregation, while (b) stealth politicians quietly and deliberatively played the game mainly to improve black-white relations and normalize racial aspects of Southern democracy.

Stealth politicians had to navigate a difficult, sometimes wayward course. Even our case-studied and surveyed leaders—oriented to racial, economic, and social progress—allow that they sometimes struggled with the challenges and compromises dictated in their regionalized calling. As will be evidenced throughout this book, certain aspects of service by public official Browder and his stealth colleagues seem uncomfortably similar to the cynical activities of traditional Southern politicos and new race-gamers.

Coauthor Browder notes that since he was a professional political scientist and campaign consultant prior to entering politics, he was better prepared than most for dealing with this part of Southern politics; however, the continuing, constant, almost casual demands of racial politics were increasingly burdensome. He says that an inner-voice nagged him during those times: "I often wondered . . . Am I a 'good guy' fighting the right causes? Or am I becoming just another Southern political hack?"

Thus we readily acknowledge the unsavory downside of traditional Southern politics in which our touted stealth politicians were embedded. We hope the reader eventually will agree that, considered within the nature of their situations, these stealthy leaders pursued acceptable compromise between "doing what's right" and "doing what works" during those historic times.

To conclude this cautionary discussion, we have acknowledged some broad unseemly tendencies and unsavory realities of Southern politics, and we have admitted the sometimes shadowy environs and ways of our stealthy politicians.

However, in our opinion, significant credit goes to those practical political leaders and activists—white and black—who helped restructure Southern elections and governance in moderate, progressive directions. They crafted a more savory and seemly politics, and the South did undergo fundamental political change during that period. Their stealthy service may have been tentative and transient, but during the 1970s, 1980s, and 1990s these politicians and activists helped close the curtain on the Old South, and they contributed greatly to the more positive aspects of a new system in this century.

An Amendment to the Race Game and Southern History

We present this thesis as a timely and critical amendment to the traditional race game and more recent Southern politics. As pointed out in the introduction, most Americans, and even Southerners themselves, have only a hazy understanding of black-white political relations in this region in response to the civil rights movement. Furthermore, scholars have ignored important realities of quiet, practical, biracial politics in the South during the rest of the twentieth century. As the 2008 presidential campaign so clearly and painfully demonstrated, public misunderstanding, ignorance, and raw sensitivities about the past woefully handicap any attempt to resolve America's continuing racial dilemma in the twenty-first century. We believe that our research will begin filling this gaping hole in Southern and national political history.

Gerald Johnson, longtime Auburn political scientist and a Browder ally, agrees that the stealth project is a provocative, daunting, but worthy effort.

> Following the provision of legal rights for black minorities in the South, what remained, and still remains to some degree in some areas, was and is the implementation of those rights. No doubt, the accommodation of mutual interests through relatively quiet quid pro quo arrangements played a positive role in this process. The attempt, however difficult, modest, and limited, to construct and tell in formal terms this untold part of history is a powerful addition to both the civil rights literature and the literature of Southern politics.[28]

Actually, according to Dr. Johnson, "Stealth Reconstruction" is simply reconceptualization of an age-old process of accommodating marginal groups for very practical reasons. However, in this case, the accommodations are different in scope because they deal positively with a newly enfranchised set of players—black minorities—in the context of sweeping social, cultural, historic, economic, and political change:

> I suspect that members of every community in the South knew about and can tell about some quiet accommodators who helped make things work during that period. But, I further suspect, most of the common talk is about the uglier aspects of the process, not to its contributions to the continuing evolution and development of the civil rights struggle and to Southern politics. Thus, "Stealth Reconstruction" can help us better understand the political history of this region.

Dr. Johnson, who now directs the Capital Survey Research Center in Montgomery, cautions about some sensitive ramifications of historical reconceptualization; he particularly warns against the depiction of "white-hat" Caucasians supplanting African Americans as the heroes of the civil rights movement. But having stated that concern, he sees this project as an important part of contemporary public dialogue:

> I think just the idea that the quiet, accommodating laborer in the vineyard contributed in substantive and substantial ways to the evolution of civil rights and Southern politics gives comfort and encouragement and hope today. The need for such service is as great now, if not greater, because the issues of Southern society are so much more subtle and complex.

Our stealth thesis, then, is an unconventional pronouncement and conceptual model that merits further consideration and investigation. We hope that the candid reflections in this chapter add credence and context to our contention, and in the pages to follow we will provide empirical evidence supporting our theoretical concept.

More specifically, we will address several important questions about stealth leadership, politics, and reconstruction during that era, hoping to raise constructive issues for the future:

1. For openers, a broad, four-part question about stealth leadership in general: Who were these stealth leaders? What did they do? What was the context of their election and service? Were they consciously playing stealth politics? And why did they do it?
2. How did their stealth politics differ from and relate to traditional Southern politics?
3. What, specifically and exactly, did they do, stealthily, in their campaigns and what was the stealthy nature of their public service?
4. How did they balance their stealth politics to appeal to black voters without alienating white constituents?
5. How did their stealth politics pay off in terms of black and white support? And public policy?

6. What were the downsides of stealth politicking?
7. Did these stealth leaders ever feel that they were exploiting black people? Or deceiving white people? And did they ever feel that they were being used—and—abused in the process?
8. What about the black activists—how did they play in this stealth process?
9. Did these stealth leaders and activists actually change Southern politics?
10. Does this stealth phenomenon still work—and what does that tell us about the future of Southern and national politics?

Before dealing with these important questions, however, we need to back up and establish historical background for the Civil Rights Revolution and Stealth Reconstruction.

2

Historical Overview

The South's Enduring Dilemma and Changing Politics

Certainly, at the dawn of the civil rights movement, the race game referenced in the previous chapter defined the South—despite its endearing charms—as a perverse, contorted regional political subculture. "Southern politics" usually meant "white Southern politics" and African Americans were nonexistent in most discussions. Mainstream analysis of the time fretted about whether whites could ever be persuaded to accept Negro participation in governance (or how Negroes could force themselves into the democratic process); few could have foreseen the unlikely phenomenon that we now suggest as a realistic course for addressing the Southern rendition of an American dilemma.

In this chapter, we will discuss the South's stubborn systemic racial problems and changing politics as historical prelude to our hypothetical stealth transformation.[1]

Systemic Problems of Leadership, Race, and Poverty

According to V. O. Key Jr.—a native Texan and perhaps the most insightful analyst of Southern politics at mid-twentieth century—the fundamental flaw of Southern history was a systemic failure of Southern political parties and leadership to address its conjoined problems of race and poverty. As he so famously articulated the thesis in *Southern Politics in State and Nation*:

When all the exceptions are considered, when all the justifications are made, and when all the invidious comparisons are drawn, those of the South and those who love the South are left with the cold, hard fact that the South as a whole has developed no system or practice of political organization and leadership adequate to cope with its problems.[2]

W. J. Cash, parallel with Key in the anthology of Southern historiography, had pitched similar, more colorful ideas about Southern politics in *The Mind of the South*. The North Carolinian particularly targeted the racist one-partyism of his native region:

> The world knows the story of the Democratic Party in the South; how, once violence had opened the way to political action, this party became the institutionalized incarnation of the will to White Supremacy. How, indeed, it ceased to be a party in the South and became the party of the South, a kind of confraternity having in its keeping the whole corpus of Southern loyalties, and so irresistibly commanding the allegiance of faithful whites that to doubt it, to question it in any detail was ipso facto to stand branded as a renegade to race, to country, to God, and to Southern Womanhood.[3]

Key accurately stated, at the dawn of the heroic drama, a daunting challenge for Southern political leaders:

> Obviously, the conversion of the South into a democracy in the sense that the mass of people vote and have a hand in their governance poses one of the most staggering tasks for statesmanship in the western world. The suffrage problems of the South can claim a closer kinship with those of India, of South Africa, or of the Dutch East Indies than with those of, say, Minnesota. Political leadership in the State of New York or California or Ohio simmers down to matters of the rankest simplicity alongside those that must be dealt with in Georgia or Mississippi or Alabama.[4]

As events would demonstrate, the systemic problems of leadership and race (overlapped and exacerbated by poverty) would inflict harsh damage throughout this region for decades to come.

An Intractable Divide Between Whites and Blacks

Even as the civil rights movement shifted into full swing, expert analysts sometimes despaired of success because of the South's intractable segregation and dysfunctional leadership. Donald R. Matthews and James W. Prothro, after extensively and statistically portraying both sides of the region's populace in *Negroes and the New Southern Politics*, worried about the future of Southern democracy. They even referenced the possibility of a racial holocaust:

> In the South today the white leader who contemplates a tentative step toward accommodating Negro demands can expect to be labeled a "nigger-lover"; the Negro who cooperates with white leaders can expect to be labeled an "Uncle Tom." Indeed, we seriously wonder whether a viable political system in the South will be possible, granted the extreme polarization of opinion, without one race being dominated by the other.[5]

Although civil rights leaders, grassroots demonstrators, and the federal government scored effective assaults on the Southern way of life, political developments during those times clearly reflected a worsening racial situation and suggested dismal prospects for bringing blacks and whites together.

In their retrospective look at Southern politics and society of the late 1960s, Earl Black and Merle Black articulated the situation thusly:

> The changing civil rights agenda, widespread white opposition to significant reforms concerning the intermediate color line, and the new black militancy had profound consequences for the major civil rights organizations . . .
>
> Just as black Southerners were beginning to participate in electoral politics in significant numbers, prospects appeared remote for successful biracial coalitions built upon issues of central concern to blacks. In no Southern state were there enough white allies to support a winning liberal politics, much less a radical politics.[6]

Indeed, the civil rights movement played out the 1950s and 1960s as a protracted civil war between advancing blacks and retrenching whites (with most leaders taking sides with their core constituencies), rather than a successful resolution of the South's historical dilemma; there was very little hope for meaningfully reconstructing the Southern political system.

Ironically, as the 1960s drew to a close, despite the United States government's having weighed in with the *Brown* decision, the Civil Rights Act, the Voting Rights Act, the National Guard, and federal registrars/pollwatchers, the national environment for black causes had definitely declined and there was little hope for a new brand of Southern leadership.

In a recounting of that era, Richard K. Scher systematically listed the problems of the declining movement:

> The civil rights movement continued after Selma and the passage of the Voting Rights Act. It continues to this day. But after 1965, it was never quite the same again, for a number of reasons.
>
> In the first place, it was a victim of its own success . . . Next the focus of the civil rights movement shifted . . . Vietnam and its accompanying turmoil began to take over the nation's headlines . . . Related to these concerns was the growing white backlash . . . Finally, the civil rights movement itself became irrevocably split . . . As a result, the direction of the civil rights movement because confused, diffused, uncertain.[7]

As for the possibility of biracial leadership, Scher notes that "some former allies of the movement joined the increasingly shrill black militants, while others became disenchanted and felt that the movement neither wanted nor deserved white support. By the late 1960s and early 1970s, it was almost impossible to tell what civil rights leaders, and the black community—Southern and otherwise—really wanted."[8]

Evidenced Impracticality of Biracial Politics and Progress

Despite historical reality, some white Southern leaders eagerly and openly sought to expand the heroic drama with biracial politics in the 1960s—and the results were disastrous.

Alabama provided a classic example of such ill-fated endeavor in . As we discussed in the previous chapter, Governor George Wallace was constitutionally limited to one term, so he ran his wife, Lurleen, for governor in 1966. Nine men (including two former governors, a former congressman, and a sitting attorney general) also lined up to challenge for the top job in the Heart of Dixie.

Alabama Attorney General Richmond Flowers and former U.S. Congressman Carl Elliott—banking on the addition of 200,000 newly-registered blacks among the 600,000 whites in the Democratic Primary—attempted to end the Wallace Era through the use of biracial coalitions.

Flowers openly sought the black vote by talking about civil rights:

> When I'd speak to black groups I'd tell them, "When I'm governor and you come to Montgomery, you're gonna get jobs, and I don't mean with mops and brooms. You're gonna get good jobs behind desks and typewriters. Not because you're black. You won't get a job in my administration simply because you're black, but you'll never be turned down for a job just because you're black." That was what they wanted to hear, and they'd all cheer and shout.[9]

Flowers was cited by the *New York Times* as "the first major white candidate in modern times to campaign directly among Negroes in the Deep South"; and he was endorsed by the Alabama Democratic Conference and most other black political organizations. Later analysis indicated that he got nine of every ten black votes in the primary.[10]

However, when all was said and done, Lurleen Wallace won the Democratic Primary with more votes (54 percent) than all nine male opponents combined; Richmond Flowers was a distant second, with only 18 percent of the record turnout.

Flowers himself acknowledged his miscalculation of the Alabama political situation:

> That was my biggest disappointment in politics. When I ran for governor, I was thoroughly confident. My polls had told me, with the

black vote I was going to receive, I could win with a small percent of the whites. That's one time I was completely wrong. I took a calculated risk and lost. I thought I had it figured, but I didn't . . . I guess I should have kept talking about the Southern Way of Life.[11]

Carl Elliott, a respected, moderate congressman of that time, likewise described his quixotic adventure in biracial politics as an ill-fated and career-killing experience; we'll let the late leader talk at length because his message has particular relevance to our thesis and case study:

> It wasn't the Wallaces I worried about as that campaign hit full tilt in April. It was Richmond Flowers. By that time, everyone knew Lurleen was going to finish first in the primary. A vote for her was a vote for George, and there were more votes for George than anyone else in Alabama. The real race was to finish a strong enough second to force a runoff. To finish that strongly, I knew I had to have the black vote.[12]

While Flowers concentrated on black votes, Elliott attempted a biracial campaign.

> Meanwhile I went about courting blacks and whites alike, refusing to go to either extreme for the votes of one or the other. I summarized my stance in a speech in Selma: "I have not come to Selma tonight to stand on the Edmund Pettus Bridge and shout 'Never!' Nor have I come to stand in the Brown's Chapel AME Church and sing 'We Shall Overcome.' There must be a middle ground for Alabamians."
>
> In the middle is just where I found myself as the black political organizations in the state moved toward endorsing a candidate. Richmond Flowers had done exactly what I'd mentioned in my speech, joining hands with black leaders in the Brown's Chapel Church and singing "We Shall Overcome" with them. And they were responding to him as the alternative to George Wallace.

Elliott's pitch for black votes was, he felt, honest and straightforward.

I didn't cozy up to them, I didn't back away either. When I made a speech in the town square in a place called Greenville, three times as many black people were in the crowd as white. When my talk was done, I shook hands with the crowd, black and white alike. Then I went inside to pay my respects to the probate judge, who hadn't come out to hear my speech. I began to thank him for the privilege of speaking at his courthouse when he suddenly cut me off.

"You," he said, as if pronouncing judgment from the bench, "have violated Southern tradition, shaking hands with those niggers."

. . .

As I was walking away, this judge came out and hollered right there in front of the crowd, "You've gone around and shaken hands with these niggers! No white man's ever done that around here before."

I turned and said, "Well, this is a new kind of day, and I'm a new kind of white man."[13]

Elliott's politics played well in sympathetic circles—he eventually was honored as the first recipient of the John F. Kennedy "Profiles in Courage" award in 1990. However, in Alabama of the 1960s, he scored little respect among either white or black voters, finishing way back in third place (with only 8 percent), struggling with painful memories of a biracial campaign, virtual financial ruin, and the end of a celebrated, productive public career.

William R. Keech, who studied varying impacts of voting and other political actions in Southern communities of that time, speculated that the problems of blacks perhaps were unfixable through electoral democracy:

The real problem is much deeper than these tactical considerations imply. The tragedy of American racial history is that it has left the Negro with more problems than men of good-will are able to solve. Votes, litigation and even the threat of violence are useful because they can influence the behavior of elected policy-makers. The most frustrating problem of the American Negro in politics is that even if elected policy-makers were totally responsive to Negro demands, it is not at all clear that they have it in their power to eliminate the inequality with which three and a half centuries of discrimination have saddled the American Negro.[14]

Thus, apparently, the concerns of early analysts about biracial politics were well founded; the heroic struggle seemed to be running out of steam.

Surprisingly, however, the Old South changed. Despite several centuries of entrenched racism and biracial electoral disasters of the 1960s, Southern politics began evolving in different manner in the 1970s.

Some may debate the merits of the subsequent pace and direction of Southern politics, but the South began—haltingly and stubbornly and constantly pressed by black civil rights groups and the U.S. Justice Department—to address its historical dilemma. As will be shown in the rest of this chapter, the system functionally adjusted in the 1970s, 1980s, and 1990s to incorporate black participation and move toward biracial progress, cultural moderation, and relatively normal politics.[15]

The South's Cultural Journey of Moderation and Convergence

While the South is still divided, racially, on important political attitudes and partisan inclinations, there is expansive public opinion research showing, with some obvious variations, a blending cultural journey of internal and external dynamics: (a) white Southerners have moderated their views about race and civil rights significantly over the years; (b) there has been substantial Southern convergence with the American nation in terms of racial ideas and behavior.

We should note up front, of course, that racial history still dominates Southern culture. J. David Woodard writes about the continuing interplay of black-white issues in *The New Southern Politics* (2007):

> Racial conflict between black and white has always been the most visible negation of whatever was commendable about the South. No matter how much one admired Southern virtues, be they the genteel manners, bravery in battle, or courage in defeat—there was always the memory of slavery, sharecropper tenancy, and white supremacy. For every word of forgiveness by a leader like Martin Luther King Jr. there was a Southern politician like Ben Tillman or Lester Maddox who needed exoneration.

The debate as to how much of Southern politics is governed by class divisions, as opposed to racial ones, continues. One thing is clear, the legacy of white supremacy was the abiding memory of life in the region, and its presence was all the more paradoxical given the deep Christian religious practices in evidence in Southern communities.[16]

This historical legacy of racial conflict is reflected in contemporary patterns of partisan affiliation, as reported by Earl Black and Merle Black in *The Rise of Southern Republicans*:

> Without question the racial divide remains the most important partisan cleavage in the South. Blacks are by far the most united of the three racial/ethnic groups. Favoring Democrats over Republicans by 87 to 10 percent, the extraordinary cohesion of Southern blacks resembles in magnitude and intensity the traditional Democratic attachments of Southern whites. White Southerners, by contrast, are now far more likely (53 to 27 percent) to be classified as core Republicans than as core Democrats.[17]

When we turn our attention to regional-national convergence, the research suggests impressive change (among otherwise mingled data and patterns of continuity). According to Robert P. Steed, Laurence W. Moreland, and Tod A. Baker in *Southern Parties and Elections: Studies in Regional Political Change*, "What does seem relatively clear is that the most noticeable nationalization of Southern politics has occurred, and continues to occur, in the region's political institutions and structures (for example, the party system, the legal system, the structures of influence in Congress)." On the other hand, they then reported data attesting to continued regional differences with regard to school prayer, religion, labor unions, and military policy. Furthermore, they said, "the role of race in Southern politics lingers on, albeit in different form."[18]

Patrick R. Cotter, Stephen D. Shaffer, and David A. Breaux more recently surveyed the Southern opinion literature, and they found comprehensive evidence of positive change. Their 2006 review showed that white Southern support for the principle of racial equality had increased over time and had reached a high level of support for this position; moreover, they concluded that South-nonSouth differences in attitudes and behaviors were declining:

> Overall, research in this area generally shows that white Southern-ers are different from their counterparts in other regions, although the differences in racial attitudes between white Southerners and others are diminishing . . .
>
> For example, in 1942, 2 percent of Southern whites, compared to 42 percent of nonSouthern whites, said that black and white children should go to the same rather than separate schools . . . During the last half century support for school integration has increased throughout the country, and differences in opinions between the South and the North have diminished, though they have not disappeared. Thus, by 1985, about 86 percent of white Southerners and 96 percent of white nonSoutherners favored white and black children's going to the same school.[19]

Cotter, Shaffer, and Breaux also found little regional difference regarding ideology and social welfare. They did detect differences in terms of toler-ance and cultural issues (crime, gender roles, morality, and school prayer), although those differences seemed to be declining.

The Pew Research Center provided an equally interesting picture of the latest generation of white Southerners, for whom the heroic drama is only a fading memory or homework assignment.[20] The Pew survey, comparing 1987–88 and 2002–03 data, showed that, while black-white differences continue, there has been remarkable convergence between white Southern-ers and nonSoutherners:

The South remains a more conservative region on racial issues, but the differences between the South and rest of the country are narrowing. Over the past generation, a declining percentage of Southern whites view discrimina-tion as rare and fewer say they have little in common with people of other races, decreasing or eliminating the regional gap on these questions.

We conclude this discussion by acknowledging serious opinion differ-ences between blacks and whites in this region. Attitudinal progress among Southerners over the past few decades has been a piecemeal process, and racism still permeates many aspects of Southern culture. But we suspect that most scholars would agree that the problem has greatly mitigated since the civil rights movement.

We maintain, furthermore, that these blended patterns of cultural moderation and convergence correlate to fundamentally changing regional politics. In the rest of this chapter, we will focus on the more politically pertinent aspects of the Southern system during the 1970s, 1980s, and 1990s.

An Established Record of Normalization and Transformation

When we shift attention from public opinion to more consequential activities, we find a full body of scholarship documenting new national, regional, and local patterns—reflecting black empowerment and, in some cases, biracial politics—in the latter decades of the twentieth century. The Southern political system shifted significantly toward the normal practices of broader American democracy.

PARTISAN AND RACIAL ADJUSTMENT: Particularly clear is a new Southern political order shaped by party and racial developments; these adjustments in turn have impacted the American political system.

Earl Black and Merle Black summarized the regional dynamics in *The Rise of Southern Republicans*:

> The old Southern politics was transparently undemocratic and thoroughly racist. "Southern political institutions," as V. O. Key Jr. demonstrated, were deliberately constructed to subordinate "the Negro population and, externally, to block threatened interferences from the outside with the local arrangements." By protecting white supremacy, Southern Democrats in Congress institutionalized massive racial injustice for generations. Eventually the civil rights movement challenged the South's racial status quo and inspired a national political climate in which Southern Democratic senators could no longer kill civil rights legislation. Led by President Lyndon B. Johnson of Texas, overwhelming majorities of northern Democrats and northern Republicans united to enact the Civil Rights Act of 1964 and the Voting Rights Act of 1965. Landmark federal

intervention reformed Southern race relations and helped destabilize the traditional one-party system. In the fullness of time the Democratic party's supremacy gave way to genuinely competitive two-party politics.[21]

Charles S. Bullock and Mark J. Rozell similarly summarized these developments in *The New Politics of the Old South: An Introduction to Southern Politics*:

> When V. O. Key (1949) published *Southern Politics*, the region was solidly Democratic. No Republican had been elected U.S. senator or governor in decades, and a generation had passed since a republican collected a single Electoral College vote. For most of a century after Reconstruction, the South provided the foundation on which the national Democratic Party rested. When the party was in eclipse in the rest of the country, little more than the Southern foundation could be seen. During periods of Democratic control of the presidency and Congress, as in the New Deal era, the South made a major contribution. After the 2004 election, the Democratic Party in the South had been reduced to its weakest position in more than 130 years. Today Republicans win the bulk of the white vote, dominate the South's presidential and congressional elections and control half the state legislative chambers.[22]

Furthermore, they note, the South's racial situation evolved dramatically.

> Key's South had an electorate in which Republicans were rare and blacks even scarcer. While he observed that "in its grand outlines the politics of the South revolves around the position of the Negro," it was not a commentary on black political influence, which was non-existent, but rather an acknowledgment that the region expended much political capital to keep African Americans away from the levers of power. Since implementation of the 1965 Voting Rights Act, black votes have become the mainstay of the Democratic Party—the vote without which few Democrats can win statewide. The votes cast by African Americans have helped

elect a black governor (Virginia's Douglas Wilder), eighteen members of Congress, and hundreds of legislators and local officials.

Partisan change and black mobilization have not been continuous but have come at different paces in various locales and for different offices. Nonetheless, the changes have been massive.[23]

Black and Black have also noted how these developments impacted the national party system:

> The collapse of the solid Democratic South and the emergence of Southern Republicanism, first in presidential politics and later in elections for Congress, have established a new reality for America: two permanently competitive national political parties. Not since Democrats battled Whigs before the Civil War has there been such a thoroughly nationalized two-party system.[24]

Stanley P. Berard forecasts important consequences not only for Southern politics but also for our national future:

> The particular mix of constituency perspectives offered by "the newest Southern politics" gives a measure of diversity to both the Republican caucus and the Congressional Black Caucus, even if that diversity does not show itself clearly in aggregated roll call votes. The prospect that biracial coalitions will continue to provide a base for electing some numbers of white Southern Democrats has implications not only for the diversity of representation in Congress but also for partisan control. Understanding Southern politics continues to be an essential element of anticipating and explaining change in Congress.[25]

BLACK EMPOWERMENT: A central factor in this reconfiguration of Southern politics, of course, has been increasing black participation and empowerment. In a recent survey statement, John A. Clark cited the transformational role played by African Americans in the region's politics over the past few decades:

The political implications of these trends also have reshaped the South from what it was at the time of Key's work. Most notable, perhaps are the increases in black elected officials (almost all of them Democrats) and the development of a competitive (and sometimes dominant) Republican Party. Both were almost nonexistent in Key's time, especially in the Deep South states. Today African Americans and Republicans have all but crowded out the formerly dominant white Democrats in many areas.[26]

The most direct and comprehensive research on black participation was *Quiet Revolution in the South: The Impact of the Voting Rights Act, 1965–1990*, by Chandler Davidson, Bernard Grofman, and a top-notch team of experts from several practices and disciplines. According to their chapter on black and white voter registration, written by political scientist James E. Alt, there has been a remarkable transformation of the Southern electorate:[88]

> Consequently, it may safely be said that the Voting Rights Act trans-formed the basis of the Southern electoral system, inasmuch as it was the vehicle for destroying the institutional barriers to black registration. . Between 1972 and 1988, a pattern of racial mobilization and countermo-bilization, now possibly in decline, produced a reasonably stable system characterized by a ubiquitous but eroding white numerical registration advantage. The decline in this advantage raised the very real possibility of convergence in white and black registration rates as a percentage of eligible white and black voters, respectively, sometime in the 1990s. If and when that happens, the transformation of the Southern registration system that the act began will be complete.[27]

Additionally, the Alabama chapter, by practitioners Peyton McCrary, Jerome A. Gray, Edward Still, and Huey L. Perry, provided especially interesting results affirming gains in the Heart of Dixie through litigated provisions of the VRA (1994):

> As long as at-large elections were in place, white majorities voting as a bloc were able to prevent black citizens enfranchised by the Voting

Rights Act from winning local office. Most changes from at-large to district elections in Alabama resulted either from litigation or, to a lesser degree, objections by the Department of Justice. Although lawsuits won by the department played a key role in eliminating at-large elections in various black-belt counties, most of the changes were due to litigation by private attorneys. These changes substantially increased minority representation on local governing bodies, both rural and urban. Indeed, black representation in our sample has now reached the level of proportional representation in Alabama.[28]

Chandler and Davidson concluded that the VRA had indeed accomplished a "Second Reconstruction":

> When we began this research, we thought it would demonstrate the success of the Voting Rights Act in changing minority representation in the South. In particular, we anticipated that many Southern jurisdictions, with a substantial black population and a history of very limited black officeholding would have adopted district or mixed plans as a result of litigation, leading to large gains in minority representation. This is exactly what we found.[29]

Bullock and Rozell provided additional assessment of black registration:

> Shortly after implementation of the 1965 Voting Rights Act, black registration jumped. Only 29 percent of the region's voting-age blacks were registered in 1962; six years later the figure exceeded 60 percent. The most pronounced changes came in states that had been most repressive with the share of age-eligible blacks registered rising from 19 to 52 percent in Alabama and from 7 to 60 percent in Mississippi. In recent years registration and turnout rates among blacks have almost equaled those of whites.[30]

They also showed the VRA's impact on Southern state legislatures:

In addition to helping elect white Democrats, the black electorate has also contributed to a growing number of African American office-holders. Figure 1.4 shows the increase in the number of black legislators in the South from a scant thirty-five in 1969, of whom fourteen served in Georgia. In 2001, the most recent enumeration, more than 300 African Americans sat in Southern legislatures. Most of the increase followed a redistricting that created additional heavily black districts. Two-thirds of the growth in black representation occurred within two elections of the 1970, 1980 and 1990 elections.[31]

And in Washington:

Creating districts with black concentrations also opened the way for the first black Democrats in Congress from the South. In 1972, Atlanta and Houston districts redrawn to be over 40 percent black elected Andy Young and Barbara Jordan. Two years later Harold Ford won a 47 percent black Memphis district. The 1980s saw the election of Mike Espy from the Mississippi Delta, and when Lindy Boggs retired, William Jefferson succeeded to her New Orleans district. The 1992 redistricting sent a dozen new black members to join the five African Americans representing the South.[32]

COALITIONAL POLITICS: Our concern in this project, of course, is bi-racial representation; and the evidence clearly supports the development of coalition politics—mainly in the Democratic Party. David Lublin explained this phenomenon interestingly in a recent textbook on the Republican South; he said that the civil rights movement had, in a sense, liberated white Southern Democratic leaders to seek biracial solutions to stubborn historical problems:

One of the wonderful political results of the changes of the 1960s is that it allowed Southerners to focus on issues besides the racial organization of their society . . . Moreover, once African Americans began voting in large numbers, Democratic candidates had extremely strong incentives to turn the focus away from race even as they quietly abandoned conservative positions on racial issues.[33]

Bullock and Rozell provided follow-up observation about the impact of biracial relationships in the new Southern politics:

> Even when black votes are insufficient to elect an African American, successful white Democrats depend heavily on this component of their electorates. This reliance makes Democratic legislators more responsive to black policy concerns and has largely eliminated the traditional Southern conservative Democrat from Congress.[34]

A similar impact was noted by Earl Black and Merle Black in the changing character of racial representation over the last three decades of the century:

> Democratic conservatism declined because it was increasingly incompatible with the theory and practice of biracial politics. The new realities affected both veterans and newcomers . . . All these Democrats understood the necessity of demonstrably supporting their party in order to promote their institutional careers and sustain their biracial coalitions at home.[35]

The transformation was not limited to Congress. Alexander Lamis found in *Southern Politics in the 1990s* that white Southern Democratic governors were appealing to both blacks and white voters during the previous few decades:

> These leaders—Jimmy Carter in Georgia in 1970 was one of the pioneers—proceeded in the 1970s and 1980s to assemble potent coalitions of nearly all blacks and those whites who had weathered the integration crisis with their Democratic voting inclinations intact. These ideologically diverse, black white Democratic coalitions became a central feature of the South's politics in the post-civil rights era.[36]

Equally remarkable, according to Lamis, was the stability of those Democratic coalitions in dealing with issues that had plagued the party for many years:

> These tensions are not new. The diverse black-white Democratic coali-
> tion that took hold in the South in the post-civil rights era has grappled
> with them for several decades and continues to do so. In the Southern
> elections of the 1990s, however, this coalition has not collapsed either at
> the voter or the leadership level . . . A moment's reflection on the details
> of the major two-party statewide contests of the 1990s as described in the
> state chapters should substantiate the continued endurance of the coalition
> as it underwent its severest test yet in the two-party era.[37]

SUBSTANTIVE REPRESENTATION: The bottom-line measure of changing Southern politics goes beyond black voting and office-holding to more substantive questions of representation: Does it make any difference in terms of the interests and lives of black Southerners?

Increasingly, research demonstrates a positive answer to this question. Political scientist Mary Herring demonstrated statistically that by the 1980s the black vote was impacting state politicians of both races in this region. Her analysis of roll-call votes in the Alabama, Georgia, and Louisiana legislatures concluded:

> Although this study presents only a static picture of three Southern
> state legislatures, it does suggest that fundamental changes have occurred
> in the political process of the American South. By far the most important
> finding is the consistent influence of black constituencies on legislative
> outcomes . . . The strategy of the civil rights movement, focused on ob-
> taining the vote, has begun to obtain significant representational benefits
> for black voters.[38]

Charles E. Menifield and Stephen D. Shaffer have provided comprehensive corroboration of state level transformation throughout the region in *Politics in the New South: Representation of African Americans in Southern*

State Legislatures. In structured, team investigation of Arkansas, Florida, Georgia, Mississippi, and Texas (along with an overview of the other Southern states), they showed definite progress in descriptive representation and mixed gains in substantive representation of African American Southerners during the 1980s–90s:

> First, as we enter the twenty-first century, it is quite clear that African Americans in Southern state legislature are enjoying some notable electoral and legislative successes. Relative to twenty years ago, African Americans comprise a greater percentage of the membership of Southern state legislatures in twenty of the twenty-two chambers studied, thereby reducing the gap in descriptive representation between the African American state populations and their presence in state legislative bodies. . .[39]

Substantive success has been less striking—Menifield and Shaffer assert "many successes, but also some disappointments."[40] They report that the black minority in this region succeeded 71 percent of the time on roll-call votes, compared to 95 percent among white Democrats and 62 percent among Republicans; and the authors suggest, based on assessments of other factors, that "the Black Caucus success level is more impressive than it might appear on the surface."[41]

Moreover, they noted a practice of effective alliances with a variety of key political players:

> Lastly, it is evident that African Americans, despite their generally liberal philosophy in a more conservative region of the nation, have been politically astute in forming coalitions in Southern state legislatures. Normally they form winning coalitions with fellow Democrats who are white, and who today exhibit basically "centrist" viewpoints relative to the white segregations of the decades past. However, on occasion, African Americans have formed coalitions with Republican lawmakers, or even backed a Republican gubernatorial candidate if discontented with their treatment by white Democratic colleagues.[42]

Some Interesting Personal Perspectives

More interesting have been the personal stories and biographies of progressive participants about how things have changed in the South as a result of the civil rights movement. The following remarks (from prominent black civil rights leaders, all native Alabamians) demonstrate imperfect but responsive change, and a certain sense of personal pride, in the new Southern politics. We'll present their positive comments first, followed by their criticisms and challenges.

The most ironic testimony comes from John Lewis, now an Atlanta congressman, a Selma-Montgomery marcher who was beaten on the Edmund Pettus Bridge, a former Freedom Rider whose family still lives in Alabama. Lewis articulated a strong message of positive change in his recent biography, *Walking with the Wind: A Memoir of the Movement*:

> No one, but no one, who was born in America forty or fifty or sixty years ago and who grew up and came through what I came through, who witnessed the changes I witnessed, can possibly say that America is not a far better place than it was. We live in a different country than the one I grew up in. The South is different . . . So many things are better . . . There is no denying the distance we have come.[43]

Fred Gray, attorney for Dr. King and Mrs. Parks and a giant of the Alabama civil rights movement, focused on legal changes in his autobiography, *Bus Ride to Justice: Changing the System by the System*:

> I have watched the appellate courts in Alabama in recent years, particularly the Alabama Supreme Court. In my opinion, we now have a court that demonstrates respect for the constitution and laws of not only the State of Alabama but also the United States of America. I feel very comfortable in appearing before our appellate courts and arguing state law questions or federal constitutional issues, and I feel that the courts will rule on the issues in accordance with the law, regardless of the parties and regardless of race, creed or national origin . . .
>
> Power has been utilized in the movement to change society from total

segregation to one which is becoming ever more just. We are not there yet, but we are moving in that direction. I believe that the success of the legal cases that I have been involved in speaks well for democracy and for the Constitution. It shows that one can use the system, abide by its rules and regulations, and change society.[44]

Similar positive and personal reflections were expressed by J. L. Chestnut Jr., a Selma native and respected pioneer of Alabama's civil rights battles, in concluding his autobiography, *Black in Selma: The Uncommon Life of J. L Chestnut, Jr.*:

> On the ride home from Opelika that Martin Luther King's birthday, though, I felt pretty good. I slowly crossed the Edmund Pettus Bridge at sunset. There was Selma. The Times-Journal. City Hall. Our law firm. I reflected back on my return to Selma on the same road in 1958. From the vantage point of how things used to be, the present is not so discouraging. When I stop and look back, I see the many barriers that have fallen and the great distance we have traveled. Remember, I started out thinking we'd be making substantial progress if we could just get a string of black-owned supermarkets in the Black Belt. It's disappointing that we don't have them, but, in context, this was a modest goal. We've gone beyond where I even dared imagine—black people and white people.
>
> I see my own life as helping to realize the dream in my world in Alabama. Though I never imagined I'd spend my whole life in little Selma, I don't know of a better place I could have taken a stand. Selma is my home. I love Selma. It's my life.[45]

Now for their criticisms and challenges, comments that soberly frame their positive assessments.

John Lewis:
> But there is a mistaken assumption among many that these signs of progress mean that the battle is over, that the struggle for civil rights is finished, that the problems of segregation were solved in the 60s and now

all we have to deal with are economic issues. This is preposterous.[46]

Fred Gray:

However, one of the most disheartening observations I have made over the years is that most of the persons who made up what we called the white power structure have never gone beyond doing exactly what the courts have ordered.[47]

And J. L. Chestnut:

We are far from the world envisioned by King in his "I have a Dream" speech. We are closer to it, but getting there will continue to be a struggle. People forget that King said near the end of that speech, "I [now] go back to the South"—meaning to implement the dream of freedom and justice for all by marches, boycotts, and other means the establishment detested. I see King, at the expense of his life, striving to realize the dream, not just pleasantly dreaming.[48]

John Fleming, a native white Alabamian and editor-at-large of the *Anniston Star*, has spent considerable time exploring and writing about the Black Belt; and he paints a similar picture of civil and subtle change in the hardcore Deep South.[49] After several days in Selma, for example, he said that the struggle for black political empowerment has been won; the city has a black mayor and a majority-black city council. He also describes contemporary race relations there as complex, healing, sometimes festering, forever evolving, never clear-cut, but something worth studying by and for the rest of us.

Today, traveling up U.S. 80 from Montgomery, along the route of the historic march, past the sprawling fields and pastures of the Black Belt, across the bridge and into town, one finds an immeasurably more peaceful Selma. It's a more civil and subtle place.[50]

Race is still at the heart of the town known as the cradle of racial intolerance, according to Fleming. "It bubbles below the surface; its undercurrents touch nearly every aspect of life." But he reports that steady progress has been made since the 1960s.

> Then, people of authority and those of the street spat the utterances of racism into the faces of fellow humans. Worse, people died for seeking equality and for helping others to achieve it.
>
> In today's Selma—a place that carries a heavy burden for the injustices and for the behavior of some of its citizens so long ago and that sticks in the consciousness of the nation as a marker of an unacceptable level of inhumanity—a sort of racial healing seems to be taking place among a festering that in many ways can be a lesson to the rest of the world.[51]

Here's another journalistic perspective—writ large to cover the state generally—from Frye Gaillard, a Mobile native and journalist who had reported the civil rights movement in his younger days:

> I write, inevitably, as a person who is white, with whatever limitations that may imply. But I also write as an Alabama native who lived through the times, who covered the civil rights movement as a journalist, and who has attempted to bring a storyteller's eye to the powerful recollections of the people in the trenches. I have tried to be fair—even to the people with whom I disagree—but I make no claim to objectivity. I am proud of Alabama's role in the story. A state once known as the Cradle of the Confederacy can now make its case as the cradle of freedom—arguably the most important piece of geography in the most important movement of our times.[52]

Gaillard's personal observation punctuates a message of harsh lessons and continuing change.

> Maybe there was something in the Alabama soil, or maybe there was a certain quality of leadership—white as well as black—that made for a powerful clash of ideas, that made us ask who we really want to be. Whatever the realities of unfinished business, the answer we are able to

give today is different from the one of fifty years ago.

All of us ought to be happy about that. But none of us should ever forget what it cost.[53]

"A Message from the Chairman" about Racial Change

Presented here, in its entirety, is a directly-relevant statement of significant change produced by aggressive civil rights action and black-white political partnering. Dr. Joe Reed (one of the region's most powerful and effective champions of biracial practicality during the reconstructive era) posted the following statement as his chairman's message on the Alabama Democratic Conference website in 2003. The message relates specifically to the ADC and Alabama; but we suspect it reflects systemic progress wrought by practical black and white leaders, working together, throughout the South.

The rise of the Alabama Democratic Conference (ADC) to a place of preeminence in Alabama has truly been a remarkable one. Founded in 1960 by a small group of committed leaders to support the Kennedy-Johnson presidential ticket, the organization has steadily grown in size, reputation, and influence to become one of the most effective voices in Alabama politics today. Indeed, few political groups can match ADC's record of success when it comes to bringing about fair and equitable representation of blacks.

Check our record. In Alabama blacks constitute 25 percent of the state's population. Black officials are well represented on most governing bodies in Alabama today. This is due largely to a comprehensive legislative and legal strategy that ADC embarked upon over the years. When ADC was founded in 1960, there were less than 10 black elected officials. In 2002, Alabama has more than 800 black elected officials statewide. Presently, black officials compromise 25 percent of the state legislature; 24 percent of the county commissions; 24 percent of local school boards; 25 percent of the state school board; and 20 percent of the membership on city councils. Black representation on the State Democratic Executive Committee stands at over 40 percent, due largely to ADC's active recruitment and influence. Also during the last two Democratic National

Conventions Alabama had one of the highest percentages of black delegates in attendance, when compared to other states.

Although getting blacks elected to every chamber in government has been one of ADC's goals, the organization's history has been marked by consistent, widespread support for hundreds of white candidates who have been sensitive to the needs of blacks and poor people. ADC is proud of the fact that few Democratic officials have assumed office in this state without directly or indirectly being influenced by the work and policies of the organization.

In short, ADC's organized network of voting members, coupled with civic pressure, has brought about significant social change. The State Democratic Party changed its racist slogan. Recalcitrant candidates stopped using racial slurs in their campaigns and began to court and respect the black vote. Without question, ADC has made politicians behave, mainly by holding to three basic operating principles: 1) there is nothing that is politically right that is morally wrong; 2) there is political strength through unity; and 3) of all crimes, the worst one politically is ingratitude.[54]

These scholarly and personal accounts—coming mainly from Southerners of both races—demonstrate that the South is a substantially different society from the old days.

White Culture and Black Politics in a Changing South

Unfortunately, the academic community has been deficient in explaining these historical developments beyond general analysis and statistical tables. It is very difficult for scholars, writing from above and afar, to explore critical human aspects—such as the personalized comments of John Lewis, Fred Gray, J. L. Chestnut Jr., John Fleming, and Frye Gaillard in the previous section—that help us make sense of positive change in the latter part of the century.

Consequently, current analysts often miss essential insights into what really happened, how, and why over the past half-century. Surely, the cooling clash of heroes-versus-villains did not magically cleanse the Southern way of life; laws and decrees by themselves did not soften the tone of Southern political discourse; and certainly the surge of black voters, in-migration from other regions, and other societal factors did not automatically translate into new styles of politics and public service in the South. Nor can we accept—as applicable across the region—case studies about the public politics of a relatively few New South leaders and black elected officials of that period.

Comprehending Southern change may require us to reconsider standard historical generalizations about Southern politics. We may have to step back, away from the pronouncements of Cash and Key, away from the stark, white-black drama of the movement portrayed by activist scholars and the media. While those works were valuable for the time, they produced a single-minded, deterministic picture that obscured meaningful patterns and potential for an alternative future. We need to view the South as a more complex region than was depicted in earlier research.

One first step toward understanding the changed South is to revisit earlier assessments of Southern culture and public life in the 1950s and 1960s. More recent scholarship has attempted such reconsideration and provides differing perspective and evidence about the white Southern mindset and black activities back then. Apparently, despite the heat of those times, the white South was not as rigidly, universally, or permanently resistant to racial change as had been assumed in mainstream accounts of the heroic struggle; and, in the other camp, as the national drama abated, black Southerners were ready to proceed in more practical pursuits.

Conflicted Complexities of the Southern White Populace

Way back in the 1960s, Lewis Killian and Charles Grigg had suggested, through the discerning eyes of Southern sociologists, that Old South society was less monolithic than normally suspected and depicted.[55] Now, contemporary research is demonstrating that Southerners of that era, while comfortable with their regional racial arrangement, were a mixed lot when it came to attitudes about the civil rights movement and the future of Southern life.

Matthew D. Lassiter is one of a growing breed of young historians revisiting conventional interpretations of Southern society.[56] The University of Michigan professor grew up in middle-class, suburban Atlanta; he says that his people, his parents and grandparents, have been ignored in most historical analysis. "There were a few white Southerners who were liberals, a larger number throwing the rocks with the rioters, and the vast group in the middle were left out of the story."[57]

Perhaps the most exhaustive and useful acknowledgment of the nuanced political world of white Southerners back then is Jason Sokol's recent historiography of that period, *There Goes My Everything: White Southerners in the Age of Civil Rights, 1945–75*. Sokol—who, ironically, was born and grew up in Massachusetts, attended Oberlin College and the University of California, Berkeley, and now lives in Brooklyn, New York—has documented, in sober yet fascinating manner, the ambiguities and antagonisms afflicting most Southerners of that time. After examining historical records, letters, and publications of the civil rights era, Sokol concluded that many whites generally and purposefully lived their lives outside the whirlwind of the heroic drama:

> Most white Southerners identified neither with the civil rights movement nor with its violent resisters. They were fearful, silent, and often inert. The prominent events of the era—the 1955 Montgomery bus boycott, the 1960 student sit-ins, the Birmingham church bombing in 1963, the Selma-to-Montgomery march of 1965, for example—often had less meaning than the changes in the texture of day-to-day life.[58]

Furthermore, they found various ways to muddle through the experience that completely altered their world:

> When the civil rights movement tore through the Southern landscape in the 1950s and 1960s, it challenged the attitudes of millions, undermined their customs, and upended their ways of life . . . In the end, few escaped its long reach. Some white Southerners attested to liberating experiences that forever altered their racial attitudes and behavior. Others found new ways to resist racial equality. Many more clung to any sense of normalcy they could salvage, at times willfully ignorant of the tumult around them.[59]

Sokol pronounced the South's race troubles as a white problem; however, he presented a picture of white Southern society of the 1950s and 1960s that was not nearly as monolithic or hardcore racist as had been depicted in the literature of the earlier era. Furthermore, preaching the possibilities of "white liberation," "biracial reconciliation," and "regional redemption," Sokol described, without condescension, a white Southern populace trying to deal with the uncertain contours of fundamental change:

> The South in the 1970s was a society remarkably similar to that of Jim Crow times in some respects, yet fundamentally transformed in others. Even for those who resisted, change continued to seep into life. At times its arrival was sudden; more often it was halting and gradual, and came in fits and starts. When tranquility settled over the sites of the civil rights movement, the work of adjusting to life in a new world finally began.[60]

Furthermore, some whites strove to mitigate reactionary politics, and others contributed as forces of progressive change during the heated 1950s and 1960s. David Chappell has highlighted this atypical white leadership in his retrospective study of racial struggles in Montgomery, Tallahassee, Little Rock, and Albany. He wrote in *Inside Agitators: White Southerners in the Civil Rights Movement*:

> Growing up during the 1960s in what must have been a typical northern white liberal family, I had an image of the white South as one big lynch mob waiting to happen. To me Bull Connor and Sheriff Clark represented the typical, not the exceptional, Southerner. Through the mass media, northern liberals reassured themselves that vicious hatreds and prejudices were vestiges of the Old South, that Dixie remained underdeveloped in the twentieth century, clinging with recalcitrant desperation to outmoded notions. We could not see that Bull Connor represented only one end of a spectrum of Southern white opinion, that there were quieter but equally representative voices at the other end. Nor could we see the vast middle, which was uncertain which way it was being led. Seeing these complexities would make the South, which was a synonym for racial trouble, too

much like our own complex reality. Ignoring them was essential to the notion that racism was somebody else's problem.[61]

According to Chappell, black veterans of the Southern movement (including Coretta King, Charles Gomillion, Ralph Abernathy, Georgia Gilmore, Johnnie Carr, John Lewis, and Hosea Williams) told him that there were white people on their side in most Southern communities of those times. He quoted Andrew Young as saying, "If it hadn't been for the kind of white Southerners you are talking about, the South today would look like Beirut looks today."[62]

Of course, many of us knew all along, or at least suspected, that the early works consisted of overdrawn generalizations; now we have contemporary research and a historical picture that differ substantially from the earlier analyses. White Southerners were not nearly as monolithically and hardcore racist as the mainstream literature suggested; in the other camp, as heated confrontations subsided, some were ready to change their ways and the course of Southern history.

Subtle Dynamics of Southern Black Politics

In addition to revising our views about white Southerners of that era, we need to appreciate subtle strategic dynamics among blacks as they charted their political course toward equal rights.

As we have noted elsewhere, various national factors negatively impacted the movement, and the heroic drama declined during the late 1960s; part of that apparent decline probably was a necessary course adjustment from cosmic movement to more routine political concerns at the community level. Dr. King himself proclaimed in his final SCLC speech (1967) and book (1967) that the national civil rights movement would have to start organizing itself for political action in a thousand different places, mastering the art of political alliances, and taking part in the smoke-filled rooms where debating and bargaining proceed.

Decades later, Stanford historian and King papers editor Clayborne Carson emphasized that same point about the importance of real-world politics to the movement:

To learn from this history, however, we must begin to understand the civil rights movement not as moralistic melodrama but as politics. Southern whites were not monolithic and intransigent but divided in ways that are similar to the division among those currently in positions of privilege and power. The ways in which Southern blacks exploited those divisions for their own benefit offer profound lessons for the future.[63]

However, most historical accounts of this "down-shifting" of the civil rights movement overlook important continuities and developments among Southern blacks at the local level. J. Mills Thornton provided useful perspective in his recent study of key racial developments in Alabama, *Dividing Lines: Municipal Politics and the Struggle for Civil Rights in Montgomery, Birmingham, and Selma*:

> In truth, an examination of the Southern communities that generated the direct-action campaigns reveals that the presumed decline of the civil rights movement is far more an artifact of the recounting of history from a national perspective than it is an accurate portrayal of the experience of Southerners during the twentieth century's final three decades. At the level of Southern municipalities, the struggle for civil rights continued to play itself out in numerous electoral contests for town councils, county commissions, and state legislative office and in the debates over measures in those and comparable bodies. In that sense, the death of the civil rights movement has been greatly exaggerated. While the national movement's influence was being curtailed, at this local level the movement remained as significant as ever. It is just that, with reenfranchisement and, frequently, after court-ordered redistricting, direct action took on a less recognizable, more ordinarily American form.[64]

Apparently, Southern black activists were just as focused on local concerns as the heroic drama; and, as national emotions ebbed, they turned to more practical political pursuits in their own communities.[65]

Thus the pertinent line of inquiry, as we reconsider these aspects of Southern history, is a combination of intriguing unknowns—"who, what, where, when, how, and why"—about regional transformation in the 1970s, 1980s, and 1990s. Did a few liberal Davids heroically slay the racist Goliaths? What major battles signaled the triumph of good over evil? How do we account for significant change in Southern politics considering regional history and the still-tense environment of white-versus-black?

As in many historical quandaries, the explanatory reality perhaps was ordinary politics—somehow accommodating both white culture and black interests—rather than mythical conflict and glorious conquest (or inglorious defeat).

The Unnoted Emergence of Stealthy Leaders and Politics

New South governors, civil rights activists, federal officials, naïve liberals, right-wing segregationists, lawyers, journalists, academics, rabble-rousers, shysters, and numerous other types dominated the regional landscape of the post-civil rights period. But we think that low-profile leaders and their moderate politicking may provide an important, heretofore missing part of the broad story of Southern history.

As discussed in the previous section, we detected throughout numerous accounts of Southern community struggles (both during the civil rights movement and afterwards), an interesting developmental pattern: less heroic drama, less villainous resistance, and more conventional politics. Furthermore, our examination of numerous locales suggests that this politics worked best when pursued by quiet, practical, biracial leaders.

Thus we hypothesize that many leaders and citizens of both races, who had learned valuable lessons through the traumatic days of the 1950s and 1960s, adopted new ideas and changed their ways to accommodate racial realities. One reality, to reiterate, was a splintered, uncertain white populace. "Some white Southerners attested to liberating experiences that forever altered their racial attitudes and behavior. Others found new ways to resist racial equality. Many more clung to any sense of normalcy they could salvage, at times willfully ignorant of the tumult around them."[66] Some were rock-throwers and liberals; but "the vast group in the middle were left out of the story."[67] Another reality was black practicality. The real movement was "not moralistic melodrama but politics."[68] Black politics centered on real issues in city councils, county commissions, and state legislatures; direct action in those forums and times took on a "more ordinarily American form."[69]

Thus, an emerging Southern leadership carefully attended to specific, localized demands of the black movement without unduly antagonizing divided white society. This proved to be an effective community strategy, at least in some areas, in the immediate aftermath of the civil rights revolution. We believe these experiences laid the groundwork for routine, essential functions of campaigning and governing throughout the region during the 1970s, 1980s, and 1990s.

The "missing" aspect of this piece of the puzzle, of course, was by design. We are talking here mainly about relatively uncelebrated politicians, not the famous New South governors and other prominent officials who played on the large stage of national attention. Most astute Southern politicians, for obvious reasons, did everything they could back then to keep their biracial activities out of the headlines; in ensuing years, there seemed to be an informal code of silence among all participants in these interactions.

Also, media and journalistic chroniclers during that period had more interesting black-white problems to write about, so the fact that biracial politics was working in some circumstances did not merit much attention in the still steamy story of Southern politics. Later analysts lacked the requisite personal experience and access to key people, documents, and information that might have provided insights about the changing day-to-day, real-world politics during that period.

Disinterested history, therefore, has overlooked the fact that many leaders, particularly white politicians and black activists functioning in areas with appropriate sociopolitical context, decided that it was time to do things differently—quietly and biracially—less heroically but with more practical and progressive results. Historians may have ignored them; but these politicians helped nurture a new Southern politics through their quiet, practical, biracial leadership.

Still the South—But "We Ain't What We Was"

Apparently, as we begin a new century, there is un-abating interest in the still intriguing but different course of Southern politics. John A Clark noted this interest in *Writing Southern Politics*, a collection of scholarship produced by the Citadel Symposium on Southern Politics:

> As the chapters in this volume make clear, the literature on Southern politics is vast and continues to grow . . . Parochial Southerners might suggest that their region is simply more interesting than others. They may be right. The South continues to be a distinctive region, owing in part to the rapid changes that have taken place over the past half century and the impact of the region on national politics.[70]

Even literary folks at the *New York Times* and publishing houses at Princeton and Harvard have expressed new-found interest in this region. *Times* editor/reviewer Patricia Cohen recently focused on the growing list of new books emphasizing change and convergence:

> Although the scholarly books published in the last couple of years focus on widely different areas—metropolitan power centers, rural backwaters, employment practices, schools—nearly all make the same point: The idea that the South is exceptional, a region apart from the rest of the country, is no longer true.[71]

Specifically citing recent books from Princeton University Press by Southerners Joseph Crespino,[72] Kevin M. Kruse,[73] and Matthew D. Lassiter,[74] Cohen wrote:

> Though the thesis discomfits some professors of Southern history, Mr.. Kruse argues "a lot of those regional differences have really dropped out the closer we get to the present day."
>
> It may turn out that what is most distinctive about the latest research on the South is its claim that the South is no longer distinctive. Mr. Lassiter's and Mr. Crespino's latest project is editing a book titled "The End of Southern History."

Harvard University Press's contribution to this re-looking at Southern politics was *The End of Southern Exceptionalism* by Byron E. Shafer and Richard Johnston, neither of whom hails from the South. In an award-winning exposition on race, class and partisan change, they proclaimed regional convergence:

> By the time of the 2000 census, there was a new politics in the American South, one simple in its outlines yet drastically different from its predecessors . . . In the process, what had been a defining regional difference in national politics, from the 1850s through the 1950s, threatened to disappear. And the possibility arose that the rhetorical question posed by the title of this chapter—Old South to New South to No South?—could be answered in the affirmative.[75]

These pronouncements echoed the sentiments of Frederick Wirt, who had captured the daunting challenge of the Mississippi movement in the 1960s and returned for follow-up research toward the end of the century. Wirt reported remarkable change in *"We Ain't What We Was": Civil Rights in the New South*:

> The combination of new economic development, new civil rights laws that opened voting to blacks, new movement of population, and new ideas about an improved political system—all combined to create a New South that observers agree is unprecedented. No one thinks that this change is complete, for blacks complain about needs that are still unmet. But it is equally clear that an understanding of the region's politics must go beyond what V. O. Key once knew and what national opinion once held. There is now a new political system with changes still under way.[76]

Race and racism are still vital matters, and much remains to be done; but this review of academic research, journalistic reporting, and personal testimony has clearly heralded substantial Southern change.

A New Racial Politics

It seems, furthermore, that blacks and whites in the South have come to terms—terms that will amaze outsiders—about living together in a new century. Our research suggests that descendants of slaves and descendants of slave owners have reconciled pressures for systemic progress with certain aspects of their cultural pasts; and the civil rights movement of the 1950s–1960s has morphed, rather curiously, into a new racial politics of black-white accommodation for a new century.[77]

In essence, then, the new order is a continuing game of racial politics—now played by both whites and blacks in more sophisticated manner without traditional perversities—in a regional system still struggling with historic black-white tension. This new approach represents a modernized, measured mixture of hard history, progressive practicality, and, most importantly, biracial accommodation.

To summarize, we have reviewed in this chapter the enduring dilemma of Southern racial problems and demonstrated that the South changed, in surprising manner, in the years since the civil rights movement. Both qualitative assessments and quantitative data show that Key's mid-century call for biracial politics had become a reality, to an appreciable degree, by the end of that century.

We have attempted to explain the changing South, at least partially, by citing some important aspects of white culture, black politics, and our hypothetical stealth leadership. We're mainly interested, of course, in how these leaders conducted their quiet, practical, biracial politics and how their actions helped transform the regional system. We present in this book our own original research about this process. Before proceeding with our research, however, we want to examine in the next chapter how other scholars have explored racial representation in Southern politics during the 1970s, 1980s, and 1990s.

3

RACIAL REPRESENTATION
IN THE SOUTH

T
o generalize about relevant research and writings of the past few
decades, we find that the analytic record is one of increased so-
phistication yet jumbled, contentious findings about Southern
leadership and racial representation. Moreover, there has been little attention or insight regarding the important practice and consequence of quiet,
practical, biracial politics.

A sporadic parade of conspicuous Southerners—New South governors,
senators, judges, journalists, courageous private citizens, and scurrilous
other personalities—garnered early notice among the heroes and villains.
Scholars and media subsequently have focused on more interesting things
that could be easily measured, such as increasing black voter registration,
the steady flow of white votes from the D-column to the R-column, and the
resultant crop of African American and Republican officials. However, there
has been limited theoretical and comprehensive attention to less-glamorous
but fundamental adjustments in Southern political life; thus not much is
known about the special service of moderate white leaders during the days
of stealthy biracial change.

The following section will address scholarly understanding—and at-
tendant deficiencies and disputes—about Southern racial representation
as reflected in the relevant literature.

Evolving Theory of Leadership, Race, and Representation

Mainstream democratic scholars trace the study of political leadership
back to long-ago discourse among European "men of ideas," such as So-

crates, Aristotle, Plato, Machiavelli, Hobbes, Locke, Rousseau, Burke, Mill, de Tocqueville, and other philosophical luminaries. These leading thinkers dominated their associates and societies with deep dialogues on metaphysics, epistemology, ethics, politics, and aesthetics.

However, perhaps the most cited and influential figure in the modern leadership literature is a woman who enjoys little renown outside college classrooms and academic circles. Also, African American scholars have been at the forefront of representational theory and research over the past few decades. Hanna Pitkin,[1] Lenneal J. Henderson/Mack Jones,[2] and Ralph C. Gomes/Linda Faye Williams[3] do not perfectly represent the evolving literature in this field; however, they are very illustrative of the concepts and concerns that brought us to where we are today. Much of the research on race, leadership, and representation within the past few decades inevitably cites or footnotes their work; equally importantly, their substantive ideas are still at the center of both academic and political debate about racial representation.

Refined Conceptualization of Leadership and Representation

In her now classic treatise, *The Concept of Representation*, Hanna Pitkin noted that previous scholars really had not focused on the representational aspects of leadership, assuming that everyone knew what it was or how it ought to be performed. Pitkin wanted to get deeper and more rigorously into the nature of the activity of representation, and she developed a rather simple but straightforward framework for understanding the various styles of activity that go into the representational function.

Pitkin proposed that representation can best be defined and understood as "acting in the interest of the represented, in a manner responsive to them."[4] She designed a typology of ways or styles in which the representative might perform that "acting."

She first examined formalistic representation, or service in terms of formal arrangements involving authorization and accountability; she next looked at descriptive representation, "the making present of something absent by resemblance or reflection, as in a mirror or in art"; then she discussed symbolic representation, "in which no resemblance or reflection is required and the connection to what is represented is of a different kind."[5]

Pitkin considered substantive representation as the essence of political leadership, with the leader "acting for" or pursuing the interests of the represented in a manner responsive to them, even if that leader is not a member of the represented grouping. After discussing the other aspects of representation, she said.

> What neither of these activities can give us, however, is representation as an acting for others, an activity in behalf of, in the interest of, as the agent of, someone else. Neither giving information about someone nor stimulating belief or acceptance in him could generally be characterized in such terms. Yet representation does sometimes mean such activity. The acting for other discussed in this chapter, differs from the representation— or symbol-making and the standing for others of the last two chapters. It differs also from the formalistic views; for, while they would see the representative as active, even as acting for others, his status as representative would be defined in terms of formal arrangements that initiate or terminate the activity, not in terms of the nature of that activity itself. We are now interested in the nature of the activity itself, what goes on during representing, the substance or content of acting for others, as distinct from its external and formal trappings.[6]

In her closing comments, Pitkin acknowledged the difficulty of fully understanding the concept of representation; and she encouraged others to criticize and advance her ideas:

> The concept of representation thus is a continuing tension between ideal and achievement. This tension should lead us neither to abandon the ideal, retreating to an operational definition that accepts whatever those usually designated as representative do; nor to abandon its institutionalization and withdraw from political reality. Rather, it should present a continuing but not hopeless challenge: to construct institutions and train individuals in such a way that they engage in the pursuit of the public interest, the genuine representation of the public; and, at the same time,

to remain critical of those institutions and that training, so that they are always open to further interpretation and reform.[7]

Pitkin's theoretical conceptualization has been criticized on several grounds (particularly its preferential emphasis on the substantive element). But it thereafter provided the central framework of analysis for most empirical research into leadership and representation. The honor roll of representational research testifies to her general ideas. More specifically, her framework of leadership style has assumed a pivotal place in the contemporary debate over racial representation.

Reconceptualization of the Black Experience

Equally important in our theoretical discussion was another interesting historical development. As already noted, the traditional literature on representation derived from ancient Western European origins, but activist African American scholars fundamentally challenged that literature in the 1970s.

Systemic racism had colored mainstream thought with a fixed pale hue throughout American history until black scholars provided academic reason and blunt demands for change. Lenneal J. Henderson, a political science professor at the University of San Francisco, and a few academic colleagues confronted that situation with an extraordinary and diverse collection of historical analysis, *Black Political Life in the United States: A Fist as the Pendulum.*

Henderson's preface directed the anthology towards those who aspired to understand or become involved in black politics. He set the tone by noting that many books had been written by whites about black politics, and he rhetorically wondered about the motivations, assumptions, hypotheses, biases, and conclusions of those writings.[8]

Atlanta University political scientist Mack Jones then put down some markers about what not to do in conceptualizing the black political experience in his essay, "A Frame of Reference for Black Politics":

The melting-pot theory of American pluralism seems to be the frame of reference most commonly used for analyzing and interpreting the black political experience in America, although attempts have been made recently to carry over the modernizing traditional-systems model from the field of comparative politics. In both instances, the researcher looks not to the black political experience for guidance in developing his conceptual scheme, but rather to the political experiences of other people. Such approaches posit a level of isomorphism between the black political experience and the experience of other groups which is denied by even a cursory examination.[9]

And, he continued:

A frame of reference for black politics should not begin with superficial comparisons of black and other ethnic minorities in this country or elsewhere, because such an approach inevitably degenerates into normative reformist speculation around the question of what can be done to elevate blacks to the position occupied by the group with which they are being compared. This, in turn, leads to the establishment of a linear model of ethnic or out-group politics and a Procrustean forcing of the black political experience into the contrived model, and in the process obfuscating, if not eliminating outright, the crucial variable in the black political experience. In developing a frame of reference for black politics, one should begin by searching for those factors which are unique to the black political experience, for this is the information which will facilitate our understanding of blacks in the American political system.[10]

So, what did Jones propose as the unique factor of the black experience?

. . . what we have is essentially a power struggle between blacks and whites, with the latter trying to maintain their superordinate position vis-à-vis the former. Since the political system is the arena in which societal conflicts are definitively resolved, black politics should be thought of as the manifestation of the power struggle between these two groups.[11]

But there was also a specifying condition: "That condition is the stipulation that the ideological justification for the superordination of whites is the institutionalized belief in the inherent superiority of that group."[12]

Finally, he said, "The orienting concepts, and therefore the frame of reference for black politics, must grow out of the above propositions."[13]

Jones thereby articulated a blunt manifesto for American academia. There could be no incorporation of black politics into established theory that relied on the experience of other people; and whatever might develop in this area, it should involve the black-white power struggle (and institutionalized racism) as a central framework of analysis. In short, black scholars were especially and exclusively ordained for reconceptualizing black politics and implementing a new theory of black participation in the American system.

Reconsideration of Political Strategy

In the decades following the civil rights movement, the most pressing questions about black participation was whether and how African Americans could play a full and meaningful role in the democratic process; the conventional debate usually focused on integrated politics versus black separatism.

While public commentary generally encouraged and lauded black-white coalition, political reality often strained the relationship between the coalescing races, and there was constant and increasing unease among blacks about the costs and benefits of interracial endeavor.

Ralph C. Gomes and Linda Faye Williams, both of whom taught for years at Howard University, comprehensively tackled the issue in *From Exclusion to Inclusion: The Long Struggle for African American Political Power*. Particularly valuable among the diverse perspectives incorporated in this edited collection were their own ideas about game theory and practical politics. While acknowledging that there had been significant historical payoffs from past coalitions, Gomes and Williams noted that blacks most often played the role of minority partners, with limited dividends, in these joint ventures:

Throughout most of the history of African American voting, these

interracial coalitions have been in support of white candidates at all levels
of government. Thus the great bulk of the African American experience
in electoral politics is made up of African Americans voting for the "lesser
of two evils" white candidate.[14]

Moreover, they reported, these coalitions often elected white candidates
whose pressing concerns were not important to the minority community;
and these coalitions increasingly splintered as elected officials pursued other
issues. In an intriguing statement of theoretical and practical conclusions,
Gomes and Williams recommended that African Americans engage in
conscious communications concerning goals, the means of obtaining them,
and distribution of the payoff received by coalition partners:

> All strategy should flow from these well-understood goals. Thus, any
> specific decision to coalesce with any particular group(s) must be based
> on a thorough, realistic, and practical analysis of whether the alliance will
> in the long run advance the goals, rather than produce some temporary
> gain but ultimately stagnation or decline in long-range interests.[15]

In elaborating on future African American goals and strategy, Gomes
and Williams specifically posed the dilemma of biracial representation as
examined in our current project:

> For example . . . it should be clearly established whether the premier
> goal is to elect more African American representatives, state legislators, and
> so forth, or whether the premier goal is to structure jurisdictions that will
> elect more progressive elected officials (devoted to advancing the policy
> interests of the poor) regardless of their race . . . This type of decision
> making should be at the root of all decisions about coalition partners.[16]

As the following discussion will demonstrate, the central issues raised
by a combined reading of Pitkin, Henderson/Jones, and Gomes/Williams
reverberate in contemporary debate and our thesis about racial representation.

Reorientation to a New Orthodoxy

Pitkin's conceptual framework, the provocative challenge of Henderson/ Jones, and the coalitional ideas of Gomes/Williams reflected changing notions about leadership and representation in the American political system since mid-century. Such new and different perspectives reoriented professional capabilities and opportunities for probing the representational process, and the academy itself underwent necessary yet difficult adjustment to the diverse norms and demands of changing America.

In the area of political science and politics, for example, new organizations and institutions focusing on race and democracy arose among African Americans during the 1960s and 1970s. The National Conference of Black Political Scientists organized in 1969 "to study, enhance, and promote the political aspirations of people of African descent in the United States and throughout the world." The Joint Center for Political and Economic Studies was established in 1970 "to provide training and technical assistance to newly elected black officials." And the Congressional Black Caucus Foundation was created in 1971 "to positively influence the course of events pertinent to African Americans and others of similar experience and situation, and to achieve greater equity for persons of African descent in the design and content of domestic and international programs and services."

Additionally, traditional academic associations—such as the American Political Science Association and the American Historical Association— developed programs specifically to expand education and opportunities for minority participation. Countless African Americans, women, and other historically disadvantaged professionals entered the profession during the 1970s and 1980s.

The combination of academic expansion, conceptual refinement, experiential challenge, and strategic reconsiderations significantly altered monocultural theory about leadership and representation in the latter decades of the twentieth century. Specifically, academic attention began to focus on diverse minority interests in the inhospitable environment of historical and contemporary society, with three central questions dominating that endeavor: (1) Can whites represent blacks? (2) Should blacks represent blacks? (3) How can we assure fair black participation in the American political system? Just as importantly, there developed a distinct professional orthodoxy reflecting sentiment that black citizens must be better represented, both substantively and descriptively, in the South and throughout America.

Empirical Research on Post-Movement Racial Representation

In the 1980s and 1990s a new generation of scholars—white, black, and other—committed themselves to studying and restructuring the political system for more meaningful representation of minority people and interests in the American system. They were particularly interested in congressional representation, which lent itself to fruitful analysis because of the available, structured nature of census data, election returns, and roll-call votes and also because of the fascinating, volatile interplay of white versus black, South versus nonSouth, and Democrat versus Republican politics.

Thus, as the twentieth century neared its end, the new generation of social scientists explored and expanded the concepts of leadership, race, and representation in creative, sophisticated, empirical manner. Their research had particular pertinence to racial representation within the South's historical and changing environment. However, these scholars split into several camps reflecting, in part, inherent personal and professional differences within the discipline and continuing political schisms of broader American society. One camp was adamantly committed to black officials representing black citizens; another group shared progressive inclinations but also entertained less-rigid notions of racial representation; and still others acknowledged race as an important factor but focused, as in the past, on political party and other conventional variables as the primary spectrum for analysis.

Unfortunately, these differing perspectives have had important ramifications, and the debate sometimes has hindered our ability to make sense of the sensitive puzzle of racial representation. To recall and redirect Mack Jones's warning of thirty-something years ago, this discussion "inevitably degenerates into normative reformist speculation" obfuscating crucial aspects of the American experience.[17] Specifically, argument over the merits of black-black representation and majority-minority districting has constrained constructive consideration of alternative factors and strategies—such as biracial politics—in changing Southern history.

Major Books on the Subject

We present here the major recent and relevant research efforts (i.e., scholarly books that dealt substantially with racial representation in Congress from the 1970s through the 1990s) in rough chronological order, noting in advance that their approaches and conclusions reflected the tensions afflicting the discipline and broader society. Typically, each scholar "pitched" a preferred version of the central question (with compelling descriptive-versus-substantive data), followed by explication of other interesting aspects of racial representation. Also, all meandered considerably in their discussions of black constituent interests, electoral schemes, representational styles, regional distinctiveness, partisan comparisons, and contextual factors.

SWAIN—CRITICAL TWEAKING OF RIGID ORTHODOXY ABOUT BIRACIAL LEADERSHIP: Carol Swain serves as an appropriate point to begin our discussion, with a controversial, multifaceted study of representation of African American interests—*Black Faces, Black Interests: The Representation of Black Interests in Congress.* Winner of the V. O. Key Award for the best book on Southern politics, Swain's study provided valuable information directly relevant to our project.

Swain critically asked: "What are black interests?" "What is representation?" "Who supports the interests of blacks on Capitol Hill?" She demonstrated very clearly, as expected, that black elected officials provided more substantial representation to black constituents than did white officials. But she also noted the practical sociological and geographical limitations to the election of black officials; more importantly, she reported that certain white politicians seemed adept at bridging the historical divide and providing effective leadership in majority-white areas with significant black populations.

Utilizing roll-call data, detailed interviews with numerous black members and a few white members, along with field observation of constituency relations during the 1980s and 1990s, Swain contended that the representation of minority interests was not the exclusive domain of black officials, and she asserted that some white Democrats performed as well or better in representing blacks than some black representatives.[18]

According to Swain, white congressmen Robin Tallon (South Carolina,

1983–93) and Tim Valentine (North Carolina, 1983–95) successfully accomplished a delicate balancing act in representing biracial constituencies in majority-white districts during that era:

> Robin Tallon and Tim Valentine are two white Democrats whose political survival in Congress has depended on their ability to balance the interest of conservative whites and liberal blacks. They replaced more conservative white representatives, and they have made important changes in order to represent the diversity of interests in their districts. Often forced to take controversial stances, they have told the whites in their districts of their duty to represent black voters, and they have reminded them that the world has changed, and with it the South.[19]

These white Southerners responded to their black constituents in varying ways, but both were demonstrably more attentive than the politicians they replaced in employment practices and voting records. They were especially sensitive to high-profile black issues, voting for the 1988 Civil Rights Restoration bill and the 1990 and 1991 Civil Rights acts. "They managed to uphold their positions," Swain said, "in spite of the vehement opposition in parts of the South to this legislation by fundamentalist groups, such as the Moral Majority, that have highly effective systems of communication."[20]

The North Carolinian's experience was probably common for white politicians in such situations because he had to reach out to the distrustful black minority from his conservative white base:

> Valentine's efforts to gain black support increased significantly after his 1984 reelection. Immediately after the election he met with black leaders and asked what he could do to let black constituents know that they too had representation in Congress. They came up with the idea of a "legislative day" for black constituents—an all-expenses-paid bus trip to the capital, where participants would meet with important national leaders. The black response to this legislative day was so positive that Valentine's office had to limit future invitations to the district's black elected officials.[21]

It was not easy representing the biracial constituency:

> Valentine compared it to "walking through a briar patch," not-
> ing that, "by the time you walk out the other side . . . you get some
> scratches on you. To my chagrin and to my disappointment, I've lost
> the friendship of good close personal friends at home because of votes
> that I've cast."[22]

Tallon, on the other hand, was elected originally and largely because of black voters, and he took care to reciprocate; in fact, his main obstacle was getting whites to accept his biracial approach:

> "Well, I can tell you, that it was difficult, real difficult. It was so difficult
> that I just backed away from it for a while, because people really resented
> (that I had defeated) this clean-cut incumbent (who had the support of
> white people) . . . Eventually, I began to reach out, but it took more than
> any one term; it took four to five years for me to feel like I had turned
> the corner, and we were all working together, as color-blind as you can
> possibly be. But, I am not so naïve to think that there's no racial polariza-
> tion. There are problems, and unfortunately in my lifetime, I don't think
> we're ever going to see that completely diminished."[23]

Swain stated in conclusion that whites could represent the interests of blacks:

> Given their constraints, Southern white representatives of districts
> with substantial black minorities do a credible job of representing blacks
> . . . Although white representatives of minority-black districts may not
> provide as much substantive representation as African Americans would
> like, the degree to which white representatives have managed to balance
> white and black interests is significant.[24]

Swain's book was a direct challenge to prevailing sentiment among progressives; and in the ensuing years other scholars reported results that both

supported and contradicted her controversial pronouncements.

RAE—ELABORATIVE COMMENTARY AND SOLICITOUS CANDOR AMONG SOUTHERN BIRACIAL LEADERS. In *Southern Democrats*, Nicol Rae did not address racial representation within the orthodoxy debate, but his research provided extensive information about how Southern politicians, specifically Democratic members of Congress, related to the changing racial situation since the civil rights revolution.

Through interviews with about thirty congressmen who served during the 1970s, 1980s, and 1990s, Rae explored an important question about the transforming South: Why did these Democrats stay with the Democratic Party? And his extensive compilation of comments from both white and black leaders was pertinent to the difficult issue of biracial politics during that period. Most often, they generalized about the broad interests of their electorate without racial connotation, but sometimes they expressed notions of equal opportunity and civil rights.

Charles Bennett (Florida) said that he was a Democrat "because the Democratic party set as its goal the uplifting of the opportunities of the underprivileged."[25] Owen Pickett (Virginia) said the Democratic Party "tends to focus on human issues—education, health care, retirement—people who cannot handle issues on their own behalf."[26] Steve Neal (North Carolina) avowed that "At the heart of our system is the idea that every individual is deserving of dignity and respect, regardless of sex or race, and the Democratic Party reflects that better and tries to enhance the human condition better."[27]

These Southern white Democrats also acknowledged, with straightforward partisanship, the role of race in unfolding Southern history. According to Congressman Lewis Payne (Virginia), "The Republicans in our state still stand for a certain status quo. Virginia had, even recently, a history of not very good race relations and didn't have a very progressive outlook on social issues. A number of us in the South feel that we've got to get beyond that."[28] Likewise, Buddy Darden (Georgia) claimed that "A lot of the racists went to the Republican party after the Goldwater campaign in 1964. That saved the Democratic party in the South and enabled them to build a coalition of moderate whites and blacks."[29]

And they were candidly solicitous in commenting about their relationships with black voters. As Payne elaborated:

> "We all share a pretty large black constituency, and we're interested in trying to do the right things to accommodate black views, in issues like the recent civil rights bill. In the first race I ran, blacks were very mobilized and were the reason I won. So long as they're all with me, it's hard for anyone else to win. I like to work with that constituency. I made sure black leaders and friends from my district got to see Nelson Mandela."[30]

Even some black Southern leaders, such as Representative Mike Espy (Mississippi) articulated the biracial message on traditional values shared by his black and white constituents:

> "I have opposed gun control and supported prayer in schools and the death penalty because I believe they are reasonable value issues. I am Mississippian . . . I was born and raised there, and I believe in what Mississippians believe in."[31]

Georgia congressman and civil rights legend John Lewis expressed more practically the changing black-white relationship by commenting, "One thing about white Southerners is that they can count, and after the Voting Rights Act, they learned to count very well." He added:

> "More and more black and white politicians get elected by biracial coalitions. You can no longer go into the black community and say one thing and then say something else to the white community if you are going to be elected and provide leadership."[33]

Rae concluded that, although Southerners remained a substantial presence in the House, things had changed as a result of the civil rights revolution, electoral realignment, and biracial politics:

Southern Democrats were now virtually unanimous in their support for civil rights, and the effects of reapportionment and black voting rights had created a greater degree of representatives and diversity in the Southern Democratic ranks.[34]

GLASER—REGIONALIZED STYLE OF WHITE-BLACK CAMPAIGNING BY SOUTHERN BIRACIAL LEADERS. James M. Glaser provided more probing insights and detailed examples of biracial representation—of the peculiarly regional variety—in *Race, Campaign Politics, and the Realignment in the South*. While Glaser's work, based on his campaign field trips with white Southern congressional candidates during the 1980s, also was not part of the debate about black-black representation, his findings fit well into our current discussion.

Glaser spent considerable time inside several Democratic campaigns (including Browder's 1989 special election), observing day-to-day developments and interviewing candidates, consultants, activists, and news people. He painted a common stylistic picture of successful white Southern politicians who courted the black vote without antagonizing their white base:

> With regard to racial issues, Democratic candidates have walked a tightrope, but they seem to be good at it. If they choose to talk about racial issues in public, they do so in measured tones and in few words. They have little to gain by articulating racially liberal positions in the press or in a debate. They have much to lose. And they are willing to test white support only so far. Most Democrats figure that they benefit when the salience of a racial issue is not raised further. A restrained, brief statement of their position on the issue is all that is necessary and need not antagonize white voters sympathetic to Democrats.[35]

And constituent blacks were cooperative with moderate Democrats:

> Black Democratic leaders appear to understand the constraints that white Democrats work under. They do not require white Democrats to take bold stands on racial issues to win their support so long as their

overall record on issues of interest to minorities is good. In the context of a discussion about the Confederate flag, the field director of the Alabama Democratic Conference told me that he did not care that Browder did not respond strongly to Rice: "We would not make that issue the litmus test for our support. It's a political issue that most (white Democrats), even liberals and moderates, couldn't touch."[36]

Glaser updated his research a decade later with visits to five additional Southern campaigns. In *The Hand of the Past in Contemporary Southern Politics*, he found that time had altered some racial and partisan arrangements but not the relational nexus of candidate style, biracial coalitions, and the racial context of the district:

> The reason congressional Democrats were able to survive the Reagan-Bush years in a conservative region, I argued several years ago, is that they were able to hold together black-white coalitions. The key was to maximize the black vote and the black share of the vote, while winning enough whites to gain district majorities. This was especially possible in places where blacks constituted larger proportions of the vote. In many Southern congressional districts, drained of blacks to create majority-minority districts, this strategy is now much less viable. But even in districts where blacks are less plentiful, the strategies continue to be pursued, and in a place where blacks constitute over 35 percent of a district's population, these strategies can work.[37]

Otherwise, Glaser's description of 1990s black-white politics was pretty much the same as before:

> One of the most important keys to maintaining the biracial coalition is the ability to address blacks and whites separately. In the language of media consultants, the technique is called "narrowcasting," targeting blacks with specific media messages that whites will not hear. Black radio and black cable television are the main vehicles for reaching black voters separately from whites. General campaigning can be segregated as well. Southern

Democrats have long taken their message into black communities through the black church and accompanied by black leaders. In doing so, they are not heard by whites and are liberated in what they can say and how they can say it. They can, in the words of a Democratic campaign consultant, communicate with blacks "surgically."[38]

WHITBY—CONFRONTING SWAIN AND AFFIRMING PROGRESSIVE PERSPECTIVE ABOUT BLACK REPRESENTATION.

Swain's controversial ideas did not go unchallenged very long. Kenny J. Whitby emphatically reaffirmed progressive perspective in *The Color of Representation: Congressional Behavior and Black Interests*. He produced strong statistical evidence that race was the central, vital factor in congressional representation and that black members were more supportive of black interests. Whitby's roll-call analysis firmly tied black-black representation to policy-making on such important matters as voting rights, equal opportunity, and governmental services during the 1970s-90s: "The high level of support among black lawmakers is unmatched by any other cohort in the assembly"[39]

Furthermore, he seemed to declare the issue settled beyond reasonable debate:

> The findings presented here have potentially important political consequences. There is more to the election of African Americans than symbolism or the color of skin. The color of Congress has implications for the quality of substantive representation for African Americans. . .At the very least those who are interested in increasing the number of historically underrepresented racial minorities in Congress should take some comfort in knowing that opponents cannot deny the importance of color in Congress based on substantive reasoning.[40]

Whitby's project did not deal directly with Southern biracial politics, but he commented on previous efforts by himself and others to characterize that relatively unexplored aspect of the representational dilemma.

> As part of their strategy to win elective office, some white representa-

tives have found it to be politically expedient to become more responsive to black interests. As discussed earlier, researchers are less certain about the exact nature of the relationship but agree that black voter participation has caused many Southern House members to moderate their conservative policy views on racial issues.[41]

As for black politicians, Whitby urged caution regarding Swain's commentary on biracial campaigning:

> Ideally, the biracial strategy is the best-case scenario and should be carefully considered by candidates running for elective office. The major defect of the biracial campaign strategy is that it discounts the significance of racially polarized voting in the United States. There is still little empirical evidence to support the conclusion that black congressional candidates can win on a consistent and long-term basis in districts that contain a majority of non-Hispanic white voters.[42]

LUBLIN—HEDGED AFFIRMATION, WITH CAUTION ABOUT STRATEGIES FOR BLACK REPRESENTATION. David Lublin's intriguing research also refuted Swain's assessment, but he expressed concern about the realistic prospects of black-black strategies of racial representation in *The Paradox of Representation: Racial Gerrymandering and Minority Interests in Congress*.

Based on statistical modeling of roll-call votes 1972–90, Lublin claimed that "African American representatives . . . provide the highest level of substantive representation in addition to descriptive representation."[43] He also showed in numerous calculations that general representational responsiveness to black interests increased along with the proportion of black constituents:

> These results strongly refute Swain's argument that neither the race of a district's representative nor the percentage of blacks in the district relates to support for black interests. Representatives from districts greater than 40 percent black show substantially greater responsiveness to African American concerns than other representatives.[44]

Lublin further specified that party impacted the relationship between district makeup and ideological representation, particularly in the South:

> Although Swain wrongly dismisses the importance of race, she correctly analyzes that party strongly influences black substantive representation . . . Southern Democrats are highly responsive to changes in the percentage of blacks above and below the 40 percent black threshold, while northern Democrats exhibit little change in their roll-call voting behavior.[45]

Speaking specifically to white-black alliances, Lublin commented on the intricacies of Southern politics:

> Unlike their northern counterparts, Southern white Democrats depend heavily on biracial coalitions to win elections. Successful Southern white Democrats perform a precarious balancing act, trying to please white and black voters. Democrats need fewer white votes as the black share of the populations grows and so they can cast more liberal roll-call votes on racial and economic issues without fear of losing reelection . . . Ironically, Southern representatives respond more to changes in the black share of the vote precisely because of the high salience of race in the South compared to northern central cities.[46]

Lublin concluded with a cautious, suggestive comment about congressional districts, policy voting, and minority interests. While acknowledging that the creation of majority black districts had increased black representation, he expressed concern about the continued viability of a strategy centered on black-black representation. Pointing to the limited potential for more black districts, he suggested that "minorities will be forced to make tough decisions about how they wish to pursue greater representation."[47]

CANON—AFFIRMATIVE SENTIMENT, WITH INTERESTING EMPHASIS ON "NEW-STYLE" BIRACIAL LEADERSHIP. In a very remarkable yet little noticed exposition, David T. Canon supported the prevailing sentiment of black-black representation while emphasizing the civic contribution of "new-style" biracial leadership, in *Race, Redistricting and Representation*.

Canon employed a variety of very useful sources for his study, adding factors such as committee assignments, bill sponsorships, floor speeches and news releases to the usual indicators of representation; his empirical scope covered several decades, with specific references to the 103rd Congress (1993–94) to flesh out observed patterns.

Blacks won election to Congress in two distinctly different ways, according to Canon. Some, whom he labeled "traditional black politicians," emphasized "politics of difference" in their campaigns and thereafter mainly represented black interests; while "new-style black politicians" stressed electoral "politics of commonality" and were oriented toward whites or balanced between the races in their service. Just as importantly, he discovered that the field of candidates determined campaign and service style more than the racial demographics of the district.

Canon went well beyond roll-call analysis to reveal that varying representational styles impacted the roles and behaviors of black politicians in Congress. Surveying numerous other indicators, he found that new-style members were more balanced in their public relations efforts, employment practices, and field office locations. Furthermore, these new-style leaders seemed to distinguish themselves as legislators in a national assembly:

> Commonality members were more likely than difference members to serve in the leadership, slightly more moderate in their roll call behavior, less likely to emphasize race in their speeches on the floor and in their sponsorship and cosponsorship of legislation, and more likely to cosponsor bills that were successful in the legislative process.[48]

Most interestingly, in a reverse-twist on a common question, Canon claimed that black members of Congress could represent white constituents; and he argued that the new-style black officials delivered better representation to white constituents than white officials delivered to black constituents in mirrored districts:

> Most white representatives from black influence districts do not spend

much time representing their black constituents, while most black members of Congress spend a substantial proportion of their time representing white constituents.[49]

BERARD—CONTEXT, CONTEXT, CONTEXT, AND LONG-TERM POSSIBILITIES FOR DEMOCRATIC BIRACIAL COALITIONS. Stanley P. Berard dealt indirectly with our broad issue of racial representation in *Southern Democrats in the House of Representatives*. He looked at the relationship between public opinion and congressional voting patterns in various contexts, including race, during the 1970s, 1980s, and 1990s.

Using survey data and roll-call votes, Berard found that Southern Democrats had changed substantially during the past few decades, for a variety of reasons, in their representational performance. Compared to historical practice, many Southern representatives had been "northernized" in the sense that they began to resemble their non-Southern colleagues in policy voting; and there seemed to be greater responsiveness to black constituents than in the past.

However, he claimed that representational response could not be explained simply by focusing on composition and attitudes of the constituency and voting behavior of the congressman—in other words, representation was contextually complicated. He reported that the observed relationship depended to a great degree on the geographical nature—urban or rural—of the area. Furthermore, he showed that the connection varied from one issue to another and that varying constituent activists probably accounted for much of the changed patterns.

More pertinently, Berard's summary observations were congruent with our discussion of biracial leadership:

> Democratic success in black belt districts in which blacks are a minority depends on the creation of black-white electoral coalitions. Maintaining such coalitions requires Democrats to engage in the balancing act described earlier: blacks must be motivated to turn out and vote Democratic, and at the same time sufficient numbers of white voters must be convinced that the Democratic congressional candidate is not 'too liberal. . .'[50]

At least through the early 1990s Southern Democrats in Congress had regularly achieved this balance by firmly supporting civil rights measures, maintaining a conservative voting record on social issues, and attempting to bridge the gap between black and white Southerners concerning the role of government in the economy.[51]

Berard also expressed confidence in a biracial future for the Democratic Party in the South:

One result of these dynamics is that Democrats will retain a substantial share of Southern House seats beyond the core of minority-majority and urban minority-influence districts that are often seen as the party's only long-term base in the region. The consequences for congressional politics are twofold. First the South will not be nearly as large a liability as many expect for the Democrats in their efforts to elect a House majority. Second, Democratic representatives from the South will continue to represent a range of ideological positions and to be a source of preference heterogeneity with the House Democratic caucus.[52]

TATE—CREATIVE INQUIRY, SOME CORROBORATION, AND BOLD CONJECTURE ABOUT THE FUTURE OF RACIAL REPRESENTATION IN AMERICA. Katherine Tate approached the issue through creative investigation in *Black Faces in the Mirror: African Americans and Their Representatives in the U.S. Congress.* Although her research focused on Congress in general rather than regional patterns, she both expanded our conceptualization and raised questions about the presumed nature of racial representation. Tate incorporated voting scores, major legislative votes, bill sponsorships, and committee assignments (for the 1993–94 and 1995–96 Congresses) to get a broad view of black legislators' political style and policy-record. She reported that, contrary to some earlier reports, black legislators had performed liberally and effectively in Washington:

The data . . . establish conclusively that Black Democratic legislators are distinctively more liberal in their voting behavior in the House, even while they are no less active in pursuing their own legislative agenda and no less successful in winning passage of it.[53]

Most interestingly as a methodological contribution to the literature on racial representation, Tate statistically probed the relationship between elected representatives and their constituents to explore whether blacks need to be descriptively represented for fair representation in Congress. She compared quantitative opinion patterns among black citizens (utilizing a 1996 national survey) and voting patterns among all members of Congress during that period. This new approach allowed a matching of the political attitudes of black citizens with the policy performance of their respective black officials and other white officials, thereby testing the essential ideas of prevailing orthodoxy.

Tate's research showed clearly that (a) black citizens were much more divided than black legislators in opinion on social and economic policy matters, and that (b) black public opinion had become more conservative over time, at least on the issues she studied, in marked contrast to the distinctively liberal politics of their black officials:

> The criticism that descriptive representation may not improve the policy representation of Blacks finds some empirical support in my study of the 104th Congress. Black legislators in the 104th did not vote on issues in the manner most directly representative of their Black constituents' views on key issues.[54]

Thus Tate's survey of black citizens found that they believed they are better represented in Congress when their representative is black, but her congressional data showed that descriptive representation did not improve the policy representation of black interests. In fact, on the specific issue of welfare reform, both white Republicans and white Democrats represented black opinion preferences more accurately than did their own black officials.

Tate's data regarding black-black representation's impact on the represented constituency were equally interesting. She found little support for the idea that such representation enhanced civic orientations among black citizens.

The evidence that descriptive district-based representation empowers Blacks is slight. Blacks are more knowledgeable about their representatives when that representative is Black, but they are neither more efficacious nor more likely to vote than Blacks represented by Whites . . . I therefore argue that in the end, it is not clear that having more Blacks added to Congress would truly improve Blacks' evaluation of Congress's performance or truly raise their levels of trust in government.[55]

Tate's findings were significantly puzzling in terms of ongoing discussion about racial representation. However, she reasoned that perfect policy congruency was only the "Holy Grail" that would never be attained, and she interpreted the patterns rather positively:

Constituents still feel fully represented despite the lack of perfect policy congruency because of all the other activities that representatives undertake in order to represent their constituents. Representation, after all is more than substantive, policy representation. It is also powerfully symbolic.[56]

Tate's study did not examine biracial leadership directly, but she conjectured skepticism about prospects for white leaders representing black interests; "Whites can win trust from Black constituents, of course, but because of history, they are necessarily going to have to work harder at establishing that trust."[57]

In her concluding chapter, Tate adamantly proclaimed black legislators' substantive representation of black interests:

Thus, while U.S. legislators are capable of speaking for a 'divergent rank' of social groups, the overwhelming, empirical evidence indicates that with respect to Blacks, at least, they normally don't. Black members in Congress have been the most consistent spokespersons for and champions of Black interests.[58]

Furthermore, she boldly maintained that the American system demands greater black-black representation in whatever manner and by whatever means necessary.

> America is a diverse nation and therefore we either change the system better to reflect its diversity, or the courts must fulfill their assumed constitutional role of protecting the interests of political minorities, including women. Such interests under the current political system can only be advanced in a national assembly that effectively mirrors the population.[59]

Research in Periodicals and Journals

Interestingly, some of the most pertinent and insightful work on racial representation has been presented in academic periodicals.

IMPORTANCE OF LIBERAL SUPPORT FOR WHITE BIRACIAL LEADERSHIP. Richard Fleisher supplied interesting evidence of the impact of contextual factors—the white liberal vote—in his analysis of constituency characteristics and congressional responsiveness.[60] Looking at various factors related to support for progressive issues among white and black members 1981–87, Fleisher concluded that some white Southern Democrats, operating in appropriate circumstances with liberal constituency support, had learned how to build biracial coalitions and represent those coalitions in Washington.

THE TRADE-OFF OF ELECTORAL AND REPRESENTATIONAL SCHEMES. Charles Cameron, David Epstein, and Sharyn O'Halloran directly examined a key point of debate—descriptive-versus-substantive representation—with sophisticated statistical analysis of the 1993–94 Congress.[61] Their research was complex and somewhat speculative; but the authors did not equivocate in their conclusive assessment that maximizing the number of minority representatives does not necessarily maximize minority representation; there is a trade-off between electing minority representatives and enacting minority-favored legislation.

THE INFLUENCE COSTS OF "PACKED" MINORITIES. Very similar results were reported at about the same time in a separate study by L. Marvin

Overby and Kenneth M. Cosgrove.[62] These scholars, after analyzing voting behavior and district racial composition for the 1993-94 Congress, found that changes in black constituency size had profound impact on Southern Democrats. Their data suggested that some of these politicians, who relied heavily on biracial electoral coalitions, were sensitive to the size of their minority constituencies; and when they lost minority constituents to racial-redistricting schemes they became significantly less sensitive to minority policy preferences.

REDISTRICTING, POLARIZATION, AND RACIAL COALITIONS. Kenneth A. Wink and Allison L. Hayes focused on the voting records of Congress members from redistricted areas in the 1990s.[63] Their data show that Southern white Democrats, who were essentially moderate, began disappearing as redistricting produced greater numbers of liberal black Democrats and conservative white Republicans. Their conclusion was that, as a result of this polarization, centrist coalitions are less likely than before.

A NEW MIX FOR MAXIMIZATION OF RACIAL RESPONSIVENESS. Most recently, Christian Grose has struck an insightful middle-ground in considering court-ordered racial districting.[64] Examining congressional representation in terms of distributive policy ("pork" projects) for 1996, 1998, and 2000, Grose asserted that, in some instances, where there is greater racial crossover voting, districts that are 40 to 49 percent black will suffice to make the election of African American legislators highly likely; and he recommends that redistricting officials pay heed to the local context of states and localities in attempting to enhance the representation of minority interests.

A Literature of Meandering Post-Movement Dissensus

Thus far, our historical overview and review of the literature have demonstrated some intriguing aspects of Southern politics during the twentieth century. Clearly, as academic observers have so thoroughly established, there was a failure of political leadership to deal realistically with the South's racial problems prior to the civil rights movement of the 1950s and 1960s. But, just as clearly, scholars themselves have failed to investigate and explain, satisfactorily, some important aspects of the South's transformation in the 1970s, 1980s, and 1990s.

Collectively, the major relevant studies (and a continuing stream of research not reported here) have provided valuable information, but no consensus about racial representation in the post-civil rights South; instead, these endeavors have stumbled along a course of meandering dissensus. Most research cited here ignored biracial developments, conditions, and strategies for change during that period except as occasional sidebars to other issues of central concern. Nevertheless, these research reports confirm some clear patterns of changed racial representation in the South. Most obviously, the South has progressed significantly since the civil rights revolution; huge numbers of African American voters now exercise their influence in the political arena, electing black officials in some areas and helping elect white officials in others. Just as certainly, Southern black elected leaders have been more responsive to black voters than Southern white officials. But the research also shows that, under some conditions, white leaders have represented black constituencies in reasonable manner. Particularly noteworthy is the changed relationship between white congressmen and their African American constituents. We have voluminous electoral data showing that blacks often helped send white Democrats to Congress; roll-call analysis demonstrates that these white representatives have been responsive in Washington.

However, beyond their occasional and easy comments about "representing everybody," we don't know very much about how these white officials engaged black activists and voters in volatile, polarized environments back home; nor are we aware of the ways that white officials served their black supporters, beyond voting, without antagonizing their base white constituency. Several of the studies reported in this manuscript hinted at these relationships in conversational and anecdotal passages; James Glaser actually reported select aspects of bifurcated campaigning in parts of the region. However, there has been no comprehensive investigation of the stealth phenomenon and its consequence for the transformation of Southern politics. Details about the private, working relationships among white leaders, black activists, and their biracial electorates might go a long way in explaining the transformation of Southern politics during the latter part of the twentieth century.

A Call for Appropriate Attention from Professional Scholars

While the academic community has enhanced its approach over the years, our review of the literature shows that scholars have not explored, fully and satisfactorily, the representational dynamics of Southern politics.

Granted, professional history has thoroughly covered the civil rights movement over the past half-century, and current interest seems unabated. Also, political science has done a thorough job evidencing black empowerment, two-party competition, and the altered voting performance of Southern officials during the 1970s, 1980s, and 1990s. However, recent research on racial representation shows timidity among historians and political scientists in looking at other important, revelational aspects of "real Southern politics" of that period, and Southern state university presses have been similarly deficient in fulfilling this aspect of their public service mission.

Thus we are left with our original, intriguing, consequential question: How did we get from the brutally contentious civil rights movement to the substantial progress of our new racial system? Nothing in the literature addresses—theoretically, comprehensively, and coherently—the causal "what" and "how" and "why" of the broad political progress that has occurred since the contentious days of the heroic drama.

Obviously, in our opinion, the new thesis of stealth politics merits further attention; however, we also know, based on the tone of current debate and discussions with colleagues, that normative, theoretical, and methodological obstacles impede research on quiet, practical, biracial politics. So we want to address these issues.

Normative Reservations

To be blunt, our focus on white officials and biracial politics as a constructive element of Southern life during the 1970s, 1980s, and 1990s does not fit comfortably into the heroic drama of civil rights history; as might be expected, there are normative reservations about our thesis and research.

As we posited in our introduction, the greatest impediment to our idea is the semi-sacred standing of the Southern civil rights struggle within our national democratic experiment. The heroic drama is inscribed in the American psyche as a moral certainty of good versus evil, of righteous souls versus racial ogres, depicted literally and figuratively in black and white images from that era and area. Scholars and journalists pay unwavering homage to the standard, ubiquitous story, and ambitious politicians generally avoid anything that strays from a common vision of the heroic drama. The civil rights movement is ingrained in our culture as an unassailable psychic monument.

However, veneration has its downsides. The most serious impact of narrow, rigid, reverent focus is a tendency to positively accentuate certain aspects and neglect or discount other important dynamics of Southern politics. As Glenn Feldman argued in *Reading Southern History*, it is difficult for historians to perform objective research and analysis with such powerfully normative perspective:

> If the historian is too close to the subject, either in time or in sentiment, objectivity is lessened. The essential integrity of the enterprise runs the risk of being corrupted—or at least compromised. Studies of repressed or excluded groups are especially vulnerable on this score because many who write movement history are more homogeneous in their beliefs than scholars in other subfields. Quite often, practitioners are attracted to this kind of history in the first place because of definite beliefs and principles— or, in less polite terms, prejudices and biases. They are convinced that the movements for greater and fuller inclusiveness were and are inherently good. Those convictions may make good politics and good social policy, but they do not always make good history. Some measure of detachment is fundamental.[65]

Civil Rights Project co-founder Gary Orfield cited similarly problematic impacts of normed constraints on the scholarship of Southern politics:

> Because of intellectual myopia, ignorance of the nature of the pre-1965 Deep South, regional prejudices, and the concentration of intellectual resources in the urban North, there have been amazingly few serious efforts to study and describe the full range of the change in Southern communities. We know more about individual neighborhoods in some of the

cities where our great universities are located than about the civil rights revolution in entire states . . . this means that we lack extremely important information about the possibility of social change through law.[66]

More recently, self-described Yankee journalist Jacob Levenson has gone so far as to identify an "artificial conceit" in our iconic commitment to the distant drama:

> Strangely, we seem to treasure those black-and-white memories, and when we drag them out, we do it with a sort of pride. It's as if they remind and reassure us that we are a people who will stare down hatred and injustice. They serve as symbols of what we'd like to think we're not.[67]

After touring the South for a book on AIDS and blacks, Levenson speculated that the country and the press often use regional images and history as a convenient box to stash problems, situations, and conditions that, while real, are actually national in scope. "It is hugely tempting to use the South as a slate for stories that as a nation we have difficulty penetrating."[68]

To paraphrase Levenson, talking passionately about the heroic drama of the 1950s–60s sometimes is a way to assert a morally correct persona without dealing with difficult issues of race today in America. Ironically, this approach seems to work for both Southerners and nonSoutherners, for both blacks and whites, as well as for scholars, journalists, and politicians of all persuasions.

Certainly—whether due to subjective norms, intellectual myopia, artificial conceit, or something else—there's little interest in exploring routine politics as a positive aspect of post-movement change in the South. Some argue that political developments have fallen far short of success in this region; the failures of the period, they insist, make any talk about quiet, practical, biracial progress outrageous and irresponsible. Others object to crediting white denizens of Dixie and their black partners with significant impact on societal progress; it may be especially galling when such ideas are forwarded by those politicians themselves.

It is equally clear, furthermore, that some progressives consider our proposition about post-movement developments inimical to their contemporary political agenda. As our survey of recent research demonstrates, for example, civil rights activists belittle the idea of "race-neutralized politics" (whether it goes by the name of stealthness in our project or deracialization in other studies). They worry that promoting effective biracial leadership will work against their push for majority-minority districts, the election of black officials for black constituencies, and the advance of African American policy priorities. Illustrative was the negative reaction, as reported by Joseph P. McCormick and Charles E. Jones, to several papers on black biracial leadership at a national conference of African American political scientists:

> Collectively, these papers fueled a fiery debate that took place during the course of the conference over the various meanings and interpretations of the 1989 elections, summarized herein. Proponents of the use for the electoral variant of deracialization bore a significant brunt of the "attack" with one scholar labeling the concept an "oxymoron," with another throwing his hands up in frustration and exclaiming, "I'm not sure what this all means." Quite clearly, as this conference came to a close, the gauntlet had been dropped at the feet of the proponents of this analytic construct to go back to the "drawing board" and reconsider its meaning and the electoral conditions under which its use as a descriptive tool was most applicable. [69]

Without doubt, professional study of the civil rights movement during those years and in succeeding decades has been a morally engaged endeavor; and various sectors view additional or alternative interpretations as discomforting challenge to their particular sentiments about history and politics. The result is a striking absence of logically intriguing investigation into important, causal dynamics of Southern political history.

We acknowledge the reservations and concerns cited in this section, but we stand by our thesis and research. Our project is not a strained rewriting of Southern history or a radical challenge to any perspective on racial representation. Our point is simply that white biracial leadership has been an important factor in Southern politics of the past few decades. In our opinion, normative concerns should not proscribe efforts to fathom the dynamics of stealthy leadership and biracial representational alliances that succeeded in a tricky balancing act and added much needed street-smarts—and real progress—to the civil rights movement.

We also believe, as do others, that political realities seriously limit majority-minority redistricting and black-black representation as a constructive course of future action. For example, at the congressional level, blacks are represented by blacks in every majority-black or plurality-black district in the Old Confederacy except for one district in Tennessee and one district in Louisiana, yet there are only sixteen African Americans among the 131 members of Congress from the South; this may be the maximum capacity under current law. However, and importantly for our thesis, a majority of the rest of the districts in this region have sufficient minority populations to play significant electoral and governing roles. More than sixty Southern districts now represented by whites have 10-40 percent black constituencies; we think that many of these areas are realistic targets for minority "political participation" and biracial progress.

Redistricting expert Harold W. Stanley clearly stated this reality in discussing prospects for more black elected officials:

> The prospects for general election majorities based primarily on black votes are restricted to very few Southern districts. The distribution of the Southern black population indicates that the election of black or black-backed candidates in most of the South hinges on biracial coalition politics.[70]

Therefore, we offer our thesis with cautious and suggestive sensitivity for normative reservations, as both a supplement to conventional history and as guidance for the future. We are convinced that our stealthy white politicians and black activists played a major role in Southern political transformation during the period of interest; and we think that this biracial leadership may positively inform and shape the future of representation regionally and nationally.

Theoretical Significance

There also are questions of theoretical significance, which can be resolved simply and concisely. To begin, were the biracial alliances proposed here substantially different and systemically consequential? For example, is there anything special about this so-called "stealth" activity—isn't it normal for leaders to conduct private politics differently from their public image? Also, white Southern politicians practiced manipulative politics for decades prior to the civil rights movement; was the furtive activity of the 1970s, 1980s, and 1990s really different? Furthermore, it is clear that Southerners were moderating their views toward race during this period; did these stealthy leaders/alliances really push the South forward or did they simply reflect changing Southern attitudes? Finally, looking to the future, does our biracial politics have any broader significance in changing America?

Our answer to all these theoretical questions is "Yes." Stealth politics was special and different, and necessarily calculated because of the region's long history in the race game. Stealth leaders are especially interesting because of the volatile nature of their constituencies, the difficulty of their historic challenge, and the success with which they performed their service. This relatively quiet phenomenon, which has received little attention from the public, media, and professional scholars, helped fundamentally change the Southern political system in positive ways. And, yes, considering trends and problems throughout society, we think that our biracial alliances have critical significance for multi-cultural America in the twenty-first century.

Methodological Issues

Methodological questions relating to stealth research are more challenging, but our discipline has dealt with such problems effectively in the past.

For example, how do we assess "quiet, practical, biracial" developments that involve ex post facto, behind-closed-door, subjectively defined machinations? In the first place, many theoretical types and academic researchers generally don't care to get that close to real-world Southern politicians. Contemporary scholars seem much happier dealing with books, journals, surveys, census data, voting records, roll-call charts, and impersonal, mind-numbing cyberspace. Also, such research is beyond the capabilities of most academicians because the central political characters of that time—both black and white—still don't like to talk about such things. Finally, once the scholar gets beyond these obstacles, there's an inherent difficulty that has split the academy for many years; i.e., these real-world political accounts defy easy quantification and scientific analysis.

Our countering argument is direct and adamant. In the first place, V. O. Key, Richard F. Fenno, and countless other scholars have demonstrated that actually engaging politicians can be very productive. More critically, the people who can provide personal testimony, factual information, and documentary evidence about this aspect of Southern history are a dying breed. While it is difficult to gather such material, the results are valuable in describing and explaining that period; and the findings should prove helpful in understanding contemporary and future politics at the regional and national levels. In our opinion, scholars are duty-bound to investigate, report, and analyze the phenomenon—despite methodological difficulties—before it is eclipsed through professional neglect and actuarial reality.

It seems clear, for example, that academic scholars should expand their professional focus and horizon to incorporate white Southern politicians more accurately in historical analysis of the heroic drama. The academic community has, for the past half-century, researched legions of heroic players: in addition to the central focus on black icons of both major and minor acclaim, we find pro-civil rights national political leaders, New South governors, justice officials and lawyers, courts and judges, churches and ministers, media and journalists, public intellectuals and educators, actors and entertainers, business leaders, labor activists, inside agitators, and, most recently, women. On the other side are the segregationist villains from central casting: ignorant rednecks, states-rights nuts, violent klansmen, local law enforcement bullies, and demagogic politicians. We know much about and have analyzed extensively the backgrounds, attitudes, activities, and contributions of all these players in the historical game of Southern politics.

Unfortunately, this is an incomplete accounting of the past half-century. Somewhere between 1970 and 2000, practical white public officials—neither heroic nor villainous—helped to quietly desegregate and moderate Southern politics. We can attest to the reality of stealth politics and leadership—it happened! But nowhere in the literature have we found any serious theoretical consideration or research documentation of this aspect of Southern transformation. It is now appropriate for professional scholars to incorporate the phenomenon of stealth reconstruction into conventional study of Southern political history.

We agree with historian Charles W. Eagles, who calls for "new histories" of the civil rights era. Eagles, writing in the *Journal of Southern History*, urges Southern research toward bolder analysis, covering both white and black participants, during the post-civil rights era:[71]

> The literature on the movement now needs, therefore, to be invigorated by new works that will challenge the established chronology, add greater detachment, and correct the imbalance now pervading the scholarship. The innovations may come from imaginative monographic work, new syntheses, and, more likely, from new bold reconceptualizations of the movement's history. From whatever source, new approaches will cause controversy and stretch the tolerance of many established scholars. To extend the debate in civil rights scholarship will require that students of the movement become more tolerant of divergent, even iconoclastic, opinions.[72]

We especially think that academicians should approach this area of study, as historian Glenn Feldman suggests, in *Reading Southern History*, with greater detachment, objectivity, and perspective in future research.[73] Moreover, we think that our own discipline of political science should engage more actively and substantively, without compromising objectivity, in the assessment of real-world racial representation. As Richard K. Scher recently complained in "Unfinished Business: Writing the Civil Rights Movement," political scientists have neglected this aspect of Southern politics:[74]

> Overwhelmingly, the literature has been written by historians, sociologists, journalists, general writers, and on-the-scene autobiographers or chroniclers. With the exception of empirical literature on the outcomes of

the civil rights movement and some analyses of how specific institutions were involved in the movement . . . political scientists have contributed very little to the literature . . . [75]

Regardless of what theoretical and normative perspectives are used, political scientists need to enter the study of the civil rights movement, and of race generally, more vigorously than they have. Race is not simply an independent variable that political scientists can manipulate to suit the needs of sophisticated, au courant statistical models they choose to employ in their research. Race is a fundamental element in American politics in exactly the same way V O. Key saw it as fundamental to Southern politics more than fifty years ago. [76]

Both disciplines need to pursue, with scholarly inquisitiveness and enthusiasm, the unfashionable idea of moderate white leadership in the aftermath of the civil rights movement. The contribution of biracial politics clearly merits serious study for balancing Southern history of the twentieth century. Just as importantly, an expanded perspective might help us deal with the perennial, stubborn question of fair minority representation in the American political system. As Lucius J. Barker, Mack Jones, and Katherine Tate observed in *African Americans and the American Political System*:

> . . . we need to know more about the behavior and responsiveness of elected white officials from districts where there are very large and discrete black and minority populations. Conversely, we need to know how black members of Congress deal with the matter of representing white populations in their districts. Given the historical and contemporary context of racial politics and race relations in this country, along with the thorny conceptual issues surrounding political representation more generally, answering this question could prove difficult for any representative, regardless of race or ethnicity. But we suggest that precisely those representatives who are able to overcome such difficulties will do much to improve both race relations and the overall quality of life in this country.[77]

We are confident—based on our combined political experience and academic research—that we have identified an important, undiagnosed aspect of the South's historic transformation. We also think that our stealth reconstructionists deserve further consideration. It may be time to try—as objectively and systematically as is possible through ex-post-facto research—to slip inside the minds, hearts, and backrooms of Southern politicians and activists who crafted the biracial politics of the post-civil rights era.

It is now our task to attempt a case study supporting the thesis of stealth reconstruction. In the next section, co-author Browder will discuss his work as an Alabama state legislator (1982–86), as Alabama's secretary of state (1987–89), and as U.S. congressman (1989–97),and we will follow up with a survey of other politicians and with discussions with activists who similarly contributed to stealthy change in the South.

PART TWO:

Stealth Research

4

THE ALABAMA SETTING
FOR STEALTH POLITICS

This case study will focus on Glen Browder's political career within the conceptual model presented in our theoretical discussion. In this chapter, he will characterize the setting of Alabama politics and introduce himself as a stealthy leader during the 1970s, 1980s, and 1990s.

I have been a mixture of academics and politics for most of my adult life. Besides my basic calling as a political scientist, I have practical background as a political party activist, campaign consultant, state representative, secretary of state, and U.S. congressman. My life as the "Professor-Politician" has been duly documented elsewhere.[1]

I was not part of the civil rights movement; however, I did occupy a unique position for contributing to Southern politics during the past half-century, and I easily satisfied the objective standards of our conceptual model of stealth leadership during the 1970s, 1980s, and 1990s. More pertinently, I have acknowledged stealthy style in my service as a driven politician during that era. As I said in the introductory chapter, I worked very hard and quietly to secure enough black support to get elected in majority-white areas; I tried to be fair, moderate, and progressive in my politics, and I didn't talk much publicly about any of this stuff.

Just as candidly, I disavow the role of righteous hero. I was an ambitious politician, not a social worker, civil rights activist, or crusading missionary. I wanted to achieve as much civic progress as was practically possible; that required, sometimes, that I dance with the devil—but I never let him take me home with him.

At the start of this case study, I want to take care of several editorial chores. First, I admit that the approach here reflects the advantages and liabilities of participant/observer methodology. Political experience has to be considered in balance with special, personal interest and memory of the era being studied. I am aware of this mixed blessing; however I think that I have maximized candor in this professional and personal analysis.

Second is a shift from theoretical considerations to practical politics and history. Thus far, we have engaged primarily in academic matters, frequently referencing other scholarly material in order to introduce our thesis, recount the historical background, and review the relevant political literature. The next few chapters will consist mainly of original research into real-world, hands-on aspects of the subject, with relatively little academic jargon or footnoting.

Third, and somewhat similar, is a style shift to personal perspective and language. I want the reader to understand that my repetitive declarations that "I did this" and "I did that" for civic and/or racial progress are statements of record rather than personal aggrandizement. The simple fact is that this is an exploratory case study, a first-person account, a heretofore untold story—and I'm the designated story-teller. So I have to dispense with modesty if I'm to provide a full and accurate assessment of quiet, practical, biracial politics.

Fourth, I rely extensively in this chapter and the following two chapters on material from the Browder Collection, consisting of several hundred boxes of documents that have been processed for public access (see *Analytic Guidebook for the Browder Collection*). This material can be reviewed for further information and within broader context at Jacksonville State University. Otherwise, standard sourcing procedures apply throughout the manuscript.

Fifth, I want to explain that, while I generally "name names" in the following case study and throughout this manuscript, I sometimes forgo reference to public officials and activists who are still active in Alabama and Southern politics. I simply exclude certain individuals from this analysis; or, in a couple of instances, I provide an acknowledged pseudonym. Our thesis is likely to generate some discussion in and of itself; and I certainly do not want to drag specific current personalities and issues into a contentious historical debate.

This is also a good time to reiterate the analytic terminology for this project that was introduced in the first chapter. "Stealth" is an academic artifact that we use in the current project to describe a style of politics and representation being examined ex post facto. Back then, we did not talk in such theoretical terms; however, we did talk, think, and conduct ourselves in a manner that conformed to this framework. I therefore will employ the term "stealth politics" for analytic purposes throughout this manuscript.

Additionally, I will use a related and more functional term—"black politics"—much as we did back then, as nonpejorative description of activities at the core of our stealthness, activities designed specifically to reach black voters and relate to black constituents, activities that were different and separate from white, mainstream politics. While public speeches often included inspiring articulations of "African American" dreams and concerns, leaders of both races, at least in private, face-to-face political settings, routinely used more succinct "black" references to their workday agenda of things such as "black campaigning," "black GOTV" [get out the vote], "black media," "black issues," and just generally "black politics."

In this chapter—dealing with the setting of the case study—I first will present the context of Alabama politics during that era; then I will discuss other political figures who blazed the trail of biracial politics in the Heart of Dixie; and I will conclude by introducing myself as a civic-oriented and race-sensitive politician trying to practice a new kind of leadership.

The Context of Alabama Politics in the 1970s, 1980s, and 1990s

By the time I entered active politics, the heroic drama was winding down to less histrionic contentions throughout much of the South. Powerful forces of change—the federal government, civil rights laws, the news media, political parties, business interests, black voters, even state and local courts—had pushed the region to the brink during the civil rights movement; and some elected officials knew that it was time to move forward. "New South" governors had taken the lead elsewhere— Terry Sanford of North Carolina, Reubin Askew of Florida, John West of South Carolina, Bill Waller of Mississippi, Dale Bumpers of Arkansas, and Jimmy Carter of Georgia come to mind. In fact, a steady parade of "New South" executives moderated Southern politics—such as David Pryor and Bill Clinton in Arkansas, Jim Hunt in North Carolina, William Winter in Mississippi, Lamar Alexander in Tennessee, Richard Riley in South Carolina, Bob Graham and Lawton Chiles in Florida, and Charles Robb and Doug Wilder in Virginia.

However, as I have shown previously, George Wallace had made Alabama a citadel of racial resistance. Although several progressives tried, it was hard for any "New South" aspirants to crack Wallaceism in this part of the Deep South. Richmond Flowers and Carl Elliott failed in 1966. State Senator Ryan deGraffenreid, who had succumbed to George Wallace in a 1962 Democratic Party primary runoff, died in a tragic plane crash mid-campaign against Lurleen Wallace in that 1966 primary. Albert Brewer (the lieutenant governor who had moved temporarily to the governor's office upon Lurleen's death from cancer in 1968) came close, but he perished at the hands of George Wallace and vicious racism in the 1970 primary. Lieutenant Governor George McMillan fell victim to a strange twist of racial politics in the 1982 primary (with many blacks supporting George Wallace's last gubernatorial campaign). Without serious Republican opposition in the general election, these critical, internecine Democratic Party primaries generally stalled racial progressivism.

Auburn University historian Wayne Flynt portrayed the Yellowhammer state during those times as both a contributor to and consequence of racial tribulation:

> It is fair to say that the bitter resistance of Alabama whites played a major role in the success of the civil rights agenda on a broad front. Subtle, less violent resistance had largely thwarted the movement. But the often violent and uniformly inept policies of Wallace, Lingo, Clark, Connor, Hanes, and others provided the movement with martyrs, publicity, recruits, and, most important of all, the moral high ground in virtually every confrontation The long-range consequence was a state deeply polarized along racial lines, one of the highest numbers of elected black officials

of any state, and a lingering residue of negative national stereotypes that proved that history is never over, history is never past, and generations unborn carry the burdens of their parents.[2]

In perhaps the most balanced treatment of Governor George Wallace and Alabama of that era, historian Jeff Frederick recently concluded his book, *Stand Up for Alabama: Governor George Wallace*, with the following paragraph:

> As Wallace's body lay in state in September 1998, news reporters and television crews crowded around the capitol to interview black and white Alabamians. Asked to define his legacy, some folks noted his 1963 inaugural address, the junior college system, or his transformation from racial demagogue to apologetic paraplegic. But more often than not, the masses who waited in line to pay their final respects to the governor could not quite come to grips with their feelings. Wallace had been their governor, and they loved him even as they were still not quite sure what to make of him. Until the state addresses the core issues it faced in 1963—issues that remain in the twenty-first century—Alabama will never be able to turn the page on the Wallace years.[3]

Nevertheless—even as Wallace was dominating the state—a temporal window of opportunity began to open for bold Alabama leaders to successfully gamble on biracial politics in the complex wake of the post-civil rights revolution. The Democratic Party still dominated electorally, so a few progressive white politicians discreetly courted the rapidly enfranchising blacks while holding onto sufficient numbers of the traditional white bases in the party primary elections, without fearing that any Republican could defeat them in the subsequent general election.

At the same time, Alabama black leaders began asserting themselves in the arena of political power. African Americans increasingly captured elective office at the local level, and they incrementally grabbed equitable presence and power on Goat Hill[4] in Montgomery. As Charles E. Menifield, Stephen D. Shaffer, and Brandi J. Brassell noted in their assessment of Southern state legislative politics during this period, there was "tremendous change" in this part of the country:

> The Deep South state of Alabama made particularly impressive strides in descriptive representation, so by 2000, African Americans were represented in the state house in proportion to the black presence in the population and underrepresented in the senate by only 3 percent . . . African Americans hold as many house committee chairmanships as their size in the state house warrants, and even more representation than numbers warrant in the senate."[5]

Of course, Alabama had long been resistant to change, and these relatively-progressive white and black leaders faced fierce opposition as they blazed their trail of biracial politics.

"Trail-Blazers" and "Lessons-Learned" in the Heart of Dixie

It is important to acknowledge that I was not a biracial trailblazer. Well before I came along, some Alabama political leaders—black and white at various levels of service and power—had already begun working together and dealing with historical problems. Furthermore, I realized that my personal window of opportunity would probably be limited by the course of Southern history. This strange and transient situation began in the 1970s, functioned widely in the 1980s, and faltered in the 1990s. Inevitably, racial, partisan, and other developments would close this opportunistic window as the new century dawned.[6]

Therefore, when I took my oath of office in the Alabama House of Representatives in 1983, I knew that I was entering a special realm. I had my own agenda of political reform and progress, but I also was prepared to pursue the challenging opportunity—at a critical juncture of time, place, events, and people—for dealing with the South's legacy of hard racial history.

Standing squarely at the geographical crossroads of the Civil War and the civil rights revolution, I knew that I would work, at least for a while, with legendary veterans of perhaps the most important social movement in American history, to help resolve continuing aspects of that struggle.

Furthermore, it was clear that black-white reconciliation was critical to my broader personal and reform agenda. Relatively few political scientists would ever experience such challenge and opportunity.

All of which leads to the point that, while I appreciated the dramatic nature of history in the Heart of Dixie, particularly the rough times of the 1950s and 1960s, my self-defined mission during the 1970s, 1980s, and 1990s called for practical working relationships with heroes, villains, and everyday politicians on a diversity of issues, not simply racial problems. I went into public service to make American democracy work better; accordingly, in the context of Alabama politics, that historical assignment would require skillful, effective, and stealthy biracial leadership.

There was a lot for me to learn about my self-assumed assignment from history books about Southern politics, or from New South politicians in other states; fortunately too, there were convenient role models—both positive and negative—for me to study in Alabama.

Of course, I learned some sobering, unpleasant lessons from reading about the experiences of Big Jim Folsom, John Patterson, Richmond Flowers, Carl Elliott, and George Wallace in the 1950s and 1960s.

More positively instructive were several white leaders who, beginning in the 1970s, blazed the trail for progressive, biracial politics. I taught about these leaders in my classrooms at Jacksonville State University, and, I utilized their experiences as a campaign consultant on behalf of various would-be politicians. Finally, as a candidate and public official, I attempted to implement the positive lessons-learned from working with these trail-blazers.

For our analysis, I'll focus on a few biracial leaders of the 1970s, 1980s, and 1990s. These were not the only politicians from whom positive lessons could be learned; but I will spare other public officials from analytic scrutiny because they are still active in Alabama politics.

BILL BAXLEY is not a good example of stealth politics—because he really didn't operate stealthily—but he was one of the first white politicians to openly solicit black votes and support black causes.

A bold, populist Democrat, Baxley championed progressive issues as attorney general (1971–79) and lieutenant governor (1983–87); and he barely missed the governorship in a controversial 1986 election. During his career, Baxley prosecuted violent white supremacists, hounded corrupt public officials, pursued environmental issues, and attempted constitutional reform. He's best remembered for finally convicting one of the 1963 Birmingham church bombers and for officially instructing a white supremacist to "kiss my ass."[7] Arguably, his aggressive pursuit of racial justice derailed his ascent to the governor's mansion on two occasions.

It was obvious to me that I had to avoid Baxley's brash ways; however, I learned from this populist that it was possible for a skilled politician to appeal to both black and white electorates and to move Southern politics in positive direction.[8]

Don Siegelman was another successful, progressive Alabama Democrat, winning elections for secretary of state (1979–87), attorney general (1987–91), lieutenant governor (1995–99), and governor (1999–2003)—an unprecedented record in state politics.

Unlike Baxley, who seemed to revel in raw political conflict, Siegelman was, for most of his career, a master of public relations, civic initiatives, biracial relations, and inside politics—an impressive and effective stealth package. He began as a champion of clean elections; he marketed an agenda of reform and progress; and he "reached out and touched" virtually every citizen—black and white—in the state. Siegelman unfortunately immersed himself deeply in Goat Hill politics; he publicly clashed with some important black leaders; and he eventually ran aground with legal problems.

Siegelman demonstrated the value of grassroots loyalists and supportive media in pressing a good government agenda; and he paved the way, both personally and politically, for my work on election reform. More generally, Siegelman's experiences—both good and bad—provided critical insights about pursuing progressive, biracial objectives amidst powerful, antagonistic interests and constituencies.[9]

Howell Heflin. My ultimate model of quiet, practical, biracial leadership during that era was the late Howell Heflin, who traveled a progressive course as chief justice of the Alabama Supreme Court (1971–77) and U.S.

Senator (1979–97). I first met Heflin at an Alabama Political Science Association conference in the early 1970s. Judge Heflin (as he was affectionately known throughout his career) was promoting judicial reform at the conference. I was impressed with his approach to achieving philosophical progress without dysfunctional political trauma. That approach has been summarized thusly in an introduction to the Howell Heflin Collection at the University of Alabama School of Law:

> During the years in which he worked for judicial reform, Heflin developed a political style that might best be described as "consultative." As illustrated above, his method was to convene, confer, and build coalitions. This nonconfrontational manner allowed Heflin and the court reformers to transform an antiquated system without making enemies of those accustomed to its delays. In 1978, Heflin won a seat in the United States Senate, weathering George Wallace's short-lived candidacy and demonstrating conclusively that he could survive in the tough world of Alabama electoral politics. Yet his fundamental approach remained that of a unifier. Throughout three terms in the Senate, Heflin aligned himself with the national-centrist wing of Southern Democratic politicians. Perhaps it was because of his bridge-building talents that he frequently found himself at the center of highly publicized events.[10]

Over the years, I grew to appreciate Heflin as an emulative leader who was well grounded personally, politically, and philosophically. As was written by his biographers, Heflin conjoined principle and politics; and he was especially sensitive to the racial history of his state and region:

> Howell Heflin was a supporter of equal rights for all citizens throughout his professional career. He handled and won many cases for blacks when he was in law practice, he made sure that blacks were included in decision processes and that they received fair treatment before the courts when he was chief justice, and he worked for civil rights in the Senate. Without question his commitment was real and reflected his deepest feelings.[11]

I noted furthermore that Heflin could be philosophically eclectic and low-keyed stylistically, yet he was very positive and effective regarding the handling of race issues.

In many ways, Heflin represented the prevailing traditions and culture of Alabama, but on some issues he went against the thinking in his Deep South state. A Southern Democrat, he was pro-defense, supported the right to bear arms, and opposed legal abortion; he also supported school prayers and opposed gay rights. Economically, he sometimes sided with the anti-tax Republicans and at other times he went with populist Democrats. And, much to the consternation of conservative elements, he generally supported civil rights and affirmative action.

Heflin himself acknowledged that his orientation confounded conventional delineation:

> An Alabama progressive in the Hugo Black tradition, Howell Heflin resists labels like "conservative" and "liberal," preferring instead to say he is motivated by compassionate moderation. Many longtime friends and colleagues consider him an "old-fashioned populist," that is a politician who identifies with and represents directly the interests of the common people. Of party leanings, he says, "Instead of being so concerned with policies that are left and right, government should be concerned with the principles of right and wrong, which come from approaching issues in measured, moderate, and compassionate tones."[12]

Heflin's voting pattern similarly defied precise characterization. As he stated in remembrance of the controversy over busing for school integration during the Reagan administration:

> I reckon I was all over the place on busing ... I voted against a lot of the things on busing that Jesse Helms and Bennett Johnston of Louisiana proposed, and I voted for some of them. It depended on the language.[13]

Overall, however, Heflin's philosophy and politics aligned in relatively progressive manner. He traversed a fitful series of racial issues, managing as best he could to deal quietly and constructively with the demands and constraints of Southern political life. As his biographer wrote: "While Heflin took a low profile with the media on these issues, he worked as a strong advocate behind the scenes."[14] Once, while helping negotiate a compromise extending the Voting Rights Act in 1982, Heflin directed his colleague, Senator Robert Dole, to quit citing his assistance on the bill that was unpopular back home in Alabama: "Don't give me any credit. I don't want to be in the newspapers on this matter."[15] In the end, Heflin and his fellow negotiators crafted a bill that passed on a vote of 87–7.

Heflin's performance on the stage of Alabama politics was lauded by many. Perhaps most interesting is a tribute from powerful black leader Dr. Joe Reed:

> I never saw him as a flaming liberal. I saw him as an extremely honest man. He was a Southerner. He knew the land. He knew the circumstances. He knew the problems that blacks experienced. I think in his own way, he would try to right every wrong that he possibly could without calling a press conference, without getting on a stump—just doing it. I think he firmly believed in the Fatherhood of God and the Brotherhood of Man. I saw him acting this way throughout his career, not out of sheer politics, but out of a commitment, out of convictions. Is this fair? Is this right? Is this wrong? He took these considerations into account more than any person I've run across in my long political career.[16]

I concluded early on that the Heflin model of quiet, practical, biracial leadership suited my personality and aspirations. Often, for example, when difficult political situations required public comment about a racial matter, I simply would pause and ask myself, "What would Heflin say?" before attempting an artful and constructive statement for the record.

Judge Heflin and the other trail-blazers might quibble with my characterization of their leadership; however, all of these political leaders (and numerous uncited others) contributed in important ways to quiet, practical, biracial reconstruction in Alabama. While I never replicated exactly their particular practices or achievements, I derived guidance from their collective experiences and employed those lessons in my own career as a stealth politician.

Profile of "A New Kind of Leader"

Boldly and arrogantly, I planned to do things strategically, positively, successfully—in other words, differently from most Southern politicians. Drawing from my personal, academic, and consulting background, and employing the lessons learned from "trail-blazing" colleagues, I devised a full strategy for entering the political arena as "A New Kind of Leader" and, through constant revision of that plan, for pursuing the course as far as possible

I thus successfully and successively assumed roles of Democratic Party activist, state legislator, secretary of state, and, by the end of that decade, member of the U.S. Congress.

I always represented majority-white areas with varying black minorities. In the Alabama legislature, my district was 93 percent white; as an elected secretary of state, my constituency was 74 percent white; and as a congressman, I represented a 73 percent white electorate. So, within this setting, biracial leadership and black constituents were serious considerations for me, especially as a Democrat, throughout my public career. I served a total of fourteen years in public office, never trailing in any campaign for public office prior to losing the U.S. Senate Democratic Primary in 1996.

As a public official, I generally pursued a moderate, centrist career. I was usually attacked by the Democrats as "too conservative" and by the Republicans as "too liberal" so I felt pretty comfortable. I concentrated on political reform, fiscal responsibility, national defense, and constituency relations; throughout my service in Montgomery and Washington, I was quietly aware of my biracial responsibilities. The quantitative record shows that I was a political moderate as a legislator. For example, I normally scored at about the 50th percentile on ideological rankings, halfway between the most liberal and most conservative members of Congress This centrism, along with my reform efforts and constituency relations, kept me in good stead with most of my white constituents. At the same time, I was carefully attentive to the African American community, scoring slightly above 50 percent during my career in Washington on the Leadership Conference on Civil Rights scorecard, a broad compilation of black and other human rights issues. I tried to be a skillful, effective leader for both whites and blacks during a time and in a setting that make me a remarkably apt subject for studying stealth politics.

Legacy of Hard History

To understand my career and the strategic elements of "stealth politics" and "black politics" in this study, the reader must revisit Southern history and the ravages of slavery on Southerners, black and white, past and present.

As *Anniston Star* publisher Brandy Ayers has explained so clearly and sensitively over the years, people elsewhere study history; Southerners live history.[17] In a sensitive, native-son essay about the South as it staggered through the civil rights movement, Ayers noted reflective comments by aging historian Arnold Toynbee about his observations as an eight-year-old boy, sitting atop his uncle's shoulders, watching the Diamond Jubilee celebration of British world supremacy on June 22, 1897:

> Well, here we are on top of the world, and we have arrived at this peak to stay there forever. There is, of course, a thing called history, but history is something unpleasant that happens to other people. We are comfortably outside all that, I am sure. If I had been a small boy in New York in 1897 I should have felt the same. Of course, if I had been a small boy in 1897 in the Southern part of the United States, I should not have felt the same; I should have known from my parents that history had happened to my people in my part of the world.[18]

History has been hard on everyone in this region, and it has been especially hard on black Southerners. After slavery, they had to build their lives from scrabble—segregated and impoverished—within a larger white environment that had problems of its own. In the course of that process, blacks established correlative institutions (families, churches, schools, businesses, etc.) incorporating the strengths and values of their cultural heritage; but

they also suffered tremendous disadvantages. The broader white government ignored legitimate needs such as education, economic development,
and law enforcement; and it was common for white leaders to leave things
alone in the black community as long as black problems did not unduly
offend or impact white society. Consequently, black Southerners developed
their own ways of doing things, ways that did not always fit the ideas and
mores of white society; in particular, black politics sometimes operated in
a shadowy arena with relatively little oversight. We should not be surprised
that reconstructive endeavors would reflect difficult interactions between
these segregated societies.

Therefore, some relatively progressive Southern politicians—both black
and white—of the past few decades have played the hand that history dealt
them. This meant that they often operated in circumspect manner to gain
white support while engaging in separate and different manner to maximize
the black vote.

It was not pretty civics. It was the continuing legacy of hard history.

Personal and Professional Background

My background came right out of the "American dream." I rose from
childhood poverty to enjoy the full blessings of American life.[19]

My dream began dismally, over a half-century ago, on the wrong side
of the tracks in Sumter, South Carolina. Sumter was like many Southern
towns of the 1940s, 1950s, and 1960s, projecting gentility and progress
despite burgeoning problems of poverty and segregation. My family was
poor by all standards, so I have few childhood memories of such gentility
and progress.

I grew up in a time and place and environment of intense national
significance—the civil rights revolution—without any apparent passion,
or personal involvement in that revolution. I was an acquiescent product
of the Deep South culture of class and caste, proceeding through the civil
rights revolution with more pressing personal concerns and with conflicted
acclimation to the Southern way of life.

Growing up in such an environment made me sensitive to social,
economic, racial, and other tensions in American life; most importantly,

however, it fueled my personal ambition and academic interests. I had been interested in the news media and public affairs in Edmunds High School (Sumter, South Carolina, 1957–61) and Presbyterian College (Clinton, Couth Carolina, 1961–65); and I worked briefly as a sportswriter for the Atlanta Journal (Atlanta, Georgia, 1966) and as an investigator for the U.S. Civil Service Commission (Atlanta Region, 1967–68). In that latter work, I served brief stints as a federal voter registrar and poll watcher in a few Southern elections under purview of the Voting Rights Act. I returned to academia for a Ph.D. in political science at Emory University in Atlanta (1968–71).

For the next decade, I focused on my family (wife Becky and daughter Jenny Rebecca) and worked as a political science professor at Jacksonville State University in Alabama. More so than any others, Becky and Jenny fostered my professional life. While neither is a very public person, they dutifully served as political spouse and daughter when I shifted my interest to politicking, and they tended the requirements of home and hearth as I plunged into my civic mission.

Academic and Political Life

Early in my academic career, I developed a professional interest in Southern history and politics, researching, writing, and teaching about regional affairs in which race mattered. I taught courses such as "Southern Politics" and wrote articles such as "Race and Representation in a Southern Community." While I had never been interested or involved in politics or civil rights issues while growing up and living in South Carolina and Georgia, I had served brief stints as a federal registrar and poll observer in the 1960s (while working as an investigator with the U.S. Civil Service Commission). I then immersed myself into academics after earning a doctorate in political science in 1971.

As a political science professor in Alabama during the 1970s, I kept a keen eye on Southern politics for myself and my students. I was especially impressed with the work of scholars such as Lewis Killian,[20] Hanes Walton,[21] William Havard,[22] Jack Bass and Walter DeVries,[23] and Numan Bartley and Hugh Graham.[24] I was well positioned to agree with the assessment of

Bartley and Graham that "the galoots were loose over much of the region," and I shared their troubling questions about the South's future:

> The South of the 1970s is not the same South that the tortured Wilbur Cash knew. Gone are the Jim Crow signs and ordinances, the yahoo legislatures with their prohibition and monkey laws, and the triumphant "nigger-baiting" demagogues; now many of the social and political dilemmas of the South are symptomatic of a national malaise. But given the region's decidedly un-American experience with defeat, poverty, and guilt, history seems to have placed a peculiar kind of hex upon her, not as an immutable curse but as a pernicious source of devilment that confounds our more rational and optimistic predictions and masks deep-rooted continuity behind the symptoms of basic change.[25]

Transferring my political science skills into the political arena, I polled extensively on political issues, and incidentally on race-related matters, as a campaign consultant. My professional counsel didn't always square with my personal inclinations, but that experience proved invaluable in helping me develop a stronger understanding of and feel for Southern politics.

While my developing analysis of Southern change was not unique, it was partisanly troubling and personally consequential. I concluded that Democratic candidates could not continue to win or lead in responsible manner simply by reaping the benefits of massive black registration. Initially, Democrats could take advantage of the expected black bonanza while holding onto their white voting majority because of tradition and habit; but, inevitably, sociopolitical developments would move conservative whites toward the Republican Party and transform Southern politics into meaningful two-party competition (probably with Republicans in the majority).

But, I reasoned, there was the possibility for positive progress in Alabama and the South if Democratic leaders could develop a biracial foundation for transformational service. Otherwise, racist demagoguery might poison Alabama politics into the twenty-first century. In my mind, considering the turbulent possibilities of those times, the future of my party and state depended upon practical leadership that would encourage black participation, minimize white reaction, and pursue moderate-to-progressive politics.

I collaborated with a solid corps of friends and supporters before taking the plunge and during the course of my political career. However, very few people—other than my wife Becky (an original vested partner in the Browder operation)—fully realized the special, mixed nature of my personally defined mission as "A New Kind Of Leader."

One member of the team who understood my broad game plan from the beginning was Dr. Jess Brown, a former student, close confidant, longtime political scientist, and oft-quoted media commentator on Alabama politics and government. Brown, now a professor at Athens State University, had a clear conception of my difficult mission in Montgomery and Washington:

> Glen Browder knew at the outset of his career as a candidate for elective office that his place on the electoral landscape would not be the ideal one. He understood that his candidacy reflected the inevitable and precarious balancing act that one must do when trying to simultaneously win elections and reform a regional culture. His personal background and academic heritage created within him a genuine desire for change in the South's economy and race relations, but his practical experiences with the rough-and-tumble of electoral politics forced him to accept a restrained agenda and to adopt a tempered rhetoric about many issues.
>
> Browder struggled often, but in a low-key manner, to build coalitions dominated by the middle of the social spectrum, while incorporating an agenda serving the have-nots of society. Browder's style of nurturing incremental change via coalition-building in the middle of the social spectrum made him neither the villain nor the hero of the established titans of Alabama's power structure. He was not enough of an overtly fire-breathing liberal to satisfy some titans inside the Democratic Party and not enough of a corporate conservative to satisfy the titans of the GOP.
>
> As the state's partisan climate changed during the 1980s and 1990s with each major party becoming more and more ideologically rigid, his place on the electoral landscape transitioned from being less than ideal to almost mission impossible.[26]

To summarize, Alabama in the 1970s was dominated by Wallace and Old South ways, but the context of the state's politics was beginning to change. Thus I embarked, with difficult prospects but considerable success, on a new kind of politics incorporating civic reform and stealthy racial progress.

Now, on with the case study. As the following two chapters will illustrate, the essential elements of my stealthy approach were (a) racially-sensitive political campaigns, and (b) moderate-to-progressive public service.

5

A Case Study

in Stealthy Campaigning

This case study focuses on Glen Browder's political career within the conceptual model presented in our theoretical discussion. In this chapter, he will discuss his electoral campaigns as a stealthy leader during the 1970s, 1980s, and 1990s.

In the previous chapter, I described the situation in Alabama and placed myself within the theoretical parameters of the conceptual model of stealth leadership. In this chapter, I will explore more activist aspects—electoral campaigning—of my career.

It will become obvious, as this examination of intent and tactics unfolds, that my political campaigns were designed and conducted to secure significant black support without driving away the white majority. Apparently, I succeeded superbly with the public aspect of my chosen role as stealth politician. The public record demonstrates that my overall career was based on civic issues, political reform, and conventional concerns; there's very little in news releases, media material, or other documents regarding any race-related actions or activities.

I never articulated an official strategy for quiet, practical biracial politics—but, as the following section reveals, it was always on my mind and in my head! My old campaign files are rife with anecdotal, conjectural, confirmative scribbling, as cited previously, and my own words, offered here as contemporary commentary, confirm my discreet intent—i.e., "I worked very hard and quietly . . . and I didn't talk much publicly about any of this stuff."

A Stealthy Game Plan for Biracial Campaigning

My scholarly and consulting analyses took on a personal focus when I started planning my own entry into political life in 1980. In preparation, I occasionally jotted down information, observations, and insights and tossed them in a catch-all folder that I called my "game plan."

For example, I noted in an early, undated scribbling that things were changing in Alabama and the South:

> Historically, Democrats (1) identify the groups in the Democratic Coalition, (2) go tell each targeted group what they want to hear, and (3) hope that totals to a majority. Republicans have done it differently and well lately. They (1) figure out the majoritarian theme/message, (2) express it in language and examples appropriate for their constituent interests, and (3) hope that totals to a majority. Contemporary social trends and modern campaigning make the traditional Democratic plan unworkable in the South.

As I plunged into active politics, I realized just how important black votes would be for my career, and my game plan began taking shape as a tactical guide for quiet, moderate change in Alabama and Southern politics. While broader, non-racial concerns were paramount, there are, throughout my files, handwritten notes in which I cited ideas about upcoming campaigns and how race figured into those campaigns and, obviously but discreetly, my future career. Numerous dated conversations with both white and black associates explored the "who, what, where, how, why, etc." of black politics. Also, several documents provided analytical, tactical, and budgetary bases for weaving race-related factors into the Browder Game Plan.

Notes and material added intermittently to the file show that I prioritized black groups in terms of their vote potential and for my personal attention. For example, at the beginning in 1980, I had listed sixteen important groups that I would have to reach to win a seat in the state legislature; by each group I had named the person to whom I hoped to assign that responsibility. Number two, right behind "Educators," was "Blacks," which I assigned to myself. When I updated my game plan file for the 1986 secretary of state

campaign, my handwritten listing had "Blacks" atop the list of fifteen group-
ings. In 1989, when I ran for Congress, I had penciled calculations for the
five top black population counties (among fourteen counties in Alabama's
third congressional district), including references to "call/visit . . . meetings
. . . marked ballots . . . $" along with names/numbers for consulting both
black and white leaders in those areas. By 1996, when I ran unsuccessfully
for the U.S. Senate against strong, relatively liberal candidates in the increasingly liberal Democratic primary, my notes outlined a detailed plan for
attracting some black leaders, splitting black organizational endorsements,
and employing independent black operatives.

Despite the obvious black element in my elections, I kept those activities
low-key and sometimes separate from regular campaign operations. Many
functions were intentionally planned as relatively quiet events targeted specifically and/or only for the black electorate. I consciously avoided situations
in which the opposition might depict me as the "black candidate." I made
sure that there were mixed faces at my events in the black community, and
I didn't spend a lot of time at all-black public meetings, arranging instead
for brief drop-ins or stand-in representatives. I tried to minimize the racial
orientation of my black media advertisements; those ads usually ran in select
areas late in the campaign.

Although I never formalized a black strategy, my campaign files include
"black" references and notes about numerous black operations; filed among
the vast documentation are a statewide analysis of the black political climate,
GOTV plans targeting black voters, and numerous budget items regarding
various black activities, organizations, and operatives. There's also a comprehensive listing of my finances for black campaigning over the years.

Additionally, the Browder Collection includes "black" folders for every
major Browder campaign, including such titles as "Blacks . . . names/notes,"
"$ Black Groups, Misc.," "Black, Sec.of State, 1986," "Dist. 3, Black/White
Voters, stats," "Blacks 1989," "1989 Campaign, Black Voter Outreach,"
"Blacks 1990," "Blacks 1992," "Blacks, Gen. Strategy and To Do, 1994,"
"Black Marked Ballots 1994," "Black Media 1994," "Black Org. GOTV
Material, 1994," Black Events, Req. for $, 1994," "Black Contacts/Con-
versations, 1994," "Blacks 1995," and "Black Politics 1996."

These historical files show that I employed a variety of tactics and operations in my actual routine for reaching black voters. As the following section attests, I relied mainly on personal relationships, organizational endorsements, and financial arrangements.

Personal Relationships and Biracial Campaign Politics

I usually consulted with a wide variety of friends/leaders/operatives regarding black issues and tactics. I initially engaged whites in my plans; then I developed black relationships that would prove critical to success in both campaigning among and serving my constituents.

The Democratic Party at that time (throughout the 1970s, 1980s, and 1990s) had become a rather successful assemblage of teachers, labor, trial lawyers, and blacks in the so-called "Coalition." So it was not hard for me to work my way into situations whereby I could then cultivate black leadership and organizations.

I eagerly sought out local white politicians and opinion leaders, especially those I had worked with at the university and in my consulting work; and, as a relative newcomer who talked about clean elections and moderate/progressive politics, I received various results. Some happily if quietly shared their experiences, recommendations, and contacts in the black community.

I then utilized white and black intermediaries and surrogates, such as fellow public officials, educational colleagues, and ministers; and I sometimes used paid operatives to work the state's black community. I tried to develop my own loyal activists rather than relying entirely on the black organizational establishment. I had discovered through experience that the black establishment was sometimes more interested in promoting their agendas than my ideas about black progress.

I got mixed response among black leaders, activists, and everyday citizens, but many of these alliances proved to be very constructive relationships. Amid all the pandering, posturing, and backroom dealings, there were clear incidents and developments of biracial progress. For example, in one of my early races, an African American friend in Anniston arranged a social get-together in a private home with some of his associates—many of whose names I had heard as educators, church members, and business owners but who were not among the political crowd normally involved in white-black negotiations and/or confrontations. It was an open, genuine, productive discussion about real issues, such as education, economic development, and the need for better communication, rather than wrangling over commitments regarding political deals and goodies. I must admit that this meeting not only impressed me with diversity in the black community—it also made me pause and reflect on the need for me to keep real "good government" at the forefront of my mind as I pursued hard-nosed practicality in biracial politics.

Among my many politically challenging, philosophically rewarding, personally useful, and downright interesting experiences and relationships in biracial campaigning were those with Ed Ewing (a white public relations expert in Montgomery), Gene Stedham (white businessman and liaison with the local black leadership in Calhoun County), Jerome Gray (field director of the Alabama Democratic Conference), Sister Mary Sue Porter Hale (local black activist from Sylacauga), Carl Silverberg (GOTV professional who worked on black turnout in the 1989 congressional election), and Roosevelt Thomas (a contracted black operative in the 1996 Senate campaign). My relationships with these individuals will be discussed here, in roughly chronological order, because they portray the political diversity, functional interplay, and interesting aspects of biracial politics during that time.

ED EWING. I owe a big debt to Ed Ewing, a quiet, savvy veteran of Montgomery politics since heroic drama days. When I was a young professor edging toward politics back in the late 1970s, Ewing and Bill Jones (then partners in the influential public relations firm, Viewpoint Enterprises) took me under their wings and taught me about campaigning in Alabama. I worked particularly closely with Ewing, who possessed impressive political credentials going back to the George Wallace administration and a long list of diverse clients—including powerful Democrats and prominent Republicans. Ewing tutored me with tactical advice, strategic counsel, and valuable contacts; and together we marched into the thickets of Alabama politics.

Those early campaigns confirmed the need for racial reconciliation in Alabama but, as might be expected, they also educated me about the limitations of academic theory and conventional niceties. Most startling was the ominous power of race. In poll after poll, and on election day after election day, I learned that racism contaminated both sides of the racial divide; this factor had the awesome power to disrupt virtually every aspect of Southern public life. I discovered, in fact, that sometimes there was no market for open, bold, biracial leadership. My polling showed that whites and blacks were so polarized in one community that my paid counsel to the white client, who actually was the best candidate for the job, was pure race-gaming: "Realistically, you're not going to get any black votes; so you may as well try to maximize your white base."

These polling and consulting experiences impacted my career in a very important way. The intensity and immensity of the race problem convinced me that there would be no easy, consensual, conclusive solution to the Southern dilemma. I would have to exercise extreme caution and commitment if I were going to contribute constructively to Alabama politics and American democracy.

In looking back on those times, it is clear that Ewing was a brilliant campaign consultant; but mainly I credit him for gifts of personal guidance and encouragement. Ed was a tough customer with a good heart. He was smart and practical and committed, and he played to win by the rules of the Alabama game. But he knew that things had to change. He emphasized that we had to live with ourselves beyond particular campaigns; and he encouraged me to pursue a new kind of politics. The practical and ethical lessons I learned under his tutelage were vital to my career as a stealth leader. Ed and I are still close friends; I occasionally consult my former mentor for input regarding public lectures and commentary.

GENE STEDHAM. Gene was a man for all seasons in my career, especially in the early years. At various times this white ex-teacher and businessman served the public as mayor, councilman, and civic leader in Anniston, the county seat of Calhoun County. But his most valuable service may have been his private relationship with the black community during some tough times of the 1960s; he had developed the working trust of blacks throughout the city and the broader region. My connection with the Anniston power-broker began when I became involved in Democratic Party activities, and it continued as I ran for state legislator, secretary of state, and U.S. congressman. We also became close personal friends.

Stedham knew, almost to perfection, the number of black votes that could be gleaned from each voting place, which leaders needed to be approached and how, and what this assignment would require in terms of political commitments and money. He took care of business himself, regularly meeting and negotiating with black leaders, making sure that things were properly planned, confirming that the vehicles and workers were in place, checking that the sample ballots were marked correctly, monitoring turnout during election day, and seeing that election-night returns came in properly and promptly.

Stedham shared valuable information, advice, and contacts over the years. He never asked for nor received any personal remuneration or recognition while handling these critically important biracial transactions; curiously, you cannot find anything in my files relating to Stedham's activities, reflecting perhaps a mixture of his own personality and sensitivity about this service on my behalf. Gene has yet to receive proper credit for his public and private service to this community.

JEROME GRAY. While Dr. Joe Reed was the boss at the Alabama Democratic Conference, Jerome Gray was the quiet administrator and field director.

The ADC operative was one of the most direct and effective players in Alabama's biracial electoral alliance, and he was never shy about what he expected when election-time rolled around. In a 1994 discussion in his office, Jerome firmly recited to me the list of complaints he had heard: "Not enough blacks on your staff . . . black inquiries not followed up . . . the vote against healthcare . . . failure to support President Clinton." Interestingly, he then went on to recommend some ideas and names, and ADC endorsed me in that election.

Gray also provided me with honest, constructive guidance beyond campaigning. Even in letters and conversations about routine events, Gray often personalized his remarks. Early in my congressional days, I got a thank-you letter regarding my contribution to an ADC annual convention, in which Gray noted my work for a civics program while I was secretary of state: "More and more, we've got to go the second mile to recruit and train our young people, as well as expose them to the affairs of government at an early age. I certainly commend you for your commitment to the Citizens Bee program here in Alabama. We need more such programs, year-round, for our young people." In a thank-you letter for a luncheon contribution, he wrote, "ADC is grateful to you for your vote in favor of the 1990 Civil Rights bill." And in an invitation to a campaign meeting, he offered, "If you can't come, you are welcome to send someone to represent you and your campaign."

Even today, I consider Jerome Gray one of the hidden treasures of Alabama politics.

Sister Mary Sue Porter Hale. Then there was Sister Hale! She was one of the grande dames of Alabama grassroots black politics, a very active former teacher, and an imposing political matron. Among her many community callings, Mary Sue Porter Hale chaired a precinct for the Democratic Party and Alabama Democratic Conference in Sylacauga.

I don't recall how we met, but she became one of my most vocal, demanding, and effective electoral supporters (or as she labeled herself in her own publications, "Supervisor for Browder Campaign"). She constantly sent me invitations to her political, church, and social events (such as the "33rd Well Earned Anniversary of Sis. Mary Sue Porter Hale, Noted Christian and MC"), along with steady requests for modest financial help for her causes. She wrote rambling personal greetings, along with directions that she meant to be followed (such as "I shall expect you to visit with me and come to my meetings" . . . "I don't want a stand in" . . ." All your black people will be there").

Substantively, Sister Hale encouraged me, with sincere admonition, to support the Democratic Party. "Brother if you don't stand up for the Democrats we are lost" . . . "So many of our people have changed parties" . . . "Several people that you and I have trusted for years have let the Democratic Party down."

I found Sister Hale a staunch ally. Most importantly from a political perspective, she delivered. She was a solid source of intelligence about what was going on in the black political community, and she jealously looked out for my interest at ADC meetings. Not coincidentally, her precinct and surrounding areas always voted for me overwhelmingly.

I still have a special place in my heart for Sister Hale, who passed away recently. After my loss in the Democratic Senate runoff of 1996, when there was no further political obligation either way, I received this note:

> The election absolutely devastated me, to the point that I am just starting to care again. I have done a lot of soul searching to figure who really were our friends. But you are at the top of my friendship list. Again thank you for being a fine Christian man. Please come to my anniversary. I love you all, and I will never, never forget you. Your True Friend, Your Big Sister, MSPH.

CARL SILVERBERG: Carl performed selected field operations on a professional basis in my 1989 congressional election. That means this white strategist from DC got paid for maximizing the black vote in Alabama.

Actually, I did not know much about Silverberg during that election because the turnout specialist worked unseen and separate from the regular campaign. However, Silverberg was a vital element in my victory. In an amazing six-page memo produced about two weeks after the election, Silverberg compiled a detailed account of field operations explaining who did what and where to produce strong black turnout for my campaign.[1] Among Silverberg's observations, with pseudonyms:

> Lora Mae Pratt in Sylacauga was very helpful and very good. Her people were organized and on the streets in the rain. It took her a little longer to accept our system, but when she did, it went smoothly.
>
> Rev. Jenkins in Opelika-Auburn was helpful, organized the area and while a little bit "expensive," delivered when we asked. He is a veteran organizer and had everything in place for us before anyone else. All his people showed up on Election Day, a rarity. He also knows how to "pad"

the list of workers so be careful next time. We had a DNC connection on the ground there, but I doubt you'd need an intermediary next time. The Rev. is that good.

The man from the office of Mayor Thompson coordinated your effort in the Southern eight counties. Rode with us, and with his wife set up the church visits on the Sunday before the election. Was reasonably candid about requests for money, who worked, and who didn't.

However, the report was not always complimentary of the black activists:

I firmly believe that Jerry Williamson in Anniston is highly overrated. . .My suggestion is in 1990, get a handle on him early, don't believe his threats, intimidation, etc. You can organize the way I did if you have to, as he doesn't own or control what he thinks or likes everyone else to think he does. None of the members of my GOTV team knew who he was, or for that matter, cared.

Silverberg's final recommendation reflected an expert's reading of this district and helped me chart my congressional course:

My outside guess of the District is that it probably isn't as conservative as Bill Nichols was, it's just that they re-elected him. Neither am I suggesting you make yourself open to attack as "that liberal college professor." I wish I had some better feel for it or some advice; but since you were the one elected statewide and then to Congress, you know it a lot more than I ever can.

Even today, I cannot explain exactly where Silverberg came from, who hired him, who paid him, or how much he earned. I suspect the Democratic Congressional Campaign Committee brought him in. But I know that this professional operative, in addition to turning out the vote, formalized valuable black input and contacts that extended through four congressional terms.

These alliances in no way exhaust the extent or nature of my biracial politics; I developed many similarly positive and constructive relations during my years in politics. However, space does not permit further elaboration beyond the few illustrative examples cited above.

Furthermore, not all my biracial relationships and experiences were warm and fuzzy success stories. Some alliances were strained; a few associations seemed to push the bounds of legality, such as the countless stream of shysters offering to get this-or-that black endorsement and turn out the black vote wherever (in exchange for help with their hefty expenses). Or the minister who asked me when I was running for congress whether I could match an opponent's job offer (which patently violated federal law). Or the newspaper guy who promised positive coverage (if we bought his exorbitant public relations package). I would discover over the years that these were equal-opportunity unpleasantries to be experienced with white as well as black operatives.

Illustrative of the "other" category was my dealings with political operative Roosevelt Thomas (a real person but not his real name).

ROOSEVELT THOMAS. He was one of the curiosities of Alabama politics, an ever-moving black activist with a quick smile and friendly demeanor—but with uncertain loyalties and shifting portfolios—while working his angles and the crowd at political events.

Thomas (who operated out of Birmingham) approached me about helping with black voters during the 1996 campaign for the U.S. Senate; and I accepted. With the primary looming in a couple of months, it was apparent that the best I could hope for was somehow splitting the statewide black vote; Thomas was recommended as the "somehow" guy. It was an awkward alliance, without much talk about philosophy, strategy, or tactics; and Thomas went to work as a free-agent, independent contractor.

Thomas apparently had had good relations with the Jefferson County Citizens Coalition in the past, and he felt the Browder campaign had a chance for the JCCC endorsement. But, even if that were impossible, Thomas told me, "I think we can pull about a fourth of the black vote statewide."

The Browder Collection shows that my campaign invested significant money in various activities through free-agent Thomas. But the campaign could not adequately monitor/control those activities, nor could it determine just what it got for its investment in terms of votes. I did get a split primary endorsement from the JCCC, but lost it in the runoff. Thomas, meanwhile, dispatched himself on unspecified missions throughout the state, and staffers cringed at periodic news reports hinting of electoral irregularities and fake marked ballots.

Unfortunately, I went on to suffer a lop-sided Democratic primary runoff defeat. It certainly wasn't Roosevelt Thomas's fault, but I knew in my heart that the unseemly endeavor was not what I had entered the public arena to do. We closed that file as an expensive, awkward, best-forgotten venture.

Overall, I enjoyed countless effectual friendships, associations, and exchanges with black politicians and activists (in addition to interactions with my own employees); in fact, many of these alliances would be considered normal, functional aspects of politics disregarding the "stealth" framework of our thesis. Unquestionably, these relationships greatly enhanced my campaigns and public service.

Organizational Endorsements and Biracial Campaign Politics

I aggressively but quietly sought black organizational endorsements and counted heavily on their get-out-the-vote efforts. Compared to such prized endorsements, black media support was insignificant, and mainstream media were irrelevant.

BLACK GOLD. For a while during the 1970s to the 1990s, African American organizational endorsements were black gold in Alabama politics.

Black organizational endorsements often could be secured without a lot of media attention and accompanying attacks from opposition candidates; and their impact could be targeted racially and geographically. More importantly, the payoff—a 90 percent bloc vote among more than a third of the Democratic primary voters and a quarter of the statewide general electorate—quite often was the key to winning the Democratic primary in the spring and vanquishing Republican opposition in the fall general election.

Mining that black gold sometimes was a study in creative, zig-zag campaigning. In my first congressional election, for example, I had to defeat seven other white Democrats and—most importantly—a strong African American politician in the party primary preceding the Democrat-Republican fight in the general election. I led the special election's first primary, followed closely by Johnny Ford, the black mayor of Tuskegee; in the run-off Ford and I then waged a high profile, gentlemanly contest—some called it a "love fest"—for the Democratic nomination. I won the runoff easily in a district that was 75 percent white.

Anniston Star reporter Jim Yardley wrote a week later that race had been the "hidden, dominant issue" in the runoff.[2] "The final vote went along racial lines, giving Browder a big win in the Third District where white voters outnumber blacks three to one. In Calhoun County, Browder swept all forty-two of the predominantly white boxes while Ford took all six of the predominantly black ones." This was true even though the African American bloc had been solidly in my camp in my election and service as secretary of state.[3] Yardley continued:

> Neither candidate did anything to fuel these feelings. Both men ran clean campaigns and avoided making race an issue. In defeat, Ford even went so far as to say the election had been a "victory" for Alabama because it had proved race was not an issue. Sadly, race was the issue.[4]

Yardley interviewed voters at campaign rallies and at the polls, and when he promised not to reveal their names, many confided that the race of the candidate was the only thing that mattered to them. Apparently, race helped pull both whites and blacks to the voting booths in the runoff.

Attesting ironically to the value of African American organizational endorsement back then was a news story by the *Star*'s Chris Smith that appeared just a few days before the ensuing general election, in which African Americans voted wholesale for me:

> While Democrats are working to ensure that black voters turn out in force for Tuesday's congressional election, Republicans have all but written off that group of voters.

The national Democratic Party, the state Democratic Party and its black wing, the Alabama Democratic Conference are exerting a strong effort to turn out black voters for Secretary of State Glen Browder.

But the Republican campaign of Opelika state Sen. John Rice has conceded 85 percent of the black vote. Rice's campaign manager, Paul Haughton, says that portion of the black vote is controlled by Joe Reed, executive director of the ADC, and will follow his endorsement.[5]

Alabama Democratic Party field worker Paola Maranan told the *Star* that she was working with black leaders to turn out black voters. She said that she had been coordinating get-out-the-vote efforts with the ADC's county chairmen in the thirteen-county district and that ADC workers would be canvassing door-to-door and handing out sample ballots endorsing me. Those same ballots would be distributed at black churches Sunday and near polling places during Tuesday's election. ADC's Calhoun County chairman, Freddie Rimpsey, said his workers were distributing 20,000 of the ballots in my home county. He said ten volunteers were working phone banks and that transportation to the polls would be provided in this area.[6]

Meanwhile, Johnny Ford was doing his part in rousing the black constituency for the general election:

Tuskegee Mayor Ford said that he expects Browder to get the lion's share of his supporters. Ford said he has made numerous campaign stops for Browder and has cut a radio commercial for him. He said that another radio commercial reminding voters to go to the polls will air sometime this weekend.

"I've been where I'm most effective and most needed," said Ford, who has made most of his stops for Browder in the southern end of the district.[7]

Such an organizational effort among African American voters was critical to stealth leaders like me; and those vital endorsements did not come easily or automatically.

THE ENDORSEMENT PROCESS. Normally, the endorsement process worked this way. Several weeks before an election, the Alabama Democratic Conference, the Alabama New South Coalition, the Jefferson County Citizens Coalition and similar groups would hold their endorsement meetings and invite candidates to appear, make a pitch, and await the screening committee's closed-door decision.

This practice, not unlike what happened with other cohesive interest groups, was the black community's way of dealing with an adverse and manipulative history. As *Birmingham News* reporters Justin Fox and Tom Gordon put it:

> In the eyes of the Rev. Lathonia Wright, Randolph County's first black county commissioner, the endorsements, sample ballots and get-out-the-vote efforts of the Alabama Democratic Conference have liberated black voters . . .
>
> "Historically, white politicians, especially the ones who promoted segregation, have thrived upon disunity in the black community. In other words, black people were not given the freedom to think for themselves politically.
>
> "The majority of the black voters in Randolph County wait anxiously for the yellow sample ballot. We flood the churches with them. We go door-to-door with them. We're not making people vote a certain way. But we are encouraging them to vote a certain way."[8]

Much of the material in the Browder Collection deals with my continuing attention to the ADC, ANSC, JCCC, their regional/local affiliates, and similar other entities. Additionally, I kept up relations with various officials, ministers, and independent operators who might be helpful come endorsement time.

Over the course of my career, I won about a dozen campaigns, both with and without the black endorsements (and I lost my final race in part because of a lack of such organizational support). There were no endorsements in my first race, in 1982, for the state legislature, since my district included only a small number of black voters; however, as the following chronology of critical races shows, these endorsements were a central focus of my campaigns and electoral successes.

SECRETARY OF STATE CAMPAIGN (1986). As a freshman state representative, I knew I was taking on long odds when I decided to run, with very little money, for secretary of state against Annie Laurie Gunter, an established state treasurer and longtime Wallace ally. So I set out to try to run the endorsement table.

It was difficult, but I gained the official statewide endorsements of both the Alabama Democratic Conference and the Alabama New South Coalition. This accomplishment was a mighty stroke for my campaign and future career, accomplished without any actual racial debate or financial obligations. I got it simply because of hard work, my pitch as an election reformer, and my promises to be "fair" to everybody. It helped, too, that I had a lot of help from key black leaders with whom I had developed good relationships in the legislature. I also picked up support from educators, state employees, labor, civic types, and virtually all the newspapers in the state. Ironically, a lot of the old Wallace crowd and local politicians helped me.

I eked out a shocking 51–49 percent victory (an outcome that wasn't official until the weekend following Tuesday's election); and then I won the general election by an almost 2–1 margin. As secretary of state, I successfully championed election reform and established myself as a bright, moderate-to-progressive leader with significant black support.

U.S. CONGRESS CAMPAIGN (1989). When Alabama's third congressional district opened up due to the death of longtime incumbent Bill Nichols, I was in good shape to make the three-month run for a special election that assumed major national attention and ramifications.

Nine Democrats and four Republicans ran for the open seat, which was viewed as a crucial test—after the 1988 George H. W. Bush regional sweep—of whether the South would finally turn GOP. As the early Democratic favorite, I was tabbed "the most liberal guy in the state" by Republican attack man Lee Atwater.[9]

Once I got the Democratic nomination, key Democratic leaders in Alabama and Washington advised me not to worry unduly about money or the black vote—they would help with things like that. It was kind of "don't ask, don't tell" on certain matters, as groups and operatives from both partisan camps invaded east/central Alabama; to this date I cannot account fully for everything that happened in that incredibly short, hectic campaign.

The plan from the beginning was for me to respectfully solicit the friendship of black organizations while deferring to African American candidate Johnny Ford as their first choice in the Democratic primary and runoff. Afterwards, as expected, the entire slate of black endorsements came my way for the crucial general election showdown with Republican John Rice.

The once-tight race deteriorated into Rice's waving a Confederate flag on a statewide public television debate, and I coasted home to victory. I served four terms with continuing, positive black relations.

U.S. CONGRESS CAMPAIGN (1994). By this time, burdened with the problems of Bill Clinton and the national Democrats, I faced white opposition in both the party primary and general election.

Democratic opponent Lea Fite challenged my party loyalties, and snatched the Alabama New South Coalition endorsement early during the primary campaign. Actually, I was warned by my loyalists that things were not going well and that a few operatives were "buying" the screening process in Mobile; by the time I showed up it was obvious that the ANSC endorsement was gone. So, I turned my attention toward the Alabama Democratic Conference state meeting in Montgomery, and handily secured that endorsement. The stage was set for a Democratic civil war, with both candidates throwing money into a political street fight. The result was a dazzling display of organizational-endorsement ingenuity and marked ballots of all shapes, sizes, and colors.

I directed intense personal attention on my own relationships, loyal activists, and local groups in the third congressional district. Fortunately, I scored big, winning 85 percent of the Democratic primary votes and getting 62 percent against the Republican opponent in a 1994 GOP revolution that saw Democrats fall like flies elsewhere in the country. Furthermore, I had once again gotten by pretty cheaply: I spent only about $70,000 in the primary and another $70,000 in the general election (at a time when the average congressional election nationwide cost in excess of half a million dollars).

As might be expected, I emerged from this election stronger than ever; but I could foresee racial problems ahead if I seriously wanted to run for the U.S. Senate.

U.S. SENATE CAMPAIGN (1996). I decided to seek the seat that was opening up due to Howell Heflin's impending retirement. But I faced strong opposition in the increasingly liberal Democratic primary from State Senator Roger Bedford, Birmingham-Southern professor/Democratic activist Natalie Davis, and Marilyn Quarles, a St. Clair County official.

Polls showed me leading the Democratic pack at the beginning, and I enjoyed almost universal support among editorialists. But I lacked strong group and financial support among the party's Yellow Dog stalwarts; and unlike my sweep through the organizational endorsements of a decade earlier, I encountered significant problems all along the way.

I had hoped that I could split blacks and the party's other liberal core constituencies. Having learned from 1994, I hired my own operatives for working the black organizational endorsements. This proved to be an expensive move—and to no avail. Both ADC and ANSC went for Bedford; Davis and I shared the JCCC endorsement.

Bedford eventually proved to be the better candidate for this primary; he was popular on the local Democratic Party circuit, well-grounded in the black community, heftily funded by trial lawyers, and an excellent, attractive campaigner. Outspent two to one in a low-participation primary (estimated 15 percent turnout), the best I could do was to force Bedford into a runoff, in which he easily prevailed 62–38 percent. Bedford would go on to lose to Republican Jeff Sessions (the present incumbent) in a close general election.

In retrospect, this defeat was perhaps destiny for me. I had hoped that the Democratic establishment would view me as the best prospect for winning the general election and would support my campaign as it had in my previous campaigns, but such was not the case. My moderate political philosophy, reformist approach to fundraising, and circumspect relationship with the black community finally caught up with me.

Changing Times. Some contend, and simple observation supports their contention, that African American politics had changed significantly in the 1990s. *Birmingham Post-Herald* political columnist Ted Bryant noted that the major black groups were beginning to split their endorsements and operate as normal interests in Alabama politics:

> The days when one leader or organization has the ability to deliver 25 percent of the vote appear to be in the past, justifiably so . . .
>
> Overall, the split endorsements, especially in the governor's race, should herald the emergence of more sophisticated black voters who make their own decisions instead of relying upon a few leaders.
>
> And that's what democracy is all about, the opinions of those few leaders notwithstanding.[10]

Associated Press reporter Phillip Rawls sounded a similar message in 2002.

> Two black political groups that once could almost guarantee a victory for a candidate in a Democratic primary suffered stinging defeats Tuesday that signal the growing independence of minority voters.[11]

Citing defeats for two powerful African American politicians—U.S. Congressman Earl Hilliard in the Birmingham-Black Belt area and Montgomery City Councilman Joe Reed—Rawls termed the development as an evolution of black voters since the civil rights movement.

Rawls also invoked explanatory comments from two knowledgeable black observers of Alabama politics. State Representative Alvin Holmes said that black voters were studying the candidates and demanding that incumbents produce substantive results: "That's the reason the New South and ADC ballots are being ignored." Dr. D'Linell Finley, a political science professor at Auburn University at Montgomery, added that endorsements were not as important as before; "You have so many groups endorsing candidates that they have become little more than splinter groups going after their favorites."[12]

Apparently, these and other developments impacted that 1996 race; that impact, and the outcome, obviously were not in my favor.

Overall, however, this accounting of organizational politics demonstrates that I had enjoyed a successful career with dependable biracial support until that final race. Furthermore, black organizations (and their endorsements) were critically important in my ability to represent black constituents in Alabama. Good organizational relations made both good politics and good policy.

Financial Arrangements and Biracial Campaign Politics

It should be obvious that the aforementioned relationships and endorsements did not operate in an antiseptic civic vacuum; and in politics, as in most other endeavors, money usually separated winners from losers. Unsavory possibilities, as described earlier, quite often became reality in the volatile mix of money and politics; I found this to be an unpleasant truism in implementing my biracial strategy over the years.

Black GOTV and Alabama Politics

In Alabama politics in the 1970s, 1980s, and 1990s, it was common practice for money to flow freely from white pockets to black organizations and then onto the streets for GOTV activities. *Birmingham News* reporters Justin Fox and Tom Gordon confirmed and explained the integral relationship between white money and black politics of that era:

> But getting out the vote takes money, and most of the money ADC spends around the state at election time comes from white candidates and white-dominated businesses and political action committees. Other black political groups, such as the Alabama New South Coalition and the Jefferson County Citizens Coalition, are in the same boat. They champion black empowerment, but depend on the white political establishment for money.[13]

Such reports tended to trouble purists, but they reflected the still powerful vestiges of segregated society and politics. Again, quoting that newspaper account:

> Joe Reed, ADC chairman since 1972, said candidates give money to his group "just like candidates employ PR (public relations) firms to get their names in the press."
>
> Politicians woo white voters through television, radio, phone banks and mailings, but in the black community the personal touch is still key, (state Rep. George) Perdue said. "There's just a difference culturally in the way we campaign."
>
> Black voters "were excluded from the political process for a long time," said state Sen. Hank Sanders, D-Selma, a former New South Coalition president. "That creates all kinds of apathies." Without get-out-the-vote efforts, he said, "the level of participation would drop dramatically."

Obviously, with cash money being thrown onto the street in sometimes ephemeral and unaccountable operations, there was always the chance of mutual abuse among candidates and organizations. Everyone had to be wary amid rampant rumors about campaign and election irregularities.

Virtually every Alabama politician was familiar, for example, with individuals, some in responsible positions with reputable organizations, who promised to do wonders for the right price; candidates had to deal with common pests who attempted to extort campaigns for petty personal gain; and everyone speculated about late-night negotiations in which support might shift from one campaign to another.

The business of endorsements, for example, created tempting opportunities for financial impropriety. In one controversial situation, a black state legislator pled guilty to attempted extortion and went to federal prison over wrongdoing during a 1988 local election.[14] In another case, a white candidate for statewide office told a newspaper that he had been endorsed by a black state organization in 1990 and gave the group $55,000; but he then heard that a county chapter had gotten a subsequent donation from his competitor, and he had to match that contribution to keep the endorsement in that area—which he did. "It's always wise to monitor at the local level," he said.[15]

Another common concern was the problem of fraudulent marked ballots, as cited in this 1994 report by the Associated Press:

> The chairman of the black Alabama Democratic Conference said fake ballots incorrectly showing the group's endorsements have shown up in three counties. "There is a massive effort to mislead the voters of Alabama," Chairman Joe Reed said Thursday. . .
>
> The ADC traditionally circulates yellow ballots with its endorsed candidates marked in each race.
>
> The ballots always show Reed's photo with the photo of the ADC's county chairman.
>
> Reed said some of the bogus ballots have his picture and are printed on yellow paper. They also have some of the ADC's endorsements listed correctly, while others are changed, making it hard for voters to tell they are bogus, he said.[16]

Such campaign practices and irregularities were and are still cause for concern. For example, the Alabama Democratic Conference filed complaints in 2006 that voters in southwest Alabama received fake ADC sample ballots with bogus endorsements for the state legislature and a circuit judge position.[17] In east Alabama, there were public charges that black ministers were being paid for endorsing a state senate candidate.[18] It is important to note that such incidents are not limited to black politics; as a politician connected with one of the black organizations has pointed out, "That's part of the political process that we did not invent."[19]

My Financial Practices

As a political reformer who hated fund-raising and lacked access to the rich special interests, I usually didn't have much campaign money so I learned to prevail most of the time with other ways and means. But I also learned early in my career that it was going to take an active campaign account to carry out my stealth political strategy.

OFFICIAL REPORTS. Browder Collection files indicate that I raised and spent a little over two million dollars in my dozen or so campaigns from 1982–1996. Although I have no idea what other entities may have done independently in that expensive 1989 special election for Congress, I scrupulously reported my contributions and expenditures; and I calculate pretty closely that I spent about 5 percent of my total budget over the years on activities separately and specifically targeted toward the black electorate.

As a practice, I made contributions to various black organizations and individuals on an irregular basis throughout my tenure in office. About half of these expenditures went to ADC, ANSC, and associated or similar black group events; routinely, the Browder campaign would purchase a table or two at annual or semi-annual statewide meetings ($500 per table) and make smaller contributions ($50, $100, $200) to periodic local events. About half of my black expenditures went to contracted activists—as little as a few hundred dollars per operative, upwards to several thousand dollars each—who worked on my behalf, mainly in the Senate campaign.

SPECIFIC OPERATIONS. An examination of specific budget transactions (and proffered packages) in the Browder Collection provides more detail about the growing cottage industry of black campaign operations during that time. Current campaigns involve much larger sums, however, the following accounts illustrate the role of money in biracial campaign politics back then.

In 1989, for example, a national party consultant suggested a GOTV plan, mainly targeted for black turnout in my congressional special election. The economy plan cost $19,440, and the best program ran up to $31,620. Neither program included phone calls ($6,000) or mailings ($4,000), which also were recommended. I'm not sure what the party actually did in that case, as it was working independently of my 1989 campaign, but the effort apparently worked. However, as a general rule, I did not expend significant amounts for special operations of this sort once I became the incumbent congressman.

In 1994, during a contested Democratic primary, a local black leader suggested that an effective GOTV plan for Calhoun and Talladega counties (two large black voting counties in my home area) could be implemented for $10,000; I passed.

Two years later, in the 1996 U.S. Senate Democratic primary campaign, a statewide organization presented a GOTV package targeted exclusively toward black voters in the Birmingham area. It included a long, costly list of options: sample ballot distribution at the polls ($6,200), door-to-door distribution of sample ballots ($5,000), ballot printing ($7,000), transportation to polls, ($3,950), and bulk mail ($14,000). That ran to a total of almost $40,000, and I again opted in other directions.

In that 1996 campaign, I ended up expending about $30,000—in a less-than-successful effort—on independent contractors in the black community. I actually paid more to black than to white operatives on the ground in Alabama that year.

The aforementioned Roosevelt Thomas topped that list, getting about $10,000 for his free-agent statewide operations. At the lower end of the spectrum that year were local operators hoping to cash in on the Senate campaign with GOTV plans that promised a lot for relatively nothing. For example, one black minister/activist offered to work black voters in Clay and Lee counties; he pitched drivers, vans, field workers, absentee ballot workers, poll watchers, door runners, phone bankers, and a local coordinator for only $600. I figured it was an exaggerated proposal, but I took him up on the offer for a negotiated $500 and even hired one of his associates for another area.

Such financial negotiations were especially common and varied regarding locally coordinated and marked sample ballots. Although statewide organizations such as ADC and ANSC tried to keep watch on their official marked ballots, there was an entrepreneurial outburst of black endorsement groups and slates in contested areas in every election cycle. Normally, these ballots were shopped around to potential candidates, who would put up whatever they could for printing and distribution expenses. The Browder Collection files include notes about coordinated slates for various groups with recommended candidate contributions of $100, $200, and $500. In the 1994 Democratic primary folder, for example, there are numerous customized ballots for supposed sponsoring organizations throughout the fourteen counties in the district.[20] Each ballot was a mish-mash of recommendations; some endorsed me, others endorsed my opponent, and still others indicated "your choice" with both names circled. Clearly many of these projects were bogus "knockoffs" designed to imply support from legitimate organizations, with perhaps minor name variations, for the contributing candidates. Just as clearly, the impact of such ballots was questionable; there was no guaranteed distribution on election day; and the only quality control was eyeballing vote totals after the election was over. But serious candidates (myself included) often felt compelled to play the game.

RETURN ON INVESTMENT. What did I get from my financial support for these organizations, individuals, and targeted campaign operations? The return was hard to specify; but I'm certain that it factored in my favor. Considering the obvious benefit of associating with key leaders and groups that comprised a significant segment of my constituency, I saw these arrangements as, overall, simply good political business. For example, spending $95,000 of a $100,000 campaign budget on mainstream activities and media might get 40–60 percent of the majority white vote; however, channeling $5,000 into the black campaign could net a return of 70–90 percent black support.

These financial investments also buttressed loyal black associates throughout the district. Nothing so pleased them (or me) as to get a letter from ADC state headquarters stating that "This memo comes to inform you that the Browder campaign is contributing $700.00 to help you get-out-the-vote in your county."

I was not the only politician participating in the black endorsement/ GOTV business of that era. According to a *Birmingham News* analysis of the 1990 election, ADC reported taking in $417,000, ANSC collected $214,000, and JCCC garnered $115,000. The primary donors were the teachers' association (AEA), the gambling business, trial lawyers, and the campaigns of white Democratic candidates Paul Hubbert, Howell Heflin, Roger Bedford, and Don Siegelman.[21] In 1992, U.S. Senator Richard Shelby—then a Democrat—apparently contributed $50,000 to the ANSC and $25,000 to the ADC before his primary race against African American

Chris McNair (the father of one of the victims of the 1963 Birmingham church bombing); Shelby coasted to an easy victory.[22]

Campaign funding was always a problem for me; but raising and spending money was a definite part of the political business. Considering my financial handicaps, I was relatively successful in terms of tactical relationships, organizational endorsements, and winning elections.

Summary of Stealth Campaigning

For the record, I enjoyed considerable electoral success during my political career, winning races for the Alabama legislature, Alabama secretary of state, and U.S. Congress. I led competitive balloting on eleven occasions against twenty-two opponents prior to a final loss in the 1996 Senate primary. I achieved this success, in great part, through circumspect biracial politics within the political context of various constituencies and districts.

I was very cautious—perhaps overly so—in my stealth campaigning. While I practiced racial fairness and publicly championed some progressive causes beneficial to African Americans, I was diligently circumspect about specifically racial matters.

I raised pertinent issues mainly in black forums and among black constituents. I attended black conferences, meetings, dinners, churches, and so forth only as suggested by black allies and as I felt necessary. I used a limited amount of black newspaper/radio advertising. In sum, I mainly ran broad, generic campaigns, and I over-relied on tactical relationships, endorsements, and financial arrangements (and of course, the magic of marked ballots) to target black voters.

I did not want to seem politically stand-offish or racially insensitive, but I had several reasons for such an approach.

First, of course, was the stealth essence of my political strategy, the central element of our thesis. I felt I had to manage my campaign in such a way as to get black support without giving the opposition ammunition for portraying me in racially divisive attacks; I then, of course, could pursue my moderate-to-progressive politics as an elected public official.

Second, I had learned a pointed and valuable lesson from black leaders themselves about respecting the special nature of black campaigning in

Alabama. Joe Reed once told me, "You can spend all your money on polling and consultants and TV commercials if you want to, but black folks talk about these things among themselves and in their churches, and they trust me and ADC a lot more than anybody else."

Finally, I had always been a personally reserved person, and I was reticent doing things that I did not feel comfortable doing—like politicking in church—things that seemed to be a perfectly normal part of black political culture.

Criticality of Context

As has been mentioned in earlier theoretical comments, an important key to stealth politics was a complicated combination of social, cultural, and political elements that factored into the racial context.

Operating in an environment of historical and continuing racial division, I attracted majoritarian white support and usually secured the bulk of black votes. My policy pitch was nonracial (with obvious catering to the white electorate on conservative issues and progressive action on selected matters of concern to blacks), and I juggled the tactics of black campaigning (personal relationships, organizational endorsements, and financial arrangements).

While the Republicans represented a formidable threat most of my career, I felt confident in my ability to marshal a biracial majority in general elections. I was mainly concerned when the racial context included serious black/liberal opposition within the Democratic Party. For example, I faced a potentially troublesome situation with African American Mayor Johnny Ford of Tuskegee in the 1989 congressional special election primary and runoff (a situation that actually turned out very positively for me). And State Senator Roger Bedford, a well-funded white populist, defeated me in the 1996 Senate primary runoff (in retrospect, a situation in which I faced impossible odds).

Campaign Record as a Quiet, Practical, Biracial Politician

Overall, then, I practiced stealth campaigning and achieved substantial biracial success within the varying context of several constituencies. Poll-

ing data and box-by-box analysis indicate that I won my elections against
Democrats and Republicans, against blacks and whites, most of the time
with strong biracial support. I probably could have continued lifelong
congressional service had I not attempted to step up to the Senate. In the
end, ironically, my cautious approach and a newly adverse contextual environment helped terminate my political career.

Jess Brown, professor of government and public affairs at Athens State
University, summarized my electoral career this way.

From the time of Browder's first candidacy in the early 1980s until
he exited the campaign field in the mid-1990s, the tenor or context of
electoral politics changed substantially. Campaign rhetoric became shriller
and partisan divisions became more rancorous in both Washington and
Montgomery. The mass media—both mainstream and the emerging genre
called talk radio—seemed to encourage candidates to become masters of
emotional one-liners about "hot button" issues.

As this environment unfolded, Browder was cross-pressured by the
demands of being an effective representative for economic interests in
his district, while also trying to placate key constituencies inside the
Democratic Party. For example, he needed to be a centrist in Congress
to protect stakeholders in his district associated with national defense or
land grant universities; but he needed to be a member with more liberal
voting tendencies on both economic and non-economic issues to placate
feminist, labor and African American factions in the Democratic Party.

At his core, Browder was not an avid partisan but a reformer. He wanted
to achieve some reform, not merely have the same debate every two or four
years. Party affiliation was part of the necessary path to achieve certain
reforms. But, bi-partisanship was also an element of his prescription for
reform, and that element was simply not acceptable to the party diehards
and single-issue crusaders. Browder understood that if campaigns were
won as a result of personal attacks, emotional one-liners, and enhanced
divisiveness between the parties, that the prospects for reform AFTER
election day were quite unlikely.

By the mid-1990s, Browder's stealthy style became less and less viable in the electoral marketplace. The changed environment rewarded "fire breathers" who appealed to the ideological extremes of one party or the other, or used character assassination as a standard tool in campaigns. During this period, there was increasingly no room on the stage for a low-key consensus builder committed to civic reform and biracial progress, but willing to achieve it incrementally. And, this was especially true in elections for high profile offices, such as contests for the U.S. Senate. Campaign politics essentially transitioned to a much more visceral state, and while Browder understood this change on an intellectual plane, he refused to adopt it as a modus operandi for his "new kind of politics."[23]

   This chapter has demonstrated that, for the most part, I approximated critical electoral aspects of the conceptual model. My political campaigns generally evidenced quiet, practical, biracial politics; and I enjoyed substantial success until losing the 1996 Senate election. Let's now shift focus from campaigning to serving. The next installment of this three-chapter case study will assess my actual performance as a stealth leader.

6

A Case Study
in Stealthy Public Service

This case study focuses on Glen Browder's political career within the conceptual model presented in our theoretical discussion. In this chapter, he will talk about the challenges and activities of his service as a stealthy leader during the 1970s, 1980s, and 1990s.

In this project, I have offered myself as a case study of stealth leadership and the practice of quiet, practical, biracial politics that helped change the South during the 1970s, 80s, and 90s. In previous chapters, I placed my career within the model in terms of political context, personal orientations, and electoral campaigns. In this chapter, I want to examine my actual public service.

Of course, analyzing that service will be somewhat more complex than was the campaign presentation in the previous chapter. Leadership, by its nature, is difficult to measure or describe, and "stealth leadership" is an even more elusive concept and practice. There was no recorded discussion back then among stealthy participants about their biracial maneuvers; there were no media accounts or research reports laying bare their somewhat secretive, oftentimes less-than-noble, yet relatively progressive maneuvering; and the Browder Collection offers no documentary material evidencing, by itself, my stealth leadership. Therefore, I have to rely mainly on retrospective self-interpretation and evaluations from other, knowledgeable participants in the politics of that period.

In the following pages, I will begin with a discussion of my strategic notions about stealth representation; secondly, I will look at my operations as a quiet, practical, biracial politician; I then will present my personalized remembrances of that era; and I will conclude with a summary assessment of my stealth leadership.

A Philosophy of Stealthy Leadership

As has been stated, I was not a civil rights champion. I generally pursued a moderate, centrist career in Montgomery and Washington. I concentrated on various civic matters, reform issues, fiscal responsibility, national defense, and constituency relations, and this performance kept me in good stead with most of my white constituents.

However, to repeat my expressed sentiment from an earlier chapter, I was prepared to deal with the South's legacy of hard racial history. I realized too that "stealth politics" was the key to my success as a new kind of leader. Quiet biracial practicality would get me through the portals of political power and guide me as an elected official along the tricky paths of my civic journey.

The Original Game Plan

In the previous chapter, I presented the "Browder Game Plan" that charted my electoral tactics for assuming political office. Pertinent to the current assessment is that the original plan mentioned nothing about ideological objectives, substantive issues, or my racial agenda. That file focused mainly on procedural matters—what I wanted to do and how that could be accomplished. I have written elsewhere that my primary motivation was civic interest and that I wanted to pursue as much political progress as was politically possible; however, there was very little in the game plan file to indicate that I was driven by any particular or intense partisan or racial agenda.

I embraced racial justice as a scholar and teacher, but, as has already been acknowledged, race was not the central focus of my early thinking. Mine was the drive of a practical reformer concerned about the general practice of Alabama politics and American democracy. However, from the beginning, I understood my own stake in the region's legacy of hard history. Although

I had never been active in politics, I had witnessed the vast black-white chasm of Southern society, up close, both personally and professionally. As a native Southerner and experienced academician/consultant, I had a pretty good handle on white politics. And since I had grown up poor among disadvantaged whites and blacks, literally on the wrong side of the tracks in South Carolina, I had at least an elementary and sensitive "feel" for black ways. The two races were physically segregated, they were different culturally, and they did not like or trust each other.

Discreetly and effectively bridging these segregated societies therefore would be very important not only to getting elected but also to my substantive work as a self-declared "New Kind of Leader." So, during my early years in the Alabama legislature, I began adding more substantive elements to my game plan. I had begun the civic journey with a solid academic grasp of principles, and I quickly developed my own practical approach to politicking on Goat Hill.

Evolving Style

My leadership style—and skills—evolved as I experienced success and setbacks on civic and racial endeavors.

I learned to build quiet coalitional power—including black and white participation—for my agenda of civic reform and racial progress. These latter two elements were inextricably conjoined in my version of Southern progress. Considering regional history, I felt that the race factor needed to be positively spun, neutralized, or at least minimized in public discussion.

To get anything done of a civic or reform nature, we had to have significant black support or at least black acquiescence; and to do anything in the way of racial progress, we had to have significant cooperation from whites. The truth was that, given our past problems and current demographics, a few noisy white reactionaries or a few black rabble-rousers could mess up everything for the rest of us. I may have overestimated the problem in some situations, but I knew—from my academic background, consulting experience, and political practice—that the opposition would do anything to thwart civic and racial progress. Therefore, I incorporated stealthy politics, adjusted for the situation at hand, pretty regularly in those days.

Normally, I began with public articulation of a universal, communitarian civic message, while I privately engaged in the push-and-pull of coalition-building among good government groups and special interests, with particular attention on courting blacks into these initiatives. I would quietly assemble the constituent leaders and activists, either physically or figuratively, challenging them on the basis of good government, and warning them that, if they couldn't solve the assignment in progressive manner, then I would proceed with my own political solution. Interestingly, both white and black politicos often responded positively to this entreaty; it avoided my pronouncement of their failed leadership, it helped deal acceptably with real, mutual problems, and it often brought good media coverage for their cooperation. This simple stealth strategy sometimes worked wonders, especially considering the history of traditional leadership and race relations in Alabama.

Eventually, my leadership ideas attracted public attention. Betty Cork, education reporter for the *Montgomery Advertiser*, noted the relative newcomer's call for more progressive leadership and racial cooperation while covering a local civic club speech in 1986:

> Alabama has not developed the leadership required to deal with the real needs of the state, Rep. Glen Browder, D-Jacksonville, told members of a Montgomery civic club Thursday. . .
>
> Speaking to the Montgomery Capitol Rotary Club, Browder said state interests are engaged in a "dog-eat-dog" struggle for limited resources. To solve the problems of the state, Alabama needs cooperation between business, labor, education, agriculture and government . . .
>
> "The essential requirement is new leadership—not simply new leaders but a new style of leadership," Browder said . . .
>
> As he has said repeatedly in talks to civic groups and others, Browder said Alabama would have to address race relations. "We may not achieve total harmony between whites and black, but we must forge a workable relationship among the leaders of the two races," he said.[1]

Disciplined Discretion

Carrying out this stealthy intent proved a demanding assignment throughout my career. I prepared myself to anticipate public pitfalls and resist repeated media inquiries about controversial racial situations, while maintaining a positive personal demeanor; I even instructed my political and office staff that, except for specific authorization otherwise, I alone spoke for Public Official Browder.

I was emphatic about my disciplined discretion on racial matters. I simply avoided talking about racial issues or tactics because anything I said would have been used against me by white and black opponents. I never raised certain topics and I dismissed probing from the opposition and media people by shifting the conversation to a broader discussion of real and important concern. When pushed on something like the Confederate flag question, I would brush it off with a comment that "I don't want to get into that kind of talk" or "That flag controversy is just something to divide us and keep us from dealing with problems like social security and education." When quizzed about racial aspects of voting or crime, I would talk about reforming election laws and drug laws to protect democracy and society at large. When asked point-blank about the role of blacks in my campaign strategy or political administration, I would proclaim that "I want to represent everybody!"

From Campaigning to Governing

As is normal in the political process, I had to transition repetitively between campaign tactics and public service. These were not totally distinct operations; however, the challenge was more complex and difficult because of Alabama history and my stealthy mission. I cautiously extended the elements of stealthy campaigning—personal associates, organizations, and money into my biracial service as a stealthy leader.

As expected, the scope of allies and activities expanded exponentially as I moved from campaigning to governing. I developed contacts and supporters too numerous to cite here during that single term in the Alabama legislature, and numerous other allies, activists, associations, organizations, and media came aboard as my standing and influence expanded statewide during my secretary of state days. Furthermore, I ambitiously and constantly recruited new, nonpolitical friends for my causes and, of course, my career.

Over time, my political science background, my deliberative approach to politics, and my evolving game plan merged into a philosophy of civic reform with an increasingly obvious element of cautious politics vital to its success. This terminology was never written or declared as a formality, but I carried this self-conceptualized philosophy of leadership and service into my role as an elected official.

A Record of Constructive Biracial Service

My general profile as a public official reflected political moderation in style and substance, accompanied by strong civic and reform inclinations, and culminating in effective public service.

The *Montgomery Advertiser* positively editorialized about that manner and performance in the last month of my service:

> Alabama should be pleased both that retiring U.S. Rep. Glen Browder will not become a fancy and highly paid consultant or lobbyist in Washington on his exit from Congress and that he refuses to rule out further involvement in Alabama politics.
>
> The state needs his particular level-headed ability to build coalitions and translate the knowledge of the academic ivory tower into practical, passable legislation. . .
>
> The Advertiser wishes Browder well upon his departure after a decade in Congress—and looks forward to a time when he might again offer his special and considerable talents in service to this state.[2]

Howell Heflin also hailed my service in a Senate speech as we both were preparing to end our public careers:

> Mr. President, I want to pay tribute today to another of the many outstanding Members of Congress who will be leaving as the 104th Congress draws to a close. That Member is my good friend from Alabama's Third Congressional District, Representative Glen Browder . . .

He approaches his job with a deliberative, studied, and professorial approach that has helped him make the right decisions for his constituents and for the nation as a whole . . .

I am proud to have been able to serve with Congressman Browder in the Alabama delegation over the last seven years. It has been a pleasure to work with him on base closure and other vital issues. He is a proven leader who will be sorely missed when the 105th Congress convenes early next year, but I am confident that we will see him in other leadership roles in the future. I congratulate him and wish him well.[3]

More pertinent to our thesis and as this section will demonstrate, I quietly provided constructive leadership on racial politics and contentious black-white relations throughout my varied and fast-paced career.

Career Pattern

Close examination reveals a definite developmental pattern as I traveled my stealthy course from the Alabama legislature to the secretary of state's office and on to the U.S. Congress.

That single term in the Alabama House (1983–86) was a "learning experience" during which I gained skills and stature as a civic leader. Besides my reform agenda, my notion of service usually inclined in progressive directions. More often than not, I worked with the Democratic leadership and majority coalition, and I loyally supported people programs, like education. I dealt positively with racial issues, supported biracial cooperation, and built trusting relationships with key African Americans—while nobody paid much attention.

It was fairly simple work, and those were enjoyable years. I basically was a local politician playing a beginner's role in important state issues and happenings in the aftermath of the civil rights movement. Black-white bickering and confrontation were constant, but we really didn't struggle with big issues of civil rights. The heroic drama had subsided, and monumental debates over racial justice took place in the federal courts and in Washington, not on Goat Hill. Therefore I was able to practice biracial politics without unduly antagonizing the traditional establishment or my people back home.

Over the course of that four-year term, I developed into a fairly prominent political figure in the legislature, particularly as my civic efforts— constitutional, election, and education reform—began to register as serious items on the state's political agenda.

My life changed dramatically when I moved into the office of secretary of state (1987-89), carrying popular support and media power as "Chief Elections Officer." That was a heady experience as I assumed statewide leadership. Unlike the simple, easy, unnoticed skirmishes in the legislature, my new assignment entailed dealing with both powerful, traditional white politicians and powerful, demanding black leaders. Fortunately, my work was pretty focused—on campaign reform—and, with some help from my friends inside and outside the legislature, we made significant progress. I served two-and-a-half years as secretary of state before the congressional seat opened.

I would describe my service as a state legislator as interesting and a learning experience, and I would describe my work as secretary of state as focused and productive. But my assignment in the U.S. Congress (1989–97), by comparison, could best be characterized as difficult, frustrating, and, in retrospect, very rewarding.

I had moved progressively into more consequential stature and environs, into the big leagues of American democracy. Powerful antagonists (Democrat and Republican, liberal and conservative, black and white, in Washington and back in Alabama) continuously pressed irreconcilable demands upon the congressional delegation. The media watched and reported every tough vote, public statement, and personal foible. And campaigns were vicious.

I had gone to Washington in 1989 as a moderate Democrat—a progressive politician by Alabama standards but a relatively conservative voice in national party politics. I was an early participant in the Democratic Leadership Council and I quickly joined the leadership of the Democratic Study Group. I also was included on important task forces of the Democratic Caucus. However, I clashed from the start with the Democratic congressional leadership and President Clinton on campaign finance reform, and I increasingly steered my own way on congressional accountability and fiscal responsibility. I charted a fundamentally independent course in 1994 by helping found the Blue Dog Coalition, a tight band of Democrats that wielded considerable influence on various issues in the Republican Congress. At the same time, defense matters (both local and national) took up more and more of my time and attention. Finally, an unsuccessful race for Alabama's vacant U.S. Senate seat in 1996 finished my long run of electoral successes. I concluded my public service in January of 1997.

Clearly, the altered environment of national politics had impacted my performance as a civic reformer and stealth politician. I found that Washington was more resistant to my version of democracy; racial politics there was more open, yet just as cynical as what I had observed in Montgomery. Unfortunately, I didn't stick around long enough or acquire sufficient standing to work much reform in Congress, and the changing times eventually eroded my capacities for stealth leadership.

The 1996 Senate loss caused me to question my civic and biracial efforts. It took several years after leaving Washington for me to reconcile the mixed impact of what I had attempted and accomplished over those fourteen years. In retrospect, I'm pleased overall, especially with my work on education, campaign, and budget reform. I like to think that I contributed something worthwhile to Southern politics.

Votes and Issues

Analysis of voting data in the Alabama legislature and the U.S. Congress documents my moderate politics and sometimes support for minority causes over the years. The voting information reported in this section is derived from several sources, and some data represent compilations using original source files. Interested readers can consult documents in the Browder Collection, or access online organizations such as Project Vote Smart (www.vote-smart.org).

In Montgomery, I was a solid pro-education vote (95 percent, as compiled by the Alabama Education Association), and I supported the business line much less often (38 percent, as compiled by the Alabama Alliance of Business and Industry). In Washington, I established a balance among education interests (64 percent, National Education Association), the business community (63 percent, U.S. Chamber of Commerce), and organized labor (65 percent, AFL-CIO). On ideological rankings, I normally scored at about the midpoint, halfway between the most conservative and most liberal members of Congress (54 percent conservative and 46 percent liberal, according to National Journal data covering social, economic, and international affairs). I supported fellow Democratic President Bill Clinton on 66 percent of recorded votes and Republican President George H. W. Bush 46 percent of the time. I was thrifty with taxpayer dollars, actually "returning" a total of $1.5 million, or 24 percent of my official congressional allowance to the U.S. Treasury during eight years in office.

Amid this balanced moderation, I was selectively attentive to the agenda being pushed by African American organizations. No quantitative assessments exist for my service in the Alabama legislature or as secretary of state, but in Congress I registered slightly above the average member—53 percent—on civil rights issues during my career (as reported by the Leadership Conference on Civil Rights, a broad coalition of black and other human rights groups). I consider this mark impressive for a liberal scorecard that counted such items as a balanced budget amendment and campaign finance disclosure as anti-civil rights legislation. By comparison, my Democratic predecessor compiled an LCCR career rating of (24 percent) and my two Republican successors have scored even lower (12 percent and 17 percent).

I had to negotiate a difficult agenda of race-related issues in Montgomery and Washington. On innumerable bills, amendments, and procedural motions, I tended to side with my black colleagues, but there were times when I factored other personal and political considerations into the situation.

I never cast a "yea" or "nay" for racist reasons or put racial blinders on my conscience, but I tried to prudently balance my racial record just as I did on education, business, and labor issues. I continuously looked for opportunities to promote racial fairness and justice; however, sometimes I took contrary positions, despite how any special interest group might score that vote.

The truth is that political life was never a simple matter of conviction and courage. I calculated each vote in terms of my general mission, representational style, mixed constituency interests, and politics. On major issues, I first looked at the broad substantive agenda, and then I weighed my own personal beliefs with constituent needs/desires and with the national interest (the classic clash of representational theory). On minor, procedural, symbolic, or "throw-away" votes, I might calculate the political baggage of the particular action.

For example, colleagues from both sides of the partisan and racial divide often attempted to attach a quota or affirmative action amendment onto a general appropriations bill for personal posturing, or for putting opponents in a tough situation, or sometimes simply for "score-card" padding. Then, in addition to the substantive merits of the amendment, I had to consider (a) whether my vote had any real bearing on the prospects for that specific amendment, (b) whether the general appropriations bill had any chance of final passage, (c) how my Alabama colleagues were voting, (d) how important the issue was to my political allies, (e) how much flack I'd catch back home, from either the right or left, and (f) how much money I'd have to raise and spend fighting a negative commercial based on that vote.

The bottom line is that I conscientiously did what I could on behalf of a progressive racial agenda; however, back then, being "balanced" was the unspoken survival requirement for most moderate white politicians who were from the Deep South and had a "D" behind their names. It's nothing to brag about; but that was how we stuck around to "do good"—as in "stealth reconstruction"—as long as we did.

In the Alabama House, for example, I loyally supported appropriations for black colleges and universities, I voted for legislation promoting the appointment of black deputy registrars, and I supported reapportionment plans for increasing black representation. But I abstained from voting on the Martin Luther King Holiday. In the U.S. Congress, I voted for reauthorization of the Civil Rights Commission, for the Hate Crimes Statistics Act, for Historically Black Colleges and Universities, and for several extensions of the Civil Rights Act. On the other hand, I opposed the use of statistical race-disparities as a defense in death penalty cases and I supported limitation on race-bias claims in death row appeals.

In fact, I have calculated that during my congressional career I voted for a full two-thirds of real racial issues on the LCCR scorecard (when the list was purged of such nonracial votes as the balanced budget amendment, campaign/lobby reform, health/welfare proposals, business-labor provisions, gender matters, gun control, and immigration).

Staffing and Services

Besides specific issues and votes, the most obvious challenge to my self-assumed role as a new kind of leader was a question of tangible consequence: how would I deal—in terms of hiring staff and providing services—with my biracial electorate. Most specifically, would I conduct myself according to higher standards of equity and fairness than traditional Southern politicians?

Such considerations were minor, at the beginning, for an Alabama state representative with no personal staff or office in a 93 percent white district. Nevertheless, I was particularly careful to respond to requests for assistance from my minority constituents, and I submitted several African Americans for positions on boards recommended by the county legislative delegation or appointed by the governor.

My activities as Alabama secretary of state and U.S. congressman assumed greater consequence, and I tried to perform my administrative responsibilities in both jobs with biracial fairness and without a lot of fanfare. As a constitutional officer, the secretary of state selected staff mainly from a state merit list, with some discretion among the top few candidates. I never articulated a racial policy, but I kept account in the privacy of my own mind. Complete, precise data by race are unavailable for my partial, two-and-a-half-year term, but a tally compiled for the legislature in late 1987 indicated that my minority employees—29 percent—surpassed the 25 percent black proportion among the Alabama public. In fact, when as secretary of state I went before the House panel of Jurisdiction, a key black legislator who constantly harangued executives about their hiring practices dismissed interrogation of me with a comment that, "He's all right—no need to go into that with him."

Of particular note is the fact that, without public notice, I appointed the first African American director of the elections division in the secretary of state's office. Jerry Henderson, an Alabama native and Atlanta University alumnus, was a Pike County commissioner who had been involved in race and electoral issues for several years. Henderson later assumed major election responsibilities in other institutions throughout the country; he presently serves as a national and international democracy consultant.

At the national level, I likewise attempted to represent minority constituents without making a big deal of hiring practices. During my eight years in federal office, blacks comprised 29 percent of the employees serving Alabama's third congressional district (which had 26 percent minority citizens). I also quietly appointed an African American to a key legislative position: Marti Thomas, a Montgomerian and graduate of Tuskegee University, served as the only official press secretary during my tenure in Washington. Thomas later served in various capacities on the Hill and in the Clinton administration; she presently works as senior legislative representative with the American Association for Retired Persons. Now Marti Thomas Doneghy, she recently revealed how she got that original press job and her thoughts about working in our office:

> I had been in Washington, D.C., already for almost two years in 1989, hoping and knocking on doors all over Capitol Hill, particularly the Alabama delegation's doors, but getting nowhere . . . But my own sense of practicality, loyalty, idealism and independence would be exactly what the congressman was looking for . . . As a native Alabamian, African American and female, I think Congressman Browder took great pride in me as his Washington-based congressional press secretary. I was his liaison to the media and it was an honor and a privilege to work for him. In many ways he spoke loudly and clearly about his stance on race politics in Alabama by his selection of me as his first congressional press secretary.[4]

I was also routinely and discreetly attentive to including African Americans in important political endeavors within my jurisdiction. For example, as a state representative (and as legislative sponsor of the Browder Education Reform Bill and as vice chairman of the Governor's Education Reform Commission), I conscientiously included African American officials in that commission and its education reform procedures. As secretary of state, I seriously incorporated African Americans in the work of my advisory reform group, the Alabama Elections Commission. As congressman, I was careful to place African Americans in important staff positions; as had my predecessor, I maintained an African American field representative and a permanent office in predominantly black Macon County throughout my tenure.

Such personnel practices were always difficult—and I encountered problems from whites and blacks alike. It was not uncommon for some white supporter to gripe about the appointment of "too many coloreds"; or a black supporter would complain because his or her favored black applicant had been overlooked for another black employee "that our folk don't know and don't trust."

Just as important as hiring was making sure that all constituents and visitors were treated fairly. As both secretary of state and congressman, I insisted that our personnel treat all citizens politely and without discrimination in telephone conversations, office visits, casework, grant considerations, and all other operations of my administrations. More personally and discreetly, I promoted fairness in job recommendations, office internships, and military academy nominations. I even monitored receptionist assignments, without formal directive, so that an African American face normally greeted visitors to my offices in Montgomery and Washington. These may seem like small and insignificant matters to some people, but not to me. I figured that black Alabamians historically have had to go to all-white offices for help, and I wanted them to know that things had changed and this was their government, too. I also wanted my white constituents to understand that this was the way Alabama politics and American democracy ought to work.

Co-author Stanberry echoed the significance of such practices from her experience as a Browder employee and her work in several other Southern congressional offices. In response to a specific question on this issue, she wrote:

> The importance of having a diverse staff cannot be overstated. When an African American constituent enters a congressional office and immediately sees people who look like him or her, it adds to a sense of comfort and at least symbolic representation. White constituents are placated because in addition to the white representative, they see a diverse staff working

together. For the interns who spend a summer or semester in an office, it offers the opportunity to work in a harmonious, biracial environment that can be carried with him/her long after the internship concludes. It helps to break down barriers and stereotypes, which is clearly a goal for those who want to move the country forward.

Again, there were no official checklists or quotas; I simply took care to make my governmental realm as equitable as possible.

Special Outreach in Black-White Relations

In addition to my voting record, hiring practices, and constituency services, I sometimes extended my leadership beyond official representational requirements into difficult areas of racial politics.

Early in my career as a freshman state legislator, I performed this self-assigned outreach by quietly contributing to the agenda and substance of Alabama politics. While my constituency was overwhelmingly white, I supported the inclusion of African American voices in important state policies, I encouraged racial fairness in processes and appropriations, and I worked closely with black leaders on constitution, election, and education reform.

Later on, I conducted social, educational, and civic outreach to keep in touch with everyday Alabamians—both black and white. Throughout my career, I regularly engaged in low-profile activities such as "Working For Alabama" (periodically volunteering as a laborer with community projects), the "Citizen Bee" (a national program that I sponsored for Alabama high schoolers, patterned after old-fashioned spelling bees), and the "Citizens Congress" (a one-day event that I convened, in which everyday taxpayers crafted their version of the national budget). Such activities not only kept me in touch with my constituents, they also helped me develop my own biracial network beyond the domain of established political organizations.

At certain critical junctures, moreover, I attempted active, out-front assignments—dealing with obvious cases of racism and racial legacies—and this outreach tested my game plan and skills as a stealthy leader. In those initiatives, I had to assume higher-profile roles to achieve progress and/or to keep volatile developments from flaring into traditional patterns of black-white trauma. These efforts usually represented a stealthy marriage of ad hoc contradictions: that is, each action involved simultaneous caution and boldness; each project was genuinely pursued despite being dangerous politically; and I preached traditional, community values while pushing progressive, biracial change in each situation. Collectively, these self-assignments reveal—specifically and dramatically—the special service that I tried to provide during those difficult times.

In this section, I will elaborate, for illustrative purposes, several incidents of such leadership.

Pollworker Training

Perhaps the most challenging and consequential situation occurred in 1988 during my second year as Alabama secretary of state.

A federal court determined that Alabama's election system unconstitutionally excluded minority citizens from meaningful participation in the administration of elections, despite numerous decrees ordering compliance by state and local officials. U.S. Judge Myron Thompson indicated to defendant Governor Guy Hunt, Attorney General Don Siegelman, and local elections officials that he was prepared to hold everyone in contempt of court.

This case was another potentially divisive development in a long tradition of black-white contention in the Heart of Dixie.

The secretary of state was not a defendant in the case, but I saw this challenge as a personal and professional opportunity as much as a political problem. Dr. Robert Montjoy, an Auburn University elections expert and friend, suggested to the court, and the involved parties agreed, that the new "Chief Elections Officer" be empowered to tackle the assignment. The other major state leaders were relieved of their responsibilities, and Montjoy and I eagerly joined forces to move Alabama toward compliance with the federal order.

It was a dicey venture, but we were well-suited for the assignment. I commanded political trust from the state's probate judges, county commissioners, circuit clerks, sheriffs, registers, mayors, city clerks, and other key officials, who felt that I would treat them as partners rather than recalcitrant racists; and I also had good relations with the major black leaders and organizations who wanted to see the plan work. Equally importantly, I enjoyed the respect of the public. The *Gadsden Times* wrote: "It's a shame it takes a federal judge to make it happen. Of course, we have no problem with the person who will administer the order. We trust Browder to make our polling places as effective and fair as possible."[5]

Fortunately, too, Montjoy's elections credentials were impeccable; he, as well, had maintained positive professional relations for many years with both sides in the contentious equation.

Clearly, the 1988 federal court order could have touched off another racial controversy for Alabama. Instead, we defined the challenge in positive, nonracial terms of electoral progress while proceeding—sometimes publicly, sometimes behind the scenes—to bring black plaintiffs and white defendant officials together for constructive, collaborative work on a real problem. Our team possessed significant backing from the federal government, we had sufficient state funding as required by court decree, and we launched a simultaneously bold yet cautious solution to Alabama's hard-history dilemma.

The secretary of state's office conducted itself ambitiously and effectively on behalf of the mission, stretching the judicial mandate whenever possible to comprehensively review and revise Alabama's election administration. During the rest of my tenure as chief elections official, we worked to devise and implement a plan for recruiting and training minority poll-workers. We contracted with Auburn University and Alabama State University (an HBCU) to assist with the program. We worked hand in hand with local officials and black leaders to produce new procedures, standards, and materials. Training sessions throughout the state significantly improved skills and weeded out deficient pollworkers; there was sensitivity instruction; voting places were upgraded for handicap-accessibility; a voter-complaint system was initiated and monitored.

As the process unfolded, I toured the state for press conferences touting the project—not as another federal order forcing integration upon local communities but as an opportunity for the people of Alabama to modernize and clean up a backward election system. The *Huntsville Times* editorialized in support of the effort:

> For the first time in state history, the method by which local election officials—or poll workers—are selected will be enhanced by Secretary of State Glen Browder and his staff . . . If state and county election officials have the insight to work together on the training mandate by doubling their efforts in recruiting and resources, they will see a significant impact on the accuracy and quality of future elections. They should see in every county an adequate supply of responsible, educated poll workers—both black and white.[6]

Consequently, local administrators diligently met the challenge and basked in the glow of positive media coverage; black organizations induced legions of minority poll-workers into the process; voters enjoyed a more efficient and responsive electoral experience; and the federal court released Alabama officials from its order.

Schoolhouse Burning

Another illustrative situation developed in late February 1994, as smoldering racial discord erupted in a small town in the middle of my congressional district.

The central incident was a dispute involving the principal of Randolph County High School and blacks in Wedowee, a rural community of less than a thousand residents. The principal threatened to cancel the upcoming prom because a biracial couple planned to participate. He backed down, was suspended, and then was reinstated by the school board.

The local newspaper, the *Randolph Leader*, attempted to steer the community in a constructive direction, but tensions mounted quickly. Both the U.S. Justice Department and the U.S. Department of Education launched investigations. Shortly, the NAACP, the Southern Christian Leadership Conference, and the Ku Klux Klan entered the fray. CNN and tons of national media pounced on the story and encamped in the town.

As the August school opening approached, the high school burned—

arson! That's when I decided to go down there and try to do something. The arson was not a congressional issue, and I could not catch the arsonist or rebuild the school. But somebody had to do something to calm racial tensions and begin some sort of healing for the community. My constituents were hurt, angry, and wondering what next—violence, more burnings by whatever nut burned the school, retaliatory burnings by reactionary whites or blacks? I knew that this situation was going to get a lot uglier, not better, on its own.

I anticipated that this would be an extended, high profile, risk-wrought assignment, so I sent my field representative, Lamar Denkins, to check things out. I instructed Denkins to contact all ministers in Randolph County churches, black and white, and start the groundwork for a biracial ministerial alliance to address this problem. Denkins was a natural for this project. In addition to his congressional fieldwork, he was a minister, military chaplain, and mental health counselor; and he knew many of the players in Randolph County. He was assisted in these efforts by Lifus Johnson, my African American staffer in Macon County, who urged the black ministers to come together for reconciliation.

My thinking was that we had to focus on what was best for the children of this community and that the best way to do that was through religious leaders and their congregations. But even that was an "iffy" course. Most of the white ministers just wanted this problem to go away . . . and there were some in the black pulpits who really welcomed the race issue. Some of them showed up only under pressure from the congressman.

Denkins rounded up twenty-six ministers—thirteen white and thirteen black. "I spent seventeen straight days down there, working with ministers and school officials, trying to defuse the situation," Denkins said. "I would set up private meetings in a local restaurant with the ministers, and Glen would come in on the weekend and talk with them." The preachers sometimes argued heatedly among themselves, he said; during one of their meetings, a Ku Klux Klan group from west Georgia left its literature in the restaurant's restroom. He added that he was never scared, "but I did receive calls and threats that Congressman Browder would be hurt politically by our involvement."[7]

The ministerial group eventually came up with a plan. They issued a joint statement, signed by all twenty-six ministers and published in the *Randolph Leader*.

> We, the united ministers of Randolph County, believe the time has come for healing to begin in our county. Our children will start to school next week and we are concerned about their welfare. A community Healing Prayer Service will be held at the Randolph County High School parking lot on Sunday, Aug. 21 at 8 a.m. The students, faculty, staff and public are encouraged to pray for our students and for community healing."[8]

These ministers then preached their message of reconciliation and healing—"for our children"—in their churches and conducted the joint sunrise service on the grounds of the burned school to help get the school year started positively.

I was unable to attend the sunrise service because of an unusual and critical weekend vote in Washington, but hundreds of Randolph County residents joined together on the school grounds that Sunday morning. They prayed for healing, they sang gospel songs, and they even hung around to help get temporary classrooms ready for the school year. I was pleased with these results. There had been a lot of concern on both sides. Those black and white preachers had never even met each other. And they'd never talked about these issues. I thought it was a very successful initiative.

Randolph Leader editor John Stevenson reported the day's activities:

> After Randolph Baptist Association director of missions Tom Stacey led the group of around 250 in singing "Amazing Grace," the audience of black and white citizens and students heard calls and prayers for unity and healing form the Rev. R. L. Heflin of Wedowee's Antioch Baptist Church, the Rev. Tom Roberts of Wedowee First United Methodist Church, the Rev. John Duncan of Wedowee First Baptist Church, and the Rev. Lonnie Houston of Peace and Good Will Baptist Church near Roanoke.
>
> Typical of the prayers offered were those of the Rev. Mr. Roberts, who asked God to "heal our community of these painful divisions," and the

Rev. Mr. Houston, who prayed, "Bind us together in Christian love as parents and children and help us to do the right thing."[9]

Stevenson noted that minutes after the prayer service ended, "the sound of hammers and power saws could be heard, as volunteers tried to beat the rain and complete the task begun last week of building stairs and landings for mobile classrooms."[10]

Rose Livingston's report in the *Birmingham News* also captured the spirit of reconciliation at the joint service:

As soon as the prayers were offered, the hammers began pounding. Sunday was no day of rest in Wedowee . . .

Now all efforts seem to be on burying the past and getting children into school. A group of 26 ministers, half of them black and half white, organized Sunday's prayer meeting at the suggestion of U.S. Rep. Glen Browder, D-Jacksonville, who was unable to attend.

The crowd sang "Amazing Grace" while gathered in front of a cleared lot where the school once stood. Several ministers, with words of encouragement from the crowd of blacks and whites, appealed for an end to the conflict. . .

Jennifer Messer, a 1994 graduate of the school, said the prayer meeting offered a message of healing the community needed to hear.

Her mother, Randolph County school board member Geneva Messer, agreed.

"I was moved by all of us being here," she said. "It shows we want to start anew and rebuild. I believe everyone wants to work together."[11]

I recently asked Denkins for his assessment of their impact, and the former aide said that, besides its calming effect, a key accomplishment of the Wedowee initiative was unprecedented community dialogue.[12]

One minister stated that he never intended to get involved in something like this, but someone had to: "We have to get the community together to solve its own problems. We can't do anything about the fire now. The community is fragmented, we've got to come together and learn to live together."

Obviously, after weeks of intense racial politics, I was happy to turn my full attention back to my congressional responsibilities. It had been a rough time for me and my constituents; but the community avoided further racial violence and rebuilt the school. Although many of the old ways still predominated in that area, most of the people of Randolph County appeared ready to start treating their neighbors as friends again.

Rural Church Arsons

Toward the end of my Washington service, a more widespread conflagration revived images of Alabama's past and threatened to ignite racial tensions throughout the South.

Old anxieties swirled in the Black Belt in 1995 as two small, rural, African American churches burned in Greene County, Alabama, just before Martin Luther King Day; another burned near Selma, Alabama, a week before the anniversary of the Selma to Montgomery civil rights march. Over the next two years, a dozen churches burned in Alabama and dozens more burned throughout the South—and most were cases of arson. Both white and black houses of worship were victimized, actually in equal numbers, but the media focus was on race and Southern history.

I did my own checking with local and state fire officials and with the U.S. Justice Department, as criticism mounted for Alabama Republican Governor Fob James and Republican Attorney General Jeff Sessions.[13] I found that church desecration was a continuing problem in rural areas and it involved a mixture of racism, vandalism, and religious issues. But I also knew that unless something were done—in terms of a positive, forceful, public discussion about both racial and religious tolerance—this situation might grow into a major black-white crisis throughout the region.

I got together with Cleo Fields (Louisiana) and we quickly forged a biracial congressional coalition—bringing together the mainly white and Southern Blue Dogs and the Southern members of the Black Caucus—to get the federal government involved in the problem. We understood, from our shared backgrounds, that racial tensions were always at the surface in many small Southern towns. We also realized that when such incidents occurred, whether acts of racism or vandalism with no racial intent, it brought out troubling divisions within the community; how these incidents were addressed would be crucial in determining the outcome.

The CBC and Blue Dogs coordinated their individual actions, conducted joint special sessions on the floor of the House, and pressed their common case for full and vigorous federal investigation and prosecution of the arsonists. We arranged a closed-door meeting with Assistant Attorney General Deval Patrick, who shared information and assured the CBC and Blue Dogs that the church burnings were being taken seriously. Afterwards, Fields said "We are pleased that the federal government is doing everything within its control"; I added that "This coalition of the Congressional Black Caucus and the Blue Dogs sends a message that that these crimes will not be tolerated."[14] Two months later, my Alabama colleague and CBC member Earl Hilliard (in whose district several incidents occurred) positively welcomed the investigation to a community forum deep in the Black Belt:

> . . . This is the home of George Wallace, Rosa Parks, Bull Connor, and Jimmy Lee Jackson. It is also the cradle of the Confederacy and the birthplace of the civil rights movement. And it's the place where Jefferson Davis took the oath of office as president of the Confederacy, but it is also where Martin Luther King introduced the doctrine of passive resistance.
>
> It is a place that has a history of racial problems, but it also has a history of solving those problems, in a confrontational manner and in other ways. I applaud those who seek the other ways. So for that reason, I welcome all of you here. This is one of the other ways.[15]

Co-author Stanberry, who was involved in the congressional action as a Browder staff member, remembers that the unusual coalition of the Blue Dogs and the Congressional Black Caucus not only produced an interracial effort to publicly address the rash of church burnings, but it also spearheaded official meetings and various informal activities. The Mobile native later wrote that the experience held special meaning for her:

> As a new employee in the Browder office and a person who hails from the South, I was concerned about the church fires for the memories it would

provoke among African Americans; I also was inspired by two groups that do not always agree on policy issues coming together to let the citizens know that they were on top of this, ensuring that the Justice Department was investigating the manner. As was the case with the Wedowee high school incident, Browder proved that it is better for different groups to work together for a common goal than to engage in activities that hamper investigations and the healing process.

The Blue Dogs and Black Caucus effectively focused federal attention on the problem, and Congress passed the Rural Church Arson Prevention Act (1996), enhancing criminal prosecution and penalties for these transgressions of America's conscience.

Of course, sorting out the role of race has been difficult and legislative action could not end rural church burnings completely. However, arrests and convictions spiked during that period, prompting the federal-state-local alliance to proclaim national victory over such outrageous behavior: "The arsonists may have sought to divide our communities by burning our houses of worship, but in they end they only helped bring them closer together."[16] More impressively, annual reports indicate that church burnings have declined in the years since enactment of the Rural Church Arson Act.

To summarize, these three situations—the pollworker court order, the schoolhouse burning, and the rash of rural church arsons—represented volatile and negative possibilities for the people, both white and black, of Alabama. Although these challenges fell outside my primary or routine responsibility, I tried to deal with the problems. I packaged ad hoc, stealthy ventures—i.e., I had to be simultaneously bold and cautious; I genuinely pursued positive objectives despite the political risks; and I preached traditional values while pushing progressive change. Each venture required a different combination of public and behind-the-scenes endeavor for community action, and I tried, through careful leadership, to help achieve civic and racial progress.

In many ways, these special outreach initiatives were simply specific and dramatic examples of the collective service that biracial leaders provided during those difficult times. My efforts in these and other cases were neither unique among politicians nor especially brilliant leadership. But I tried to do it as a stealthy policy and practice. I looked for ways to be constructive with private, personal influence or public, official intervention when I thought I could help in progressive manner. Sometimes it worked minor miracles; sometimes it made a bad situation better; sometimes it just ticked people off.

Thus far, I have focused on votes, issues, staffing, services, and outreach as an effective stealth leader. The following account—a point-by-point discussion which I compiled for this project based on my own remembrances—depicts some of the intricacies and difficulties of such efforts in the real-world politics of Alabama and Washington during those times.

Racial Remembrances of Alabama and Washington

It did not take long in Montgomery for me to realize the challenge of my self-assumed mission in a state burdened with the legacies of hard history. While notions of "A New Kind of Leader" and "stealth politics" might sound glamorous, I would struggle mightily in my game plan for civic reform, racial progress, and career success in the 1970s, 1980s, and 1990s.

I will attempt to describe, retrospectively and analytically, the biracial politics and personalities of those times. Historical context has already been presented in previous chapters; however, the following section more personally elaborates race relations from inside the system back then. Some of my remarks are blunt, reflecting both positive and less-than-positive aspects of biracial politicking; I report them in full because they convey valuable, nuanced insights into service as a stealth leader.

Black and White in Goat Hill Politics

I refined my game plan extensively as I dealt with the dynamics of public service in Alabama politics. Apparently, too, many others figured out they had to accommodate a new racial system in the post-civil rights era.

Most white leaders of the 1980s knew that a new day had dawned in their state. They may not have liked it; for sure, many hated it. But they accepted the reality of a new, biracial politics. While everybody understood that racism and racist politics would continue into the future (not simply

by purposeful action but because of the difficulty of quick fixes for historical dilemmas), many white elites realized that there had to be significant
adjustment in Alabama, whether through changing attitudes, affirmative
action, or even simply institutionalizing racial considerations in routine
politics and government.

The Democratic establishment—including Governor George Wallace
and the lieutenant governors who served during this period, Bill Baxley,
Don Siegelman, and Jim Folsom Jr.—fairly easily embraced the new way
of doing business; and House Speakers Tom Drake and Jimmy Clark both
wielded their presiding gavel in partnership with the small but determined
Black Caucus.

At the same time, a powerful, liberal confederation of blacks, teachers,
unions, and trial lawyers—known as the "Coalition"—took over Alabama
state party politics in the 1980s. Of course, other Democratic white politicians never accepted or changed; they continued to rant and obstruct; some
switched parties; many inevitably faded from the scene.

A Messy Clash of Civics vs. Race

Before my first year in the Alabama legislature was out, I experienced
a historical trauma that defied stealthy resolution. In 1983, under intense
federal pressure to correct past discrimination, the legislature was forced
to redistrict itself and undergo an immediate, reapportioned election even
though the incumbent legislators had just been elected the previous year.
The Democratic Party decided to "hand pick" its nominees—rather than
undergo a complete primary process—for the quick special election. The State
Democratic Executive Committee called a nominating session for October
1, 1983, and the liberal "Coalition" laid plans to ideologically cleanse the
state legislative body. As a member of the SDEC, I found myself in an ugly,
brutal, intraparty brawl pitting electoral civics against racial progress.

Unlike the challenging situations discussed in the previous section, there
was no room for quiet, practical, biracial leadership during the "Saturday
Morning Massacre" in Birmingham. It was a public "bloodletting" of incumbents versus incumbents, veterans versus newcomers, liberals versus
conservatives, whites versus blacks, males versus females, and friends versus

friends. Amid angry recriminations, the SDEC dismissed eleven sitting, shocked Democratic state senators and state representatives, all of whom had been duly elected by their constituents less than a year earlier. Ironically, even two recalcitrant blacks were dumped by the "Coalition." I generally favored my incumbent colleagues or abstained when it was incumbent-against-incumbent, but more often than not I sided with the "Coalition" on many painful choices. My most gut-wrenching personal decision was mentor John Teague over good friend Lister Procter. I had worked as a consultant for both of these white senators in earlier years. My toughest political vote was for black challenger George Grayson over white colleague Dwayne Freeman in a Huntsville area House district; the legislative/Democratic leadership argued convincingly that the federal judiciary and the Justice Department would object to a white politician being picked for the new black-majority district. After all the uproar, there were four new African American legislators (increasing the black membership from fifteen to nineteen) and a half-dozen relatively progressive white Democrats; collaterally, the redistricting produced a similar smattering of angry Independents and opposition Republicans in the 140-member legislature.

Clearly, this high-profile "hand-picking" was a direct clash between civics and race, messily complicated by history, ideology, friendships, grudges, and brute politics. It ripped asunder, at least temporarily, my carefully crafted stealthy game plan and foretold extended heartburn for the Democratic Party. I bled emotionally for my part in this incident, which represented a conflicting amalgam of personal considerations and political outcomes. Most importantly, it violated my ideas about small-d democratic representation while expanding racial representation in the Alabama legislature. I'm not sure how I would handle the situation if I had it to do over—I'm just thankful I'll never have to do it over.

The Beginning of a Two-Party System

The Democrats followed up the 1983 legislative hand-picking with another controversy in the 1986 gubernatorial primary. After investigating alleged Republican crossover voting, a special party panel replaced primary front-runner Charles Graddick with liberal party favorite Bill Baxley, thereby inspiring disgusted general election voters to hand the governorship to Republican Guy Hunt and thus birthing a real two-party system in the Heart of Dixie.

In many ways, the new GOP leadership resembled traditional Alabama politicians. Almost all the newcomers were white, and they prioritized limited government, low taxes, a favorable business climate, and pro-family/morality issues. Especially in the beginning, the Republicans had fewer outright racists in their ranks; and the old-line business types dutifully accepted change in principle. But some of the political practices of the new day rankled them—and they vociferously attacked the Democrats for race-based political dealing. Also, the insurgent Republicans relentlessly assailed ethical shortcomings of the Democratic establishment. Later defections of disgruntled conservative Democrats regimented and normalized racial, political, and philosophical divisions between the legislature's Democratic establishment and the growing Republican caucus.

As a civic democrat, I agreed with the Republicans on numerous matters regarding proper legislative procedures and various reform matters. But I was a Democratic Party team player, with responsibility for governing rather than posturing, and I stuck with my team.

Expanding Black Leadership

Another notable development in Alabama during those years was that the black leadership quickly expanded beyond its "heroic" core. While the civil rights movement was still a potent rallying cry, and while most black leaders in the state still derived their electoral support from the combined base of religious and civil rights organizations of the 1950s–'60s, new organizations arose as bases of black power and influence. The Alabama New South Coalition and Jefferson County Citizens Coalition began to challenge the Alabama Democratic Conference in local and statewide politics. Black elected officials increasingly were more secular, independent, and professional as politicians and leaders. Educators and lawyers prevailed among their ranks rather than the ministers and activists of the old days.

After working with and forming extensive relationships with African Americans in Montgomery and throughout the state, I concluded that—

other than obvious historical differences, their commitment to the black community, and "neo-heroic" posturing—most black leaders in Alabama were like white leaders in Alabama: they were politicians eager to assert their new influence on important public policy. I found that blacks were no more nor no less noble and no more nor no less political than their traditional adversaries. For the most part, they were interested in the same things as moderate white politicians—improving the state's education system, economic development, jobs, and social services, while also looking out for black constituencies, other disadvantaged people, some powerful special interests, local areas, and pet causes. At the same time, they were just as inclined as white politicians toward personal power, patronage, and perks.

Pervasion of Race and Racism

Nevertheless, it seemed to me that the race factor pervaded daily life in Montgomery; black-white tension directly or indirectly impacted just about everything that happened on Goat Hill during that era. Black legislators struggled constantly—and aggressively—to deal with their policy and political disadvantages in a system where obvious racial considerations—and some racism—still prevailed. Likewise, many white legislators resented the attitudes and ways of certain black colleagues—particularly those individuals trading on historical mistreatment for personal political advantage and private gain.

Indeed, I learned first-hand that crass racial politicking was a biracial phenomenon in Alabama. There were endless racial clashes over important public policy—the organization of the legislature; the division of money for education, highways, law enforcement and other functions; appointments to various colleges, boards, and commissions; and resolutions about various hot-button or even non-controversial issues. Quite often there were private slurs from both sides; discussion on the floor sometimes grew unnecessarily heated as nonracial matters escalated into racial issues. Sometimes, whether the issue involved race or not, it was resolved to a great degree in some private, backroom manner of racial accommodation.

Few of us were surprised or seriously concerned about this situation; after all, politics is politics; also, we knew it was a well-deserved nuisance from our aforementioned legacy and we simply lived with it. But it was a real part of biracial politics—and it added to the challenge of my practical assignment—during that period.

I was surprised at the extent of black politicians' disinterest in and outright antagonism to my civic legislation, such as education, election, and constitutional reform. I had figured that African American politicians might be natural allies in these efforts, but in reality they were not very interested in these matters of great concern to some of us white leaders and the outside progressive community. The black leadership had only recently gained a place at the table of power; and they questioned whether such reform efforts were white attempts to undo their hard-fought political gains. Quite often, for example, they viewed ideas about increasing school standards as excuses for penalizing black teachers and students; and they saw proposals about cleaning up voter lists as legal disenfranchisement of the growing minority electorate. So I usually had to work hard to sell them on my reform initiatives—and not always successfully.

Inevitable Problems of Biracial Cooperation

Furthermore, I encountered problems in my stealthy approach because of disagreements, and even friction, between myself and some of my African American colleagues, likely due, I reasoned, to personal ways and differing political ideas on both sides. I acknowledge that I brought my own white manner and biases to the table, so I understood why some of them seemed un-amenable to my stealthy entreaties. I guess they had reason to question such discreet maneuvering as insulting to them and their race. Also, my biracialism—at least its more obvious aspects—could have been seen as a seasonal interest; I naturally tended to concentrate my attendance at black events and my financial contributions during election campaigns.

I also found that my version of stealth partnership just didn't work with some African American leaders. It was hard to work quietly and biracially with a guy who screamed 'racism' twenty-four hours a day. More disappointing was the fact that certain black leaders and activists, even though enshrined in heroic history, turned out to be less than heroic in the post-civil rights era. Some succumbed to the same tactics and temptations as run-of-the-mill white Southern political hacks. I dealt with them in particular situations and on isolated issues, but they seemed more interested in their own personal and political gain than racial reconciliation. I had to accept the fact that some people—both blacks and whites—were not interested in stealth reconstruction.

Politics and Race in the National Capital

My academic and political background in Alabama prepared me well for service in the U.S. Congress. Of course, there were major differences between Alabama and Washington, and I had to deal with some tricky angles immediately upon moving from Goat Hill to Capitol Hill.

Obviously, the issues in Washington were more comprehensive and consequential—the American economy, national security, and international relations. The personalities and egos were bigger—President Bush, President Clinton, Speaker Wright, Speaker Foley, Speaker Gingrich, Majority Leader Gephardt, Majority Leader Armey, and various icons who went simply by the title of "Mr. Chairman." And the constituent pressures were greater—fighting the federal government for people back home, telling the local community that their military installation might close, and raising large sums of campaign money.

Most importantly, I found that civic and racial challenges in Washington were formidable.

Moderation, Centrism, and Reformist Struggle

I settled into the congressional system as a moderate, centrist politician with good government and reform inclinations, and I worked bipartisanly during my tenure in Washington. I usually sided with the Democrats; however, I discovered that, just as in Alabama, the Democratic establishment was not very enthusiastic about my good government or reform agenda. Throughout my DC service, therefore, I struggled to organize and promote civic issues unpopular with my party.

In Alabama, I had been a key player on the relatively progressive team that ran the show. Even then, as a member of the majority faction which included both whites and blacks, it had been difficult to push and implement good government initiatives. In Washington, I took my seat as an "outlier" in the neverland of Southern white Democrats who often found ourselves in the crossfire between our own party and the opposition Republicans. The GOP takeover in 1995 pushed the Blue Dog Democrats further to the sidelines. Throughout, I constantly jockeyed among various organizations and issues of black-white consequence at home.

Under those circumstances, prospects for meaningful reform were virtually nonexistent.

A More Subtle and Sophisticated Race Game

It was also clear that race and racism were alive and well—although more subtle and sophisticated—in the national capital. Earlier, while discussing Alabama politics, I acknowledged the constant, dominant, routine role of racial considerations in the Heart of Dixie. However, white leaders in Alabama often pursued progressive government in private concert with black leaders, a candid, cooperative, personalized relationship that was facilitated by our shared legacy. But race relations were distant and strained in Washington.

I found the course of biracial politics in the United States Congress to be more public and showy but also more impersonal and cynical. Both Democrats and Republicans, white and black alike, professed color-blind and civil rights principles; but pertinent transactions often resembled the same insider game of crass, race-based wheeling-and-dealing for public acclaim and special interest power. Maybe I looked at all of this through the eyes of a white Southern sentimentalist, but sometimes racial politics in our national capital seemed just a refined rendition of what happened back in Alabama.

Continuing Dilemma in Congressional Politics

Interestingly, I found it more difficult to pursue my kind of leadership in Washington than back in Montgomery. As a Southern white politician in DC, I carried history and stigma amid alien pressures that made my job much more burdensome.

Most white Southern politicians—particularly Democrats—who seriously wanted to provide positive biracial leadership and enjoy career political success knew that an essential part of successful politics was an objective, instrumental, coldly calculating regard for race, racism, and constant scrutiny. All the while, as we vigilantly avoided and opposed racist politics, we knew it was there in the heart of a significant portion of our people, both white and black.

I sometimes looked at my colleagues from other sections of the country, from areas without the black-white factor and thought to myself—they've got an easy job. I even said to them occasionally that, "You don't know what politics is unless you represent and have to secure mixed, majoritarian support from a constituency made up of a former slave-owner society and a former slave-society—that is still fighting that fight."

It bothered me that I had to deal with the old race dilemma so stealthily and clinically in a congressional body that had racial problems of its own; it bothered me even more that I was unable to accomplish more of my mission as "A New Kind of Leader" in American democracy.

The Partisan Alternative

Eventually, along with most white Southern Democrats serving in Washington, I had to consider the options as Republicans grew stronger in the region; the problem was a fairly common topic of discussion among the Southerners.

Why didn't I just switch to the Republican Party? I concluded I would be more comfortable continuing my mission of pursuing civic reform and biracial progress within the Democratic Party. Part of that was philosophical. My background and ideas inclined me toward the Democratic Party (although I admit I sometimes got fed up with the left's issues and attitudes and treatment). But at least half of my sticking was "stubbornness"—I considered myself more than an opportunist and I just did not want it on my political tombstone that I switched parties to hold on to some stupid office and power and perks.

Besides, I knew that, with the moderate, reform course I had chosen, I would have the same trouble with the Republicans that I had with Democrats. The core right didn't like me any more than the core left. And the moneyed special interests in both parties had no strong feeling for my kind of politics.

Changing Times and Politics

Toward the end of my career, as Alabama and the country proceeded toward a new century, I realized that the times and politics had changed considerably since I had crafted my game plan for leadership in the 1970s.

Consequently, just as in Montgomery, traditional politics and racial contentions in Washington complicated the national aspect of my civic mission. By the mid-1990s, it was much more difficult for me to pursue civic reform, and I knew that my adventure in stealth politics was about to come to an end.

When I left the U.S. Congress in January of 1997, I was not sure whether I had contributed anything significant or constructive to American democracy. I and my good government allies had tweaked congressional ways a little here and a little there; and I had tried, at least in my individual style, to provide positive biracial leadership as a national politician. But I had been unable to achieve the civic centerpiece—campaign finance reform—of my congressional agenda; and the impact of our budget work would not become apparent until I left office. My stealth leadership ended in the 1996 Senate primary, and it took years before I would feel comfortable about my efforts in Washington.

Memorable Personalities in Stealthy Racial Politicking

I rubbed shoulders with genuine civil rights heroes and some villainous holdovers during the 1970s, 1980s, and 1990s. I profiled some of my role models and campaign counselors in previous chapters, so I will now talk about a few memorable personalities in my stealthy experiences as a public servant in Montgomery and Washington. This list (arranged in rough chronological order) includes both black and white individuals; some were big-name officials, others were low-key operatives, and a few are still active in politics. Of course, these leaders were not all quiet, practical, biracial politicians; the value of this listing is that it reveals the varied nature of relationships and the flavor of the environment within which I attempted my stealthy public service.

RAY MINTER. There's no way to present my stealth politicking without mentioning Ray Minter, my former student, campaign aide, and chief assistant in Montgomery and Washington. With an impoverished background and with professional experience as a high school government teacher, Minter was my close friend and philosophical partner.

Most importantly, Minter shared my positive sentiments about democracy. But the Piedmont native also functioned as my administrative right-hand and political bulldog. He had an easy-going personality and he got along with the good old boys; he was a natural for street politics and sophisticated negotiations, thus he worked well on the campaign trail and in the corridors of power.

Minter, who also had grown up among poor whites and blacks, understood and practiced stealth politics for his new-kind-of-leader boss. I trusted all my employees to be fair and impartial, but I tried to keep them out of "politics" as much as possible. Whenever I had to have an important political problem fixed pronto, I usually turned to Minter to get it done; this was especially true in sensitive racial transactions. For example, when the Browder operation had to do something quick, tough, and/or sketchy in race-related political matters, "That was a job for Ray Minter." When it was time to explain some unpleasant racial reality to a disgruntled supporter, "That was Ray's job." When personnel matters took an untoward racial bent, "That was Ray's job." And when reapportioning for our district ran awry in the race-racked Alabama legislature, "That was Ray's job."

Explaining things, arranging deals, distributing money, cussing out people who needed cussing out—all discreetly—Minter did everything required to make my special version of politics work for me, racial progress, and American democracy.

I've jokingly said that Ray could go to jail for some of his activities on behalf of our mission. But the truth is, he deserves much of the credit for whatever we accomplished.

Minter retired as deputy commander at the Anniston Army Depot in 2008. He now lives in the rural Rabbittown community.

JOHN TEAGUE. One of the most useful models for my career and my work as a stealth leader was state legislator John Teague.

I had worked as an early campaign consultant for Teague (a Democrat from nearby Talladega County), and we formed a close personal relationship when I entered the Alabama House and John climbed into the president pro tem's position in the Alabama Senate. Teague served in the Alabama House and Senate during the 1970s and 1980s; he eventually lost the 1986 Democratic primary race for the nomination for lieutenant governor. Today, Teague is a contract lobbyist in Montgomery.

Teague was a consummate Alabama insider who knew how to deal discreetly, amiably, and effectively with virtually everybody—Democrats, Republicans, liberals, conservatives, educators, business leaders, labor representatives, men, women, blacks, and whites. Bill Clinton was the best politician I ever dealt with in Washington, and John Teague was the best in Montgomery. Everybody came to Senate President Teague for help sooner or later; he had the knack of helping you even when he had to turn you down. For example, he'd say, "Well, Glen, your House bill is not going to pass over here because Senator So-and-So has a problem with part of it, but after this session ends you and I will go by his office and work something out so that it can pass in the upcoming special session." You usually walked away realizing that he just told you "No" in a way that made you grateful to him.

John Teague also had great relations with his fellow legislators and knew how to work things out—especially between blacks and whites—by negotiating compromises along the way. For example, he and black Rep. Fred Horn passed controversial, landmark legislation in 1983 allowing black deputy registrars to expand minority voter rolls. For their efforts, the two shared the Lyndon Baines Johnson Political Freedom Award presented by the Alabama Democratic Conference.

Teague thus was able to help me push my bills through the legislative process, including some reforms that were not really popular among black politicians. In those dealings, I learned that quiet diplomacy, good personal relations, and practical politics inside the system can be just as effective as substantive merit, dramatic speeches, and external political pressure.

My relationship with John Teague and the lessons I learned from him were critical to just about every aspect of my agenda as a new-kind-of-leader and successful biracial politician.

GEORGE C. WALLACE. I learned, in time and through personal dealings, that George Wallace would be a valuable partner in my "new politics" of civic reform and biracial progress. During that last term (1983–86), Governor Wallace lived through his own mortal hell of self-realization about his role in state, national, and world history. Therefore, he wanted to help poor people, he wanted to help black people, he wanted to improve the education system, and, irony of ironies, he was prepared to raise taxes as necessary to provide needed social and governmental services.

I would visit him in the Governor's Office, at his private quarters in the Governor's Mansion, or by telephone, to talk about this or that issue. He rambled a lot, especially about how we needed to help poor people and black Alabamians. And he would say to me, "Glen, I want you to do what you think is the right thing to do!" Then, he'd turn to one or more of his aides and say, "Do what we need to do to get this taken care of!"

George Wallace Jr. recently reflected on his father's relationship with me:

> Glen Browder was one of my father's favorite people. He admired the intellectual and philosophical approach Glen brought to public service. I have often thought that had they been peers in the sense of being from the same generation that my father would have sought him out to be one of his confidants. As is so often the case, political figures have those around them who are very helpful in a number of ways, but tend to lack a clear vision of the bigger picture, and how that affects our posterity. Glen Browder had that capacity; my father recognized it early on in his relationship with Glen, and thus began a friendship my father always cherished.[17]

I refuse to comment any further on George Wallace's racial past—partly because the governor truly agonized over his role in black and white pages of history. Governor Wallace suffered inner pain that dwarfed the crippling injuries from his would-be assassin. He no longer demonized his enemies—he had his own demons and they tormented his very soul those last few years. He pushed progressive legislation and he sought forgiveness from black Alabamians for his segregationist past. After extreme physical and emotional suffering, he realized at least partially the grace of redemption before his death.

I also realize that, ironically, the reformed demagogue had personally fostered my fledgling career as a biracial leader.

PAUL HUBBERT. Dr. Paul Hubbert has been the most powerful unelected leader in Alabama for the past several decades. As executive director of the , his influence extends comprehensively across the spectrum of politics and policy. Since overseeing the merger of the white and black teacher unions in the 1970s, he has been the central figure in Democratic Party activities and state government. Despite losing the gubernatorial general election in 1990, Hubbert is often called "the real governor" in Montgomery.

Hubbert was a close political friend and advisor from the time I set foot in Montgomery. As an ambitious young political scientist, politician, and reformer, I was a natural player in Goat Hill politics, and I hooked up with Hubbert on numerous progressive issues. At the same time, the AEA chief executive nodded positively and patiently as I pursued my own nimble course of stealth politics.

I think Paul Hubbert and I hit it off so well because we were somewhat alike personally. We both grew up poor and benefited from education; and, while both of us enjoyed the game of politics, we basically were more interested in practical progress rather than personal or high-profile political gain. We could plot and argue, privately and publicly, in a positive manner—then come together on what was good for Alabama. Or at least that's the way I saw it.

The AEA boss, like Governor Wallace, was therefore a very productive ally for my twin agendas of political reform and racial progress. Hubbert enlisted in the governor's education reform movement, giving me a solid connection with Joe Reed, other black politicians, black activists, and black educators throughout the state. Later on, these alliances proved vital to me in convincing reluctant politicians to go along with election reform; later still, these ties helped send me to Congress.

Throughout it all, I was able to pursue my reform and racial agendas without a lot of brutal conflict; much of the credit goes to Paul Hubbert's buy-in to my stealthy style and mission.

DR. JOE L. REED. Joe Reed is a remarkable entry in our reconstruction story. He was a critical figure in both the heroic drama and subsequent stealth transactions, and he continues today as one of Alabama's foremost politicians.

Reed is head of the Alabama Democratic Conference, associate executive secretary of the equally powerful Alabama Education Association, vice chairman of the Alabama State Democratic Executive Committee, and a former Montgomery city council member. He has been the predominant black political leader in Alabama for decades.

Irascibly righteous, powerful, and with a demanding personality is how I describe Reed. In both formal communications and face-to-face exchanges, Reed alternatively helped my career and pressured me to further black objectives in Alabama. He was quick with political advice, and it was usually on-target and compelling. Most of it understandably inclined toward his advantage.

Reed constantly invited me to attend black meetings, dinners, and celebrations, suggesting often that "you ought to buy a table for this event, and we'll get some of our people to sit with you." He also could be pointedly direct about such invitations, as when warning me that "If you can't come to our endorsement meeting, we cannot endorse you." Additionally, he regularly urged me and other white politicians to make use of black media in campaigns: "We believe that such advertisements and use of black-owned and -operated media will not only further your campaign in the black community, but will also further economic justice and parity and will go a long way in assisting us in assessing the candidate's commitment to equal opportunity for all people."

Reed was persistent and insistent on black-related matters and issues. On one occasion, he chastised me regarding a recommended appointment for which I, as secretary of state, was considering another applicant: "When you take somebody to the dance, you expect them to dance with you!" But he also was supportive; once, during a critical, closed-door redistricting fight, he spoke up and said, "Browder's been good to us, and we ain't gonna hurt him."

Dr. Reed today continues his work in Alabama politics—still pushing hard in the Alabama Democratic Conference, the Alabama Education Association, and the State Democratic Party Executive Committee. Of course, he now has to share the stage with younger, more diverse, and independent black and liberal leaders. There's a lot of open speculation—among both his friends and enemies—about whether his time has come and gone. In typical fashion, Reed is defiant: "What you have to ask yourself is, can you still dance? I think I'm still a pretty good dancer."[18]

Joe Reed could be pushy and brusque. But he always treated me right, he never lied to me, and he has paid his dues to Alabama.

DR. RICHARD ARRINGTON JR. I did not have close ties with Birmingham Mayor Richard Arrington, who had been a fixture in Alabama politics during the 1970s, but we developed a positive working relationship during the 1980s and 1990s.

Reed and Arrington were markedly opposite. The former was a feisty personality, a teacher unionist, and civil rights activist; the latter, a college dean and biologist, was more subdued and even academic.

I normally saw little of Mayor Arrington in my Montgomery and Washington politicking. Our exchanges mainly consisted of routine political discussions and pleasant conversations at meetings of the Alabama New South Coalition (which Arrington helped found) and the Jefferson County Citizens Coalition (which he personally created and ran in Birmingham). Arrington apparently acquiesced in my "quiet, practical, biracial politics" early on; he also played an interesting role in my eventual exit from public service.

In 1996, as the Democratic primary neared, I figured that I had to split the black vote because there was strong competition from Roger Bedford, a powerful white state senator, and Natalie Davis, a white female political scientist/party activist in Birmingham.

Early in the year, I visited Dr. Arrington. We covered a few issues, then we talked about campaign plans. I think he understood my situation and he was responsive and helpful. Thereafter we conducted our affairs via mutual associates. I lost the ADC and ANSC endorsements to Bedford. But with Arrington's tacit approval, I gained a split endorsement from the JCCC.

Throughout the primary and runoff, Browder operatives worked the mayoral connection as best they could. Arrington counseled the campaign; he supplied key names; he hosted a community leaders reception; he authorized a written endorsement; he prepared an endorsed mailout; he cut a radio spot. Most importantly, he personally prepared a lengthy, handwritten memo outlining a complete campaign plan of events, sample ballots, radio advertising, and targeted box-by-box statistics for black voters in the Birmingham area. Interspersed throughout these directives were several interesting remarks: "Tell them to call me if they have questions . . . I suggest an ad with your candidate's voice and my voice as testimonial . . . In addition to Coalition sample ballot distribution in Jefferson County, I urge your candidate to distribute our ballots under the name of the Alabama Citizens Coalition in Tuscaloosa, Montgomery, and Huntsville."

Arrington is now a Birmingham businessman and part-time educator. Looking back, I realized that the former mayor was in a tough situation in which he, like myself, was striving for practical progress within an environment of biracial volatility; I appreciated the help of the former fellow college professor.

JOHNNY FORD. Johnny Ford, then mayor of Tuskegee, has been one of the most recognized, charismatic, adaptable African American leaders in Alabama history. He worked for Robert Kennedy, supported George Wallace, served for years as a Democratic public official, switched to the Republicans, and most recently declared himself an independent.

Johnny Ford and I, along with a slew of other candidates, ran for the

Democratic Party nomination for the open seat for the Third Congressional District in 1989; I beat him in a runoff. That election captured a lot of attention, not only because of the possibility for a black congressman but because of the amicable relationship between the two of us. I knew—and it was a practical part of the campaign game plan—that there was never a serious Browder-Ford race since African Americans comprised only a fourth of the district.

We played our pre-ordained roles in very effective concert. The media called the runoff a love-fest; and after my victory, we set about defeating Republican nominee John Rice. Ford warmly hosted me in Tuskegee, escorted me around the black church circuit in a long white limousine, and generally blessed me as the right choice for U.S. Congress.

> Glen Browder is a friend, a good and fair man . . . We need leadership that listens, that is responsive to our needs, that cares about all of the people . . . leadership we can trust! Glen Browder will give us this kind of leadership, and I intend to work as hard as I can to see that he is elected as our next congressman.[19]

The Browder-Ford association greatly expanded my circle of black friends and my grasp of diverse concerns in the lower end of the Third Congressional District. Our paths never crossed competitively again, and we are still on good terms.

HANK SANDERS. Henry "Hank" Sanders was and still is a powerful African American politician in Alabama. He's most noted as a prominent member of the Alabama Senate from Selma and as one of the primary founders of the Alabama New South Coalition, which now competes with the Alabama Democratic Conference in state politics. (Additionally, Sanders is known as the husband of Faya Ora Rose Toure, perhaps the most fiery black activist in the state.)

I did not work very much or closely with Sanders while we both served in the legislature. But I knew that he was there when I needed some advice or help from an African American partner in any effort that was beneficial for blacks and whites in Alabama. Hank was friendly and straightforward, and his word was good. He also knew that we sometimes had to play a stealthy game because there were still too many people wanting to be "heroes" and too many others willing to be "villains." Most white members of the legislature back then knew that you could work in good faith and constructively with the soft-spoken and savvy Selmian.

Sanders had won his seat during the 1983 Democratic Party hand-picking which was such a painful experience for me; he returned the favor in 1986, as his ANSC endorsed me for secretary of state (as did the rival ADC). He also was helpful on several of my reform initiatives of the mid-1980s, such as education reform and election reform. Even today, I feel like if I needed support for a good cause, I could call on Hank Sanders.

Over the years since then, Sanders has traveled the tough road of Alabama politics, earning both praise and scorn. From my perspective, he ranks among the positive architects of stealth reconstruction.

ALVIN HOLMES. Democrat Alvin Holmes undoubtedly is one of the most unforgettable, vilified, and valuable personalities in Alabama state legislative history. Every legislative body needs some version of this volatile black politician to entertain, annoy, challenge, and expose elite shenanigans in the state capitol.

Of course, whether you viewed Holmes positively or negatively depended on whether he was on your case or jumping on somebody else's back. Holmes generally was a pain in the rear for everybody during my service, but he proved to be politically astute and successful for his constituency and he served a useful societal purpose. A part-time history professor at Alabama State University in Montgomery, he quite often asked questions that needed to be asked and he launched attacks that needed to be directed at powerful leaders and governmental institutions.

Occasionally Holmes and I ended up on the same side of issues, and we associated peaceably at black meetings and other events. But it was difficult dealing stealthily and productively with Holmes because he constantly played the race card—sometimes for ridiculous reasons. Many white legislators, particularly Republicans, hated him; whites of the Democratic

Coalition tolerated him; and even black legislators sometimes simply shook their heads and laughed or frowned. A common comment was, "That's just Alvin being Alvin!"

I remember a few good exchanges with Holmes. Once, while the House was considering my Crime Victims Compensation Bill (which fined law-breakers to provide financial help to innocent victims of violent crime), he jumped up to the debate microphone and started railing against the legislation as just another way "to stick it to black folks." I quickly corralled him and explained that most violent crime victims in Alabama were black, and they needed financial help for medical bills and missed work; he said nothing to me in direct response, but he did not proceed with his rant at the microphone.

Most of the time, however, I knew to avoid Holmes. He had no appreciation of my assignment as a stealth leader, and he was not the kind of practical politician that I could work with except when necessary. A couple times, he threatened to do everything he could to defeat me; I guess eventually he did so.

An interesting update: the Alabama legislature, during its 2007 organizational session, bestowed upon Alvin Holmes the honorary title of "Dean of the House" for his thirty-two years service in that body. The bipartisan resolution noted that Holmes "has gained national and international respect as a tireless champion of the causes of the poor and disadvantaged."[20]

EMORY FOLMAR. As the reader has probably noticed, most of the political leaders and activists in this account of Alabama and Southern politics were Democrats. My Democratic affiliation and chosen mission of civic and racial progress naturally inclined me to work mainly within my own party. However, I never was a highly partisan politician, and I often partnered with Republicans on specific initiatives, particularly on civic matters. One of these GOP leaders was, somewhat surprisingly, Emory Folmar, now retired, but back then chairman of the Alabama Republican Party and mayor of Montgomery.

I had consulted early in my career as a professional pollster for close associates of the mayor, and we developed a trusting relationship. But neither could fully and publicly embrace the other because our parties and politics were miles apart. While I worked well with African Americans and within the progressive Democratic coalition, Folmar fought bitterly with his black opposition in Montgomery and against Democrats statewide. Interestingly, however, we sometimes pulled in the same reformist directions. We both believed in election reform and this helped me on a couple of important occasions. I suspect that he put out the word that I was "OK" when I ran for secretary of state in 1986. He also played a critical role in getting the Republican Party to support progressive change in state campaign laws. Democratic Party Chairman John Baker got battered and bruised in dragging our party to campaign reform, but without Emory Folmar, we probably would never have passed the Alabama Fair Campaign Practices Act in 1988.

Thus the Browder-Folmar connection fell clearly but awkwardly into the stealth category on election reform. We formed an odd couple of politicos, and we went through our entire careers without any official, public association; but our stealthy personal relationship left a lasting, positive imprint on Alabama political history.

JOHN LEWIS. John Lewis is an American icon. The Atlanta congressman's career spans many of the confrontational events and struggles of the historic, heroic drama. I remember him, however, as a man who helped people and brought them together rather than dividing the races.

The first encounter between us was an interesting personal footnote during the tense days of civil unrest and "Black Power." If memory serves me correctly, I first met John Lewis in the 1960s when he was a young leader of the Student Nonviolent Coordinating Committee (known as "the shock troops of the revolution") and I was a young investigator for the U.S. government (considered by some within SNCC as part of the civil rights problem). To be honest, I was uneasy about my assignment to probe somebody at SNCC as part of the job security clearance process. I was a coat-and-tie-wearing white guy with a Southern accent and it was quite an ordeal locating my subject in black Atlanta during the hot days of "burn baby burn." I pushed the buzzer at a locked, intimidating doorway, and a gruff, phantom, electronic voice from somewhere said, "What do you want?"

After identifying myself, the door opened, and I proceeded up some dark stairs to be encountered at the top by an Afro-haired guy who didn't look very friendly. But John Lewis was indeed very friendly and responsive; as I would learn over the years, he is an incredibly genuine person who really believes in racial reconciliation.

Lewis has been an effective player in Southern politics over many years because he is as much preacher as politician. The son of an Alabama share-cropper, he embodies spiritual reconciliation both publicly and privately. This approach has facilitated his successful dealings over the years with practical, progressive white Southern politicians.

We worked together on numerous common concerns in Washington. Additionally, we partnered on various projects and issues of special interest to Alabama—such as designation of the Selma-Montgomery National Historic Trail and the rash of church burnings in Alabama and across the South.

When I ran for an open U.S. Senate seat in 1996, Lewis wrote:

> Over the last seven years I have seen Glen Browder in action. He is an able, smart, and dedicated member of Congress. He is a man of compassion, commitment and principle. Glen is also committed to building a more tolerant and understanding nation, a truly interracial democracy.[21]

I lost that race, but I am especially proud of this commendation from an American icon and fellow Southerner who knew the value of discreet but positive biracial service.

JIM CLYBURN. Jim Clyburn is a good inclusion on this list because he very clearly demonstrated the peculiar course of black-white relations during our period of concern in Southern history. Consider the following anecdote: It seems that two boys, similar in age, grew up during the 1940s and 1950s in the same small town. They went through the public school system and graduated from high school at about the same time in that town. Interestingly, both eventually would run for statewide public office—secretary of state—in the same year; one would win narrowly while the other would lose narrowly. More interestingly, eventually both would run for, get elected to, and serve together—as members of the same party—in the United States House of Representatives. Incredibly, they met and introduced themselves to each other, for the first time in their lives, on the floor of Congress.

That is a true story. Jim Clyburn and I both grew up in Sumter, South Carolina, but we never knew each other there. Clyburn attended all-black Lincoln High School and I went to all-white Edmunds High School. Clyburn stayed in South Carolina while I moved on to Alabama (the respective states of our electoral careers), and we ended up serving together as congressmen in our nation's capitol.

Beyond this strange anecdote about common backgrounds, there were striking parallels between us. Most obviously, we both overcame the handicap of our backgrounds to launch successful political careers. We started our public lives in state government before going to Congress. Neither was extreme in philosophy or behavior. And we worked, quietly and biracially, for political reform within the system. I was a relatively conservative Democrat and Clyburn was from the relatively liberal side of the party; but we both reached across party, racial, and philosophical chasms—without a lot of fanfare but with considerable success—on important issues.

Although we never met until that day on the floor of Congress, we were able to bridge the historic racial divide rather effortlessly and we worked together on several important political problems in Washington. Our relationship was more than a political opportunity—I sensed in Clyburn a kindred spirit in practical, biracial service. Perhaps it helped that we grew up—together yet apart—back in South Carolina!

Jim Clyburn and I will never know where that special relationship might have led, since I'm no longer in Congress and our lives are separated by different careers and hundreds of miles. However, we still talk, whenever our paths cross, about Sumter, American democracy, and the American dream.

BILL CLINTON. There's not much new that can be said about Bill Clinton, but the charismatic leader must be mentioned, at least briefly, in any discussion of stealth reconstruction in the South.

Ironically, Bill Clinton was a consummate leader who performed his biracial magic out in the open—because he was so good at it. I had watched Clinton from the beginning back in Arkansas, and I consider Clinton the best politician I ever knew or observed.

We were never close personally or politically, but we came along at the same time. We both practiced biracial politics in our respective states; and we both demonstrated practical leadership styles in addressing stubborn problems of hard history. I always felt that Clinton understood the trials and tribulations of Southern politicians, and the president personally tried to help, whenever and however he could, as white and black leaders in his native region quietly struggled with racial challenges.

In fact, I was convinced at the time that the Man from Hope was America's best chance for dealing with the racial dilemma. President Clinton embodied skills and commitments that served our region well; he knew how to reach out and touch both whites and blacks and bring them together in positive manner. Had he not been distracted by personal problems, it is likely that Clinton indeed would have led America across the biracial bridge to the next century.

In some ways, on a much larger scale, Bill Clinton was like the stealth leaders covered in this manuscript. He alternately pressed progressive initiatives and accommodated traditional barriers. I would resist calling him a real stealth leader, because he was a national figure and he was certainly not quiet—but there are interesting similarities in terms of practical, biracial politics. Moreover, Clinton's performance can inspire and guide contemporary biracial leaders.

Of course, there were many, many others—white and black, including a few women—who might be cited in depicting those interesting and consequential times, but space prohibits a full inventory.

To generalize, the philosophy, record, and remembrances presented here provide useful context for what happened in the 1970s, 1980s, and 1990s. Careful readers should have seen in this chapter a multitude of complex, normative experiences as I pursued my game plan and mission of public service. In my difficult chosen course as a stealth leader, I worked positively and effectively with a wide variety of cooperative leaders and activists; but, also in that process, I sometimes struggled with whites, I sometimes struggled with blacks, and I sometimes struggled with myself.

Looking back over the past few decades, Dr. Jess Brown at Athens State University explained that his former professor's strategy worked well for an agenda of electoral reform and enhanced racial understanding in the 1980s, but it became less and less effective during the 1990s.

> Two factors essentially undermined or reduced Browder's ability to nurture quietly a limited reform agenda. At the beginning, he mastered "Southern politics" and worked well with personalities and political networks as diverse as George Wallace, Joe Reed, Paul Hubbert, and Emory Folmar. But conditions changed during his approximately fourteen years in elective office. First, state-level politics in Montgomery witnessed a much higher level of interparty competition after the 1986 governor's contest. By 1990 and thereafter, partisan divisions at the state capitol began to harden, and it became much more difficult to interact effectively with leaders in both parties. Second, Browder became an actor in the national Congress by the late 1980s and left the arena of state legislative politics. As he joined the much larger and more complex institution of Congress, his ability to make progress on his agenda was reduced. He lacked the personal ties to leaders in Washington that he had enjoyed with leaders in the much smaller arena of Montgomery.[22]

Unfortunately, Brown said, important stakeholders in Alabama needed a congressman focused on an agenda that did not include electoral reform and biracial harmony.

> In sum, as the partisan environment in state politics changed radically, and as Browder's political forum shifted from Montgomery to Washington, the capacity to build political bridges for a limited civic agenda—such as electoral reform and racial progress—diminished considerably.

Substantial Success as a Quiet, Practical, Biracial Leader

So, as I look back over my entire career, how do I wrap up this case study? I think that the material in these three chapters—accumulated through retrospection, documentary research, media reports, and personal interviews—accords with the conceptual model of stealth leadership and politics. On the whole, I think that the evidence supports the generalization of substantial success in quiet, practical, biracial service.

Civic, Racial, and Political Contributions

Now, I'll step aside and let a few associates provide their assessments of that service.

First, here's current Alabama Lieutenant Governor Jim Folsom Jr. Folsom—who previously served as governor, lieutenant governor, and member of the Public Service Commission—expounded in loose, free-ranging manner about his JSU professor, campaign consultant, and friend. His remarks have been excerpted and edited slightly for conciseness:

> Glen has contributed quite a bit in different ways.
>
> He has more awareness of ethical standards, and he's much more conscious of public perception than the average politician. He was serious about things, but not in a way of selling his soul.
>
> He also made a major contribution as a reformer who has achieved actual reform in a very pragmatic way. Nine out of ten other politicians could have proposed the things that he proposed and probably would never have gotten to first base with it. He was very diplomatic and did things in a non-obtrusive, quiet way. And he could get all the good-old-boys to go along with his program.
>
> Glen's left a great legacy and a great reputation.[23]

George Wallace Jr., who served as Alabama state treasurer in the 1980s, pointedly referenced the racial politics of that period.

> Glen Browder was one of those quiet practitioners of bringing people together and he is one who helped build trust between the races. His

interaction with blacks during this period helped black folks understand that there were whites of good will, and a dedication of purpose to help improve their lives. He became the example by his actions, of what our state and people needed to do at that time in building bridges as the transformation occurred all around us. I believe Alabama and our nation are better because of the services and sacrifices Glen Browder has made. He always envisioned something larger than himself, and his service reflected the best within us.[24]

Kelvin Cunningham, the first African American to serve as chairman of the Talladega County Commission, voiced a similar tribute to his former JSU professor.

On the state level, he was able to bring calmness to the legislature. His ability to work with people from all walks of life is extraordinary. As secretary of state, he was the most innovative one to hold that position. His mark in that position has a lasting effect on the people of this state. As a member of Congress, he was a breath of fresh air . . . Professor Browder never caused attention to himself when working to create a better Alabama. He would seek out those he thought willing to sit down and work for a common cause. He knew that certain individuals were serious about making circumstances better. He moved in a very quiet but direct manner. His ability to work with blacks, whites, Democrats and Republicans made him a very special public servant.[25]

Marti Thomas Doneghy, who got her breakthrough job in Washington as press secretary in the Browder office, said that some of my votes were a bit conservative for her personally, "but as time has moved on, I can't remember what those votes were." She talked about leadership in difficult times.

Congressman Browder's contribution to Alabama politics and American democracy is that his decency and quiet, low-key, hardworking tenure at the state and congressional level was a flash point for change in the state on many levels, particularly good governance and race.[26]

Current U.S. Rep. Artur Davis (who never studied under nor worked with nor served with me) provided a unique personal characterization.

> Browder's defeat makes him, to some observers, just another tantalizing "might have been," another candidate who tried for the brass ring either too soon or too late. I think of him more grandly, as the first politician I met who inspired me to public service. The occasion was a banquet for honor students in Montgomery County in April of 1986; Secretary of State Browder was the keynote speaker, and I remember to this day the challenge he sounded that night. He argued that those of us who lamented Alabama's stagnation had our own obligation to improve this state, by taking whatever steps were within our personal power. Glen prodded a room full of overachievers to consider politics or civic life as worthy options. I left the banquet with an award as the top male honor student in Montgomery County. I also left with a conviction that politics needed to be more than a spectator sport. For planting this seed, and making it plausible, Glen Browder has always been one of my political heroes.[27]

End of the Road

Perhaps the most interesting assessment is obtained by coupling the endorsement letter sent out a decade ago by U.S. Congressman John Lewis and recent remarks by Dr. Joe Reed, both of whom were profiled earlier. In his endorsement letter, reproduced here in its entirety, Lewis noted the commitment to building "a more tolerant and understanding nation, a truly interracial democracy."

> May 15, 1996
> Dear Dr. Reed:
>   I am writing to urge you and the Alabama Democratic Conference to endorse Glen Browder for Alabama's open U.S. Senate seat. Glen has been a valuable member of the House of Representatives during the past seven years and would be a great asset in the United States Senate. Additionally, I believe Glen has the best chance of retaining the seat of

retiring Senator Howell Heflin and helping the Democrats regain control of the U.S. Senate.

As you know, I am not a stranger to the state of Alabama. I grew up on a small farm just outside of Troy in the Southeastern part of the state. My mother still lives on that farm and I return there often. It was there in Troy that I first tasted the bitter fruits of segregation. It was there that I first heard of, met, and became involved with Dr. Martin Luther King Jr. and the struggle for civil rights. I dedicated my youth and have dedicated my life to helping build what Dr. King called "the beloved community," a community at peace with itself. As a matter of fact, just yesterday the House passed a bill, HR 1129, to designate the route taken by civil rights marchers between Selma and Montgomery a National Historic Trail. I introduced this bill and it was co-sponsored by Congressman Browder.

Over the last seven years I have seen Glen Browder in action. He is an able, smart, and dedicated member of Congress. He is a man of compassion, commitment and principle. Glen is also committed to building a more tolerant and understanding nation, a truly interracial democracy.

Glen Browder's career is filled with examples of his commitment to civil rights and equal rights for all Americans. Here in the Congress he has supported the extension of the Civil Rights Act and funding for historically Black colleges and universities, as well as an increase in the minimum wage, the student loan program, head start, the school lunch program and other programs of interest to the African American community.

Recently, Glen was instrumental in organizing a meeting between members of the Congressional Black Caucus and primarily white Southern Democrats to take a stand against the wave of recent church burnings across the South. This group met with Assistant Attorney General for Civil Rights Deval Patrick to get a report on the progress being made in the investigation and to urge that everything possible be done to solve these serious crimes.

Earlier in his career, first as a state legislator and then a secretary of state, Glen has supported programs and legislation that would increase minority participation, involvement and representation in the political process.

Glen Browder is a good man with a proven record of support. It is critical that Alabama Democrats choose the best candidate to retain control of the Senate seat currently held by Senator Heflin. I believe Glen Browder is that man.

So while I now represent the city of Atlanta in Congress, I still take pride and interest in the state of Alabama. Glen Browder would make an outstanding Senator. He is someone you can talk to and someone you can trust. I hope you and your organization will see fit to endorse him for the U.S. Senate.

Sincerely,

John Lewis

Member of Congress[28]

Of course, the Alabama Democratic Conference did not endorse me for the U.S. Senate in 1996, and my political journey terminated in the Democratic primary runoff.

Dr. Reed discussed that endorsement, and conveyed the changing environment for stealth politics in the 1990s, in a recent interview for this book.

Glen Browder was a good secretary of state and a good congressman. No question in my mind, Glen would have won that U.S. Senate seat if we had backed him in the primary. He would have been, should have been a great senator. I told some of our folks that we may have made a mistake . . . But we had a couple of important things he didn't vote for.[29]

I moved on, long ago, to a productive life after politics. I'm proud of my public service. I probably should have been more supportive of minority issues back then, and I acknowledge that my circumspect approach to racial politics helped terminate my public career. But there were other factors that figured into my service and exit from public office. One was my original civic motivation, and another was my trending political independence, both of which served me well but eventually estranged me from core party groups and financial interests. Additionally, the physical distance between

Washington and Alabama separated me from political leaders, news media, and large populations in other parts of the state, which came into play during that final statewide campaign.

But the critical factors were context and timing. I enjoyed my career in Alabama politics and American democracy and I like to think I contributed something worthwhile with my quiet, practical, biracial service. But the truth is that "stealthness" was a transitional phenomenon. Stealth leaders helped reconstruct traditional ways; but our kind was destined to fade away as a new era of racial customs and partisan politics swept through the South.

In the next chapter, we will expand our attention to other public servants who pursued somewhat similar careers and made comparable reconstructive contributions throughout the South.

7

THE BROADER SCOPE
OF STEALTH LEADERSHIP

I n our introductory chapters, we proposed a thesis of "Stealth Reconstruction" and a conceptual model of stealth leadership. Then we produced an illustrative case study of Glen Browder's stealthy career. Now we want to explore the broader scope of stealth leadership and politics.

We have already discussed general concepts of leadership and racial representation, so here we simply note that the literature on the roles, styles, behaviors, and other aspects of public service have been expanded considerably by numerous scholars over the years.[1] Of particular interest for our project is the work of Richard Fenno, who reported that representational patterns in at least one Southern congressional district changed considerably between the 1970s and 1990s to reflect important political and demographic developments.[2]

Additionally, macro-patterns of change among white Southern leaders of the era of interest have been well documented, particularly in terms of congressional politics. The standard approach has focused on the growing minority vote and its influence on public officials, as observed mainly in representation.[3]

We also reported a beginning body of research into contextual aspects of the relationship between Southern white members of Congress and their black constituencies. Several studies have presented useful statistical and narrative findings demonstrating how these Southern politicians were adjusting (or not) to the new realities of racial representation. Interestingly, some reports suggested that white officials could acceptably represent black citizens while others purported that only blacks could or should represent blacks.[4]

All of these works were valuable additions to the literature on Southern politics and history following the heroic drama. However, the statistical studies too often treated broad patterns mechanistically, as if the Voting Rights Act of 1965 easily and automatically calibrated upward white representation of black interests; most scholars did not routinely converse with real human Southerners about the difficulties and struggles of practical politics. Except in a few recent studies, seldom did anybody extensively probe the individualized, localized, and interactive relationships between white Southern politicians and their black constituencies.[5] Consequently, the available research insufficiently depicts the intricate dynamics of an evolving South.

Now we will begin a more systematic examination of the stealthy dynamics that so changed the traditional South described by Cash and Key. We will look at prospective stealth leaders throughout the region, and, as with the Browder case study, we will focus on their setting, orientations, campaigns, service, and impact as the critical elements of our conceptual model.

The Survey and Its Focus

We envisioned a simple, unscientific, exploratory survey of a select handful of Southern ex-officials, not for precise statistical analysis but to help flesh out our image of stealth leadership (at least from the perspective of those white leaders) and our ideas about stealth politics (again, the white version of stealth politics) throughout the region during that period.

The survey focused on the concept of "stealthness," which we earlier defined as "quiet, practical, biracial politics" that challenged and helped change the traditional course of Southern history. We viewed stealthness as a representational style in which the public official pursued broadly conventional objectives and projected a popular and effective public image on most issues, thus allowing flexibility in dealing constructively with contentious racial issues. We wanted to determine just how these leaders incorporated their own substantive inclinations with discretion as they broke with the central racial tradition of Southern history. We realized that we would have to cast our research net creatively and carefully, since every stealth politician was an individualized combination of purposefulness and inadvertence; each practiced varying manner and degree of quietness and practicality, perhaps even without considering such matters.

Survey Respondents

We decided on former members of Congress as our subjects, because (a) we had extensive experience and expertise in the congressional arena; (b) there already existed a body of literature upon which we could base our project; (c) there was a ready list of regional individuals from which we could select apt nominees; and (d) we thought that we could convince some of our former colleagues to participate in a controversial academic project.

The particular individuals were selected because they had been successful Southern white politicians in majority white areas (at least 51 percent white) with significant African American populations (at least 20 percent black). And they had demonstrated substantial support for minority issues (compiling 50-plus percent career voting records on a civil rights scorecard).

It turned out, due primarily to our definitional factors, that all of our respondents were white male Democrats. They came from Arkansas, Florida, Georgia, Mississippi, North Carolina, South Carolina, Texas, and Virginia; their combined congressional service covered the period 1964–2005.

We contacted twenty potential participants during the spring of 2007, and thirteen respondents bravely and graciously provided written answers to numerous items regarding their biracial campaign practices and service efforts. They are listed alphabetically below, along with their respective district black percentages (according to the U.S. Census) and civil rights voting scores (compiled from the website of the Leadership Conference on Civil Rights). These numbers vary from year to year, so the displayed percentages should be viewed as approximated ranges and averages.

NAME, STATE, AND TENURE	% BLACK	%LCCR
Bill Alexander, AR (1964–1993)	20–30%	64%
Michael Andrews, TX (1983–1995)	20–30%	77%
Butler Derrick, SC (1975–1995)	20–30%	74%

Martin Frost, TX (1979–2005)	20–40%	84%
Martin Lancaster, NC (1987–1995)	20–30%	55%
L. F. Payne, VA (1988–1997)	20–30%	53%
Pete Peterson, FL (1991–1997)	20–30%	59%
Owen Pickett, VA (1987–2001)	20–30%	57%
Roy Rowland, GA (1983–1995)	30–40%	55%
Ronnie Shows, MS (1999–2003)	40–50%	56%
Robin Tallon, SC (1983–1993)	40–50%	71%
Lindsay Thomas, GA (1983–1993)	30–40%	59%
Tim Valentine, NC (1983–1995)	40–50%	62%

Survey Methods

This survey presented several methodological issues related to written, self-administered, retrospective assessments.

First, since the stealth project is a new and controversial endeavor, we anticipated that our former colleagues would be somewhat reticent. Most of these ex-politicians continue to be active in some civic calling or manner; we figured they might be reluctant to repeat unpleasant experiences with academic and media types. Our project posed a particularly daunting challenge for Southern ex-politicians, who tend to shy away from nosy journalists and pointy-headed professors dredging up the "sins" of an earlier South.

Second, there are always serious problems in getting politicians to provide candid responses to complex, sensitive questions; we recognized, as ex-politicians ourselves, the natural tendency to put a generalized, positive spin on personal political history.

In short, we accepted that no simple survey can begin to capture or communicate the full nature, problems, and pitfalls of biracial politics during that era. We knew that we would have to read between the lines, behind the lines, and, in some cases, off the record in determining the biracial realities of Southern history.

Most importantly, we would have to probe and assess intricate variations of stealthness—"stealth by design" and "stealth by coincidence," "admitted stealth" and "silent stealth," "full stealth" and "partial stealth," "continuous stealth" and "intermittent stealth"—because all of these endeavors figured into the "de facto stealth leadership" that helped explain Southern reconstruction during that period.

Accordingly, co-author Browder personally called all prospective participants by telephone, introduced the research, solicited their participation, and sent cooperative participants the theoretical introduction to our study and a questionnaire. They were asked to fill out the questionnaires either electronically or in hard copy and return them to us. The respondents were told in writing about the groundbreaking nature of this research, the importance of candor, and that they could designate any portion of their commentary as "not-for-attribution"; otherwise everything was quotable.

The questionnaire was structured in two sections designed to explore, directly, the concept of "stealth politics" and, indirectly, the practice of "quiet, practical, biracial politics." We asked first about the nature and activities of their "biracial relationships" and then we probed the more sensitive issue of "stealth politics." There were twenty-three mainly open-ended items, and respondents were encouraged to elaborate. For the most part, the respondents wrote frankly and richly about their biracial experiences and perspectives. (As is common in reporting such studies, we slightly edited some responses, without altering their substance.)

Mixed Affirmation and Uncertainty (with Some Denial)

The collective data and commentary of this survey, considered along with the Browder case study material, provide valuable information for our theoretical inquiry. The general findings support the actuality of stealth leadership and political/systemic change during that period; furthermore, we conclude that these findings are worth pursuing in other forums of Southern politics.

In the following pages, we will present the survey results and discuss how specific findings comport with our thesis of stealth reconstruction. We begin with our respondents' mixed reaction to stealthness as a concept.

Acknowledging the Stealthy Past

We had anticipated that some of the respondents might respond cautiously to interrogation on such sensitive personal orientations, so we structured the questionnaire to elicit useful information through both direct questioning and other, indirect, less loaded items. Fortunately, we found that while some struggled with the concept of "stealthness," they all were forthcoming in elaborating their special biracial leadership through the alternative inquiries.

As the completed questionnaires floated electronically back to our offices, we detected various strains of excitement, curiosity, and intro-spection about our project. Some welcomed the opportunity to discuss seriously and openly things that had intrigued or bothered them over the years; several actually wrote notes or verbally expressed thanks to us for beginning this research. Others questioned the proposition and terminology in describing their individual experiences. A few offered helpful suggestions about the overall thesis of stealth leadership, politics and reconstruction.

Unsurprisingly, it was difficult for the former members of Congress to provide a distinct "yes" or "no" response to our blunt, open-ended research inquiry about stealthy orientations. For the record, we determined that almost half directly acknowledged stealthy leadership; almost half expressed uncertainty about their stealthness; and a couple denied that they had been stealthy politicians.

Subjective Self-Assessments

The major purpose of the survey was to explore the validity of our stealth proposition, so we designed our questionnaire to probe the mindset that they brought to Southern politics. We provided our former colleagues with an introductory discussion of the thesis, and, in the second half of the questionnaire, we directly asked them several questions about stealth aspects of their politics.

While we had given the respondents an option of selective anonymity, all submitted their completed questionnaires for full attribution. However, it was obvious from their written comments that our old friends had chewed hard on the stealth idea.

The exact wording of our most direct question was: "Would you agree that you practiced some manner or some degree of 'stealth politics' as we described it in our thesis of Stealth Reconstruction?" About half of the group affirmed their stealthness and clearly explained their stealthy ways. The second half never specified a direct yes or no, but they indirectly implied various stealth practices in talking about their biracial politicking. For example, several respondents quibbled with the stealth terminology, but they then elaborated stealth-like activities in dealing with blacks in their campaigns and public service; and they exhibited stealth-like attitudes in challenging traditional Southern politics. We concluded that some of these reported activities and attitudes—while not "secreted" from public view—were silently, partially, intermittently, or coincidentally stealthy within the framework of our analysis.

We present here, in rough alphabetical order, pertinent remarks of all our congressional respondents to demonstrate their varying, substantive, and cautious ways of dealing with our direct stealth question.

BILL ALEXANDER (ARKANSAS): "I was always open in my efforts to be fair with all my constituents, and Arkansans were ready to be supportive when I entered politics."

BUTLER DERRICK (SOUTH CAROLINA): "Yes, I practiced stealth leadership to accomplish some civil rights objectives . . . and I never 'flaunted' this stuff in the face of the white community."

L. F. PAYNE (VIRGINIA): "I worked very hard to reach out to the black community in an increasingly open manner throughout my ten years of service . . . and I never said anything in any group that was contradictory to statements or actions elsewhere."

PETE PETERSON (FLORIDA): "Yes, I think 'stealth politics' is an appropriate description of the process albeit at the time I did not think of it in those terms. Clearly, my objective was to act as a credible leader, catalyst, and mentor rather than a political mouthpiece for the community. Indirect, quiet community involvement in seeking solutions to problems was for me a more effective approach."

OWEN PICKETT (VIRGINIA): "I did not know at the time that I was engaged in 'stealth politics' but I tried very hard to respond to the needs of citizens across the board in my district."

ROY ROWLAND (GEORGIA): "Was what I was doing stealth politics?

... There was not very much that I did in the black community that was different from the white community. I went to black churches and white churches, I went to black reunions and white reunions, and I met with black and white officials."

RONNIE SHOWS (MISSISSIPPI): "Sure I did it. It got me elected. Every elected job I ever had was for a majority-white constituency, and if I hadn't played stealth politics I would not have gotten elected to anything."

ROBIN TALLON (SOUTH CAROLINA): "Yes, I practiced stealth politics. I recognized that it was the reality of representing my district, and I did so to get elected and stay in office."

LINDSAY THOMAS (GEORGIA): "I am not really sure that I feel comfortable in calling my approach 'stealth politics'. . . . I felt simply that the problem of race was more couched in the minds of individuals than in the laws of the land, that it would take time for these prejudices and relations to change and that the best approach was one of steady progress over time to which I was fully committed. In the ten years that I served, I found that my approach was recognized and accepted by the citizens of my district . . . So I just don't know if this was called a 'stealth approach' or not."

TIM VALENTINE (NORTH CAROLINA): "I do not think that we practiced stealth politics as such. That is to say we did not have a plan or policy to try to hush-up or deny our appeal to black voters. It's also true that I wouldn't normally, if ever, sprinkle a speech to a white Kiwanis Club with references to the last NAACP meeting I had attended."

Perhaps MARTIN LANCASTER (NORTH CAROLINA) provided the most interesting response to this question. Lancaster, a redistricting victim after eight years in office, submitted a comment that acknowledged limited stealthness and ironically underscored the logic of stealth politics in certain settings: "Yes, but not much. I was pretty transparent in my relationships with the African American community and felt comfortable with that approach since I had a Democratic district with 26 percent black vote. However, when my district was changed to lean 55 percent Republican, my transparency came back to bite me!"

The clear "nay-sayers"—Texans MARTIN FROST and MICHAEL ANDREWS—are particularly noteworthy at this point because they caused us to slightly refine our conception of stealth politics and our analysis of the data obtained in this survey.

Frost, proclaiming that "Texas is different in some respects from the rest of the South," was adamant about his unstealthy approach to politics: "I publicly identified with the black community from the very beginning and never tried to operate in a stealth manner . . . I never hid my interest in black voters from the white community . . . Over a period of years, my white constituents just accepted the fact that I was pro-civil rights and found other reasons to be for me."

In Andrews's Houston district, there was an apparent downplaying of race, and he likewise questioned the relevance of the stealth premise. "I am not sure I agree. Houston is a big racially diverse urban area. There is diversity in every leadership area—professional and political. Because of that, large cities may have, by their demographics and economies, moved faster toward a larger recognition that political leaders had to respect the influence of the black community . . . There is always a balancing act between diverse groups—in blue-collar areas with labor organizations versus the business community, causing friction and creating political conflicts. In fact, I spent more time balancing these interests than I ever did along racial lines."

The Frost and Andrews submissions confirmed that the ranks of Southern reconstruction included non-stealth-oriented players. However, it should be noted that both Frost and Andrews served atypical, multiracial constituencies; their Texas districts included large, growing numbers of both black and Hispanic voters in addition to white voters. Obviously, stealth politics was a less meaningful and useful model for certain Southern progressives in more diverse areas where multicultural demographics and extra-racial issues outpaced the traditional race game of Southern politics. Accordingly, while we used some of their information that appropriately referenced biracial politics, we excluded Frost and Andrews from the ranks and analysis of stealth politicians.

Combining our best judgment from academic research and political experience, we designated most of our cooperative former colleagues (eleven of the thirteen respondents) as de facto "stealth leaders" and certain aspects of their work as "stealth politics" within the framework of our reconstruction thesis. These designated stealth politicians had been originally selected for this survey because they met the objective criteria of our theoretical model (i.e., electoral success in majority-white districts with significant black minorities and relative responsiveness to minority issues); and, whether by direct self-definition or indirect self-elaboration, their subjective responses essentially confirmed their "quiet, practical, biracial leadership." We do not claim that these former members of Congress were full-fledged embodiments of stealthness; however, the eleven that we have designated for study sufficiently approximated our theoretical notion of stealth politics. Our conclusion is that all of them sometimes played the Southern race game, either purposefully or inadvertently, in some manner of stealthness, for generally positive reasons.

Elaborated Explanations of "Why" and "How"

When probed beyond the direct question, our designated stealth leaders quickly and easily extended their discussion into the "why" and "how" of their stealthy work. Even those who had expressed uncertainty or qualms about the formal idea of stealthness proceeded with pertinent and valuable remarks reflecting the origins and specifics of their transitional service in the race game of Southern politics.

Perhaps the most forthcoming practitioner of the game was ROBIN TALLON, an engaging representative from South Carolina's Black Belt who ironically combined both stealthness and openness throughout his congressional career. He wrote on his questionnaire that he had often been asked how he managed to win elections with favorable voting scores from such disparate entities as the Chamber of Commerce, the AFL/CIO, and the NAACP: "I usually replied that it was simply by representing my district."

Tallon, a self-acknowledged stealth politician who credited much of his success to solid, consistent black support, said that conservative whites probably didn't realize the extent of his black initiatives, and "the people who mattered in the white community knew that 'stealth politics' was a reality in order to build seniority for the Sixth District."

Other respondents offered varied specifics about "why" and "how" they conducted their particular brands of quiet, practical, biracial politics.

PETE PETERSON (FLORIDA): "Whenever possible, I did not address issues as 'black or white' in the first instance. In dealing with issues that were oriented strictly toward the black community, I would always try to demonstrate that what we were doing was for the greater good of the community as a whole."

OWEN PICKETT (VIRGINIA): "My hands-on, person-to-person activities in the black community got very little publicity outside this community and I do not remember ever being 'called to task' by conservative whites for this activity."

L. F. PAYNE (VIRGINIA): "Sundays were days that I spent almost exclusively with the black community attending as many as five church services, often speaking and attending picnics, church dinners, etc. This was rarely publicized except by word of mouth."

RONNIE SHOWS (MISSISSIPPI): "You do what you have to do. Especially when I was first elected, I kept a low profile on some things. For example I didn't say anything about the rebel flag issue or go to state Democratic Party events; and in Mississippi, you couldn't endorse anything that Jesse Jackson was for or say that you would vote for Bill Clinton."

BUTLER DERRICK (SOUTH CAROLINA): "You always had to be careful that the white community, at large, did not think that you were 'in cahoots with those radicals.'"

When challenged by white constituents about their responsiveness to the black community, our respondents apparently explained themselves as best they could. TIM VALENTINE (NORTH CAROLINA) said that he didn't recall ever being asked by any white voter why he was attentive to the black community, but his voting record as a fiscal conservative helped him get along with the whites: "Many times (and the record will show this) I voted with the Republicans. I was an active member of the Conservative Democratic Forum. My voting record and my political philosophy were well within the range of acceptability as far as most white voters were concerned."

ROY ROWLAND (GEORGIA) mentioned the King Holiday vote: "I simply said it was a non-issue and would pass regardless of my vote and I saw no good reason to not be responsive to 35 percent of my constituency." BUTLER DERRICK (SOUTH CAROLINA) faced similar questions about supporting

African American and former U.S. Marine Ron Dellums as chairman of the defense committee: "I explained that I had worked with him for many years. That he was not a communist, but a 'full-blooded' American."

Right . . . or . . . Wrong?

We further explored the thinking of our designated stealth leaders by asking whether they had ever pondered the moral appropriateness of such race-based politicking. They reported, with varying elaborations, that they did not seriously question whether their approach was right or wrong; and, when probed specifically, they said it did not occur to them that they might have been deceiving their white constituents or exploiting the black community.

Pete Peterson (Florida): "No, I did not ask myself that question. I did however often consider whether I was being totally honest in dealing with some of the more complex and sensitive issues where it was necessary to reduce the issue to simple terms that could be readily understood by my constituents."

Robin Tallon (South Carolina) wrote in terms of practical, tactical politics: "I recognized that it was the reality of representing my district and whether or not we were going to have seniority in Congress." Owen Pickett (Virginia) talked about representational responsibility: "My philosophy was that once elected I had a responsibility to represent all constituents in my district fairly and impartially." Butler Derrick (South Carolina) reasoned historically that "I saw it as a means of accomplishment that would be of great benefit to their generation and generations to come."

L. F. Payne (Virginia) said that conservatives viewed him as not being "pure" enough in the politics of the past, but "I always felt that reaching out to the black community was a good thing and hopefully was helpful in promoting better attitudes and understandings of all races." Ronnie Shows (Mississippi) was pretty direct: "I think it worked both ways. Certainly we were used and we used them too. Overall, it was positive because we were able to do some good things."

These comments have provided valuable evidence about the orientations of our designated stealth leaders. They either directly defined or indirectly elaborated themselves as stealth practitioners of some sort, and they pursued their leadership courses in varying ways for positive reasons. In the following section, these leaders recount extensive—but not always harmonious—engagements in the biracial political process.

Positive Memories of Biracial Relations

Without exception, our colleagues expressed positivism (and very few negative comments) about their relationships with black activists and constituents.

Crisp comments of "good," "strong," "comfortable," "very close," "mutually supportive" described their biracial associations; most asserted that those relationships improved as they served in public office.

LINDSAY THOMAS (GEORGIA): "I was very comfortable with the relations I had with the black community. I was open and honest as I had promised to be and there never was a serious racial issue that arose in my district during the ten years that I served. I will hasten to add that the good relations I enjoyed did not come from any careful strategy that I or my staff devised. Rather, I believe, I built on the good relations of the member I followed in Congress and the fact that there was an exceptionally capable and experienced array of black leaders in my district. These leaders had long before developed a strategy of cooperation and steady but measured progress on racial matters rather than a strategy of confrontations and demands that polarized the black and white communities."

PETE PETERSON (FLORIDA): "I was able to maintain a very strong, supportive relationship with the black community throughout my political career . . . If anything, my relationship with the black community actually grew stronger throughout my relatively short political career. I greatly respected what they were trying to do for their communities under incredibly difficult circumstances while dealing with abject poverty, drugs, and crime. Since departing the Congress, I have maintained many of the relationships that I made during the period of my representation."

RONNIE SHOWS (MISSISSIPPI): "Very good. All of my political career has been a close relationship with the black community. And over that time I began to see and feel what their frustrations were about."

Martin Lancaster (North Carolina): "I had a close working relationship with the black community throughout my civic and political life. I enjoyed strong voting and financial support from that community as well. In fact, I would still be in Congress if redistricting had not surgically removed practically every black voter in my district in order to create a majority-black district!"

L. F. Payne (Virginia): "We began as strangers and ended as friends."

The account of Tim Valentine was especially instructive. He said that, on a scale of 1–10 (or worst possible to best possible), "My relationship with the black community went from 1 in my first congressional campaign in 1982 to 7 or 8 in my last in 1992." Valentine explained that he shocked the black leadership by winning his first Democratic primary runoff against a formidable black candidate. "I made it my business to get along with my black constituents, to convince them that I, a white man, could and would represent them in word and deed." Eventually, he wrote, the black electorate became the mainstay of his electoral support.

Bumps in the Biracial Road?

Inevitably, there would be "bumps"—or difficult interactions—in the twisting road of biracial politics. We found no meaningful link between these bumps and stealthness. However our respondents proved to be storehouses of interesting information—most of it relating to routine difficulties, personal gripes, and a few entertaining anecdotes—about their particular situations during that era. These stories are pretty generic for politics everywhere, regardless of the racial or regional angle; but we present them here as further fleshing-out of the stealth model.

Butler Derrick, for example, provided several interesting comments about black-white interactions in South Carolina. In one response, he noted a constant need to mediate and mitigate racial tensions in both camps. "There were two very radical, for the time, civil rights leaders that I was able to work with. I tried to make them understand that nothing was accomplished by 'burning the schoolhouse down.' It was touch and go, but fortunately they were intelligent men and only tried to 'burn' one time. On the other hand, many white people saw African Americans as a threat to their jobs and social status . . . I tried to help the white community understand that blacks were not a threat and that they could trust the black community."

Derrick also recounted, somewhat humorously, a couple of incidents illustrating the recurrent requests for white politicians to cover black "expenses" in Southern politics.

"I remember an old minister who had gone to a great deal of trouble to work out the number of votes I needed to carry a precinct. He said he would be glad to help me 'in the name of good government' for 25 cents a vote. Of course, I explained that we did not do this.

"On another occasion, the State Democratic Party sent about $1,500 over to help pay for gas, etc., to get voters to the polls. I called three leading ministers to my office and asked them to split the money and use it for expenses. There was a fight and one of the good reverends left with a bloody nose. Of course, this was an exception. Most were interested in what they could do to bring about better government."

By scouring the completed questionnaires, we have compiled a representative list of "bumpier" aspects of biracial politics cited by our respondents. (Exercising editorial discretion, we present them without attribution.)

- Bridging the racial divide sometimes seemed to be an understandably impossible assignment. "The biggest obstacle in dealing with the black community was, of course, their inherent distrust of white people generally and white politicians in particular. How could white people expect any different reaction given the history of race relations in our country for over four hundred years?"

- Attempting such an assignment entailed a disproportionate time commitment for white politicians. One respondent said, "A huge amount of my personal time was required to maintain my presence in the black community; and I did not have sufficient time to follow through on some of their issues because of other official duties." Another said, "I attended black churches over half the time, interfering with attendance at my own services." A savvy, seasoned politician who retired rather than seek reelection in a majority-black district, commented that he was in black churches three out of four weekends toward the end of his service, "and I just couldn't keep that up forever."

- There was growing pressure to be more attentive to black political demands. "It was a struggle to balance all of my representative responsibilities and 'be right' on black issues 100 percent of the time, which was the general expectation."

- They also were constantly expected to cater to minority ministers. "The ministers of course expected to be a part of the decision process if they were going to use their 'good offices' to move forward; and you had to be careful that they did not think you were usurping their powers . . . and you had to avoid showing favoritism among them."

- It was also tough determining which minority leaders were representative of the community. "It was sometimes difficult identifying who really spoke for the black voter in a particular community, realizing that the loudest was not always the most respected or listened to most by the voters in that community."

- Some so-called "consultants" or "contractors" claimed excessive influence in the black community and tried to extract excessive money from white candidates. "There were always people wanting to get on the campaign payroll who did not bring anything to the table."

- A few dissidents made life especially tough. "There was a small group of activists who felt I never did quite enough for the black community and were often vocal about it."

- Then, there was the problem of reactionary whites. "Some white people didn't want me working at all with the black community."

- Finally, the middle-of-the-road white leader had to be supercautious in public comments. "I constantly had to 'tip-toe' around sensitive issues to avoid racially offending somebody on one side or the other."

While the positive version of biracial relations reported here seemed sincere and provided fresh commentary, it may also reflect the natural tendency among ex-politicians for favorably remembering certain aspects of personal history. The reported bumps added interesting color to the story; but these difficulties suggest normal political complaints rather than anything theoretically central to stealthness. Based on our experience, off-the-record conversations, and research presented elsewhere in this manuscript, we think that this particular accounting is an interesting but incomplete rendition of biracial politics in that period. So we report it without claiming any special consequence for the stealth thesis.

Fortunately, the ensuing questions provoked more specific responses relevant to our purpose. The next section will show that our leaders and their black allies broke with tradition in this part of the country by engaging substantially and effectively in the political process.

The Relatively Progressive Agenda of Biracial Campaigning and Public Service

The dealings between our officials and their black constituents were not radically different in form or process from what other studies tell us about campaigning and serving the public. However, these accounts assume special significance in the context of our stealth thesis and conceptual model of changing Southern politics.

Their representational styles varied; however, most of our surveyed leaders reported that they conducted important activities—administered either within or separately from their formal campaign or service institutions—targeted specifically for the black community. The significant finding is an extensive agenda of relatively progressive activities rather than the exploitative ways of the traditional Southern race game.

Biracial Campaigning

In their pursuit of black voters, our respondents said that they relied heavily on personal/individual relationships, community organizations, and money.

Most importantly, at least at the beginning of a campaign, they aggressively solicited the personal allegiance of influential individuals in the black community, including church ministers, public officials, civil rights activists, the media, various professionals, and friends. In fact, there was probably no closer working relationship in Southern politics than that between stealthy white politicians and black ministers.

As **BUTLER DERRICK (SOUTH CAROLINA)** noted: "The black ministers were the most powerful group in the black community. They would be in charge of getting their parishioners to the polls; and many would distribute literature and speak for you from the lectern on the Sunday before election day. I stayed in constant contact with them, sometimes speaking to their congregations and sometimes joining in for their 'picnic on the grounds.'"

RONNIE SHOWS (MISSISSIPPI) offered an example that communicates the special importance of person-to-person biracial politics in that era. In one of his early races, for the state legislature, Shows trailed the white incumbent in the first primary by a thousand votes; and he lost the black community that he had worked hard to carry. So he approached the key black activist who had been avoiding him and asked for her help in the runoff: "I waited most of the day outside her house until she came home. I asked her if my opponent ever came to her house, and she said he sent somebody. I asked her if he ever put up signs or handed out campaign cards in her community, and she said no. Then I told her that she and her people were voting for an official who was supposed to represent everybody and he didn't have enough respect to come and ask for their support. She didn't say anything, but she asked me for my pencil and wrote my name on her ballot. I won that runoff by a thousand votes, and that lady's granddaughter was my first page as a Mississippi state senator."

The next major element of biracial campaigning was organizational assistance. It was essential that any serious candidate secure the informal support of black church-related groups and formal endorsements of as many entities as possible from among civil rights organizations, party-affiliated committees, community clubs, professional associations, labor unions, educators, and the media.

TIM VALENTINE (NORTH CAROLINA) submitted an especially revealing account of his initial endorsement experience in a meeting with the Committee on the Affairs of Black People in Durham: "These were closed-door sessions, usually in a black church in the city. Tough questions were asked and straight answers expected. A white person in one of these meetings usually felt hostility. Years of pent-up frustrations came to the fore. I, as well as other white candidates, were sharply and aggressively questioned separately and alone (while others waited in a 'holding pen' nearby). I was never conscious of any media people being present . . . My first appearance before this group was in 1982. I will never forget that event. I thought I knew what I was in for but I did not. Over four hundred years of ill use and discrimination poured out in the form of questions and statements—sometimes expressed in earthy language. On this occasion I felt as if they were saying to me: 'Why the hell are you alive!' I hasten to add that relations improved as we got to know each other better."

Finally, financial considerations permeated all of these aspects of bi-racial campaigning, mainly because of the importance of paid operatives, friendly media, GOTV, and "miscellaneous expenses" geared to the black community. Precise dollar numbers were unavailable, but our respondents estimated that they spent between 15 to 40 percent of their total budgets for activities relating to the black electorate (a range that roughly approximated the black proportion of these districts).

Each of our respondents enumerated personalized combinations of these tactical activities in describing their efforts in the black community.

PETE PETERSON (FLORIDA): "Of course, many campaign activities were targeted toward the black community . . . Community fish fries were a staple of every campaign and I used the town hall format for many of my campaign events in the black communities to ensure clear, focused and effective communications and to rally them to join our GOTV activities. During campaigns I frequently attended black church services, which were a very effective mode of communication; and I aggressively sought endorse-ments from black religious leaders throughout the district. While it was not considered a campaign 'activity' there was an absolute campaign prerequisite to have a solid sharp cadre of black campaign workers with me all the time. Their advice and counsel was invaluable."

MARTIN LANCASTER (NORTH CAROLINA): "In every campaign I had multiple campaign events targeted on my friends, supporters, and rank and file voters in the black community. In every campaign, I brought prominent black leaders (often black congressional leaders) into the district for campaign events. I always had minority chairs in each county and in the district and always had minority campaign staff proportionate to the black population in the county and district."

ROBIN TALLON (SOUTH CAROLINA): "I knew that I would get 98 to 99 percent of the black vote, so the concern was voter turnout. We organized the district down to the precinct level with phone banks. We organized the black precincts with our own precinct chairmen and volunteer workers to man phone banks on election day and get people to the polls . . . We had poll watchers in every majority-black precinct, served refreshments to the voters in the larger black precincts and had another person to be in charge of our signs and campaign materials distributed in every black precinct. These individuals were usually members of these communities themselves."

L. F. PAYNE (VIRGINIA): "Politically, the black community controls about 25 percent of the vote, which I felt I could capture by being helpful and responsive . . . But to truly reach the black electorate, you had to attend many black events, churches, clubs, social events, etc. I also made appearances before the Voters League for an endorsement that was communicated widely; and the GOTV effort ensured that blacks would come to the polls to vote."

OWEN PICKETT (VIRGINIA): "I kept in touch with the black community by attending church services where I stayed through the entire service and mingled with the congregation. I did this probably 90 percent of the Sundays during my service in Congress."

What did their black allies ask for in return for their assistance and endorsements? Apparently, their motives were pretty conventional. Some wanted the politicians to hire black staffers and provide constituent services to black citizens; but apparently most just wanted to be part of the process and to secure better representation of black issues and the black community.

PETE PETERSON (FLORIDA): "Interestingly, it was quite rare for any black leader or citizen for that matter to ask me for a specific benefit in return for their support. If anything, their requests were generally in the form of simply asking for recognition, fairness, and access to government agencies/programs. There were of course, many who wanted assurance that my positions on leading issues of the day were not too far removed from their own, particularly when it came to civil rights, funding for education, abortion, gun control, labor and agriculture issues."

ROBIN TALLON (SOUTH CAROLINA): "In the beginning, in seeking the endorsement of the Sixth Congressional District Black Caucus, I pledged that my staff would reflect the racial diversity of the district. I ended up with more than 50 percent of my staff being from the black community. This included my chief of staff. I also pledged that I would be a congressman for many of my black constituents who felt that they had never had a congressman who represented their interests."

ROY ROWLAND (GEORGIA): "The only specific request that I recall was to hire some blacks on my staff. . . I had several blacks on my staff. In fact, two of my district offices were headed by black females."

LINDSAY THOMAS (GEORGIA): "It was never put to me in the form of a specific question on a specific issue. There was the question of the Martin Luther King Holiday that was an issue in my first campaign and I clearly stated that I would support the Holiday and followed through on my commitment."

L. F. PAYNE (VIRGINIA): "No quid pro quo."

RONNIE SHOWS (MISSISSIPPI) said, however, that sometimes these relationships were more materialistic: "It depends on who you were dealing with. The majority of black preachers and activists wouldn't take a dime for helping you and some of them were my best friends. But some of these people made their living off of white politicians and even said if you didn't pay they would help the opposition. The longer I was in office and the higher profile office I would run for the problem became worse and worse."

Constructive Public Service

All our respondents reported that these campaign activities easily continued into their service as public officials. They hired black staffers and served black constituents; they opened the political process and governmental offices to the black community; and they addressed issues of concern to black citizens through their votes and in other ways.

PETE PETERSON (FLORIDA): "There was a seamless transition from the campaign to constituent service. I always had highly qualified and energetic black staff assigned to my Washington and district offices so I was assured of good analysis and advice on issues of interest of the black community. I also stayed in close touch with my black supporters through frequent personal visits to schools, churches, workplaces and through frequent town hall meetings, flyers, and the conduct of routine constituent service activities. I suspect a casual observer of my district activities would have found it difficult to tell when I was on a campaign swing or just doing my job."

MARTIN LANCASTER (NORTH CAROLINA): "My representation of all segments of my constituency was as fair to every segment as I could possibly be. I sought out the views of leaders in the minority and was receptive to contacts made by the minority community . . . In whatever endeavor I was ever involved in (from the Red Cross to the county library board) I always advocated for proportional representation of the black community on the boards and in leadership positions."

TIM VALENTINE (NORTH CAROLINA) probably spoke for numerous white Southern colleagues who felt that they had to prove themselves to their black constituents. As has already been reported, he made it his business to convince them that he could and would represent blacks: "I hired black staffers in my district and Washington offices. I was seen in the black community. I was available. We were dead serious about constituent services. We answered our mail. My door was open to all whom I represented. I supported all civil rights legislation . . . In short, I tried to conduct myself so that African Americans would have to understand that we intended to treat them with dignity and fairness."

RONNIE SHOWS (MISSISSIPPI) apparently took extensive steps to reach out to African Americans in his operations as a state official and U.S. congressman. "I used to attend all their events, their churches, and their revivals; I put them on boards; and I gave them responsible positions on my staff. Some people thought I had too many blacks and I told them I hired the people I thought could do the job. I also told them that the black community comprised between 40–45 percent of the voters in my district and I got at least 90 percent of their votes . . . and if they didn't like it, that was not my problem."

Other members seemed to serve their black constituents with an individualized style that emphasized impartial service and minimized race-conscious operations. According to ROY ROWLAND (GEORGIA): "I hadn't really thought about it, but I guess my relationship with the black community was about the same as it was during my time in medical practice . . . As a physician, I had contacts with many blacks on a very personal basis, I always treated everybody with the same respect and care. That was true in my public service as well."

Likewise, BILL ALEXANDER (ARKANSAS) said: "My family taught me to be friends with black people . . . Just treat people fairly and don't make a big deal out of it."

OWEN PICKETT (VIRGINIA), who earlier informed us that he had attended black churches almost every weekend in his district, provided a particularly striking account of personal service to his minority constituency. "Black leaders mainly wanted access and an open line of communication to make sure their views were heard and fairly considered. I have had black ministers call me in Washington and request that I join them in prayer on the telephone when an issue of particular interest to them was coming up for a vote."

A Different Kind of Race Game?

It is apparent that these leaders conducted many of the same campaign and service activities as did traditional politicians (and they experienced similar bumps along the way) in a system with peculiarly regional and racial dynamics; however, unlike their predecessors, they seemed to play the race game—quietly and practically—for relatively progressive purposes and objectives. Some conducted separate activities for their divided racial constituencies; others simply accommodated black-white differences in their routine activities. But, compared to the traditional race game of Southern politics, they were differently oriented; and their actual leadership was a different exercise of players, issues, rules, and outcomes. Theirs was a politics of responsive public service for both black and white citizens.

Our overall conclusion is that all of these leaders figured out—whether purposively or not, separately or not, happily or not—how to successfully court and serve their black electorate without arousing undue ire from their white majority. The next section suggests specifically and generally their reconstructive imprint on Southern politics.

The Perceived Impact of Quiet, Practical, Biracial Service

The former congressmen expressed varying ideas about stealthness, but they were adamant about the positive impact of their biracial service. Their own collective account was one of progress in everyday politics and long-term, consequential change in the Southern system.

Political Progress

It is very evident that our surveyed leaders took pride in their contributions to the changing politics of that era. Whether talking about their "firsts" on behalf of blacks, their stands on controversial issues, or their patterned fairness in representation, the respondents considered themselves positive biracial leaders in an uneasy time for both blacks and whites.

BUTLER DERRICK, an avowed stealth leader, listed some risky aspects of a career that stretches back to the turbulent 1960s in the South Carolina Black Belt: "When I ran for the state legislature in 1966, I was the first candidate to ever go to African American homes and shake hands, and discuss problems with members of that community. First in South Carolina to appoint a black to a public school board, to the election commission, etc. First in the county to publicly acknowledge that both races would be better if the schools were integrated . . . In Washington, I supported equal job opportunities, one man, one vote. Issues that would help them have greater input, such as creating black districts. Worked hard to see that they received the support from the government to which they were entitled. Supported African American advancement to committee chairmanships and other positions of influence in the Congress . . . And I did these things without 'shoving it' on the white population."

ROBIN TALLON, another South Carolinian, stressed bold initiatives during his self-defined stealthy run in politics: "The black community was always a priority for my office. As an example, in my first term in office, I successfully lobbied our senior U.S. Senator, Strom Thurmond, chairman of the Senate Judiciary Committee, to support and report out of the Judiciary committee the Martin Luther King Holiday legislation . . . Also, I came out publicly for removing the Confederate flag from the state capitol. I felt that if a significant percentage of the population was offended, then it made sense to remove it and get on with other issues that affect everyone's everyday life."

PETE PETERSON (FLORIDA), who surmised that the stealth thesis was an accurate characterization of his service, articulated a mindset that probably was pretty common among Southern white politicians during the latter years of that era:

"I was always keenly aware of my obligation to represent the interests of my constituents—particularly my black constituents for I felt that they had historically been unrepresented in the district. As a result, almost as an auto response, I would find myself evaluating legislation, government agency activities, environmental decisions and other government actions for their potential impact on the black communities or black people in general. Legislative issues associated with civil rights, agriculture, environment, transportation, jobs, housing and education were the prime areas of concern among my black constituents and I worked to improve legislation wherever possible to ensure that black communities got their fair share and a fair shake."

Virginian L. F. PAYNE, who seemed unsure about how to classify himself in terms of our stealth thesis, was definitely positive about his biracial mission and record: "I told my constituents that my job was to represent all citizens and consider all points of view; and we had a total open door policy, which wasn't the case in the past. I tried to let the black community especially know they were being heard and represented."

Mississippi two-termer RONNIE SHOWS enjoyed good biracial relations before losing in a redrawn district. He expressed mixed feelings about his service in a changing Southern politics: "I feel very positive that we were able to do some good things. We worked hard to help the working middle class, whether black or white. I think a lot of white politicians took black voters for granted, so I tried to deliver for them and gain their trust over my thirty-year career. But the higher the office the less your constituents know about who and what they're voting for; and it ends up being a contest of outspending your opponent. The only time I didn't get strong black support was in my last election; and the only thing I regret is losing to somebody who didn't share my ideas about issues and service."

Systemic Change

Generally speaking, furthermore, our former colleagues seemed to understand and cherish their roles in changing the fundamental nature and course of Southern history.

For example, MARTIN LANCASTER (NORTH CAROLINA), who had acknowledged a slight degree of stealthness, probably exemplified the common sentiment among many white Southern politicians of that era. "I think the manner in which I represented the people without regard to race set a positive tone for the district."

Georgian LINDSAY THOMAS was ambivalent about the stealth concept, but he acknowledged a strategy of racial cooperation and measured progress rather than confrontation. "I represented a traditional Democratic district with adequate moderate support in the white community that never put me on the cutting edge on racial matters. Quite frankly, I never had to worry about these matters with the support base that we had. Certainly there were extremists who would have polarized the communities had they had the chance, but they simply never gained the traction that the responsible leaders in both communities had and maintained. I guess I was just lucky . . . However, if you call my style 'stealth' then I would say the biggest upside was that it allowed a constructive environment in which we could concentrate on the issues that affected everyone's daily lives."

ROBIN TALLON (SOUTH CAROLINA), a strangely self-defined and open "stealth politician," took the view that he was helping fellow whites as well as the black constituency. "On balance, I think it all evened out. I explained along the way that if we want to improve one of the poorest districts in the nation, everybody needs to be involved. And I enlightened many within the white communities on the need for them to work with the black communities. As John F. Kennedy said, 'A rising tide lifts all ships.'"

PETE PETERSON (FLORIDA), another acknowledged stealth leader, emphasized his efforts to moderate the racial dialogue of Southern politics. "I truly hope that my service will be remembered as having positively impacted the democratic process . . . I believe I was also able to tone down the 'I'm right and you are wrong' character of debate within racially divided communities."

Finally, **BUTLER DERRICK (SOUTH CAROLINA)**—drawing from his broad perspective as a proud citizen, long-time public official, and stealthy practitioner in the state that fired the opening shot of the Civil War—philosophically mused about Southern absolution. "I like to think that I was doing what was best for the country . . . that I was helping to remove the 'mill stone' of segregation and inequality that had hung around the neck of the South for so many decades . . . I think we made the African American community feel more a part of the process; and we helped make the white community understand that they had a common interest and benefit in progressive government."

When all was said and done retrospectively, our simple survey conveyed a picture of varying stealth service among selected politicians of that time in this region. Despite mixed reactions to our particular conception of their leadership, these former members of Congress attested to the reconstructive nature, activities, and accomplishments of quiet, practical, biracial leadership throughout the South.

Summarization of the Exploratory Survey

This survey was structured to help assess the idea of stealth leadership and politics by exploring pertinent aspects of political setting, personal orientations, electoral campaigns, public service, and systemic impact among selected Southern white politicians throughout the region during that era. Several closing comments and ramifications seem appropriate.

First—considered along with the Browder case study—this report suggests very strongly that these stealth leaders contributed in important ways to reconstruction of Southern politics between the heroic drama and more contemporary developments.

Clearly, something was happening in that period that has been missed in conventional analysis. In addition to the heroic drama, in addition to spectacular mass registrations of African American voters, in addition to striking increases in black elected and Republican officials, in addition to the usual, celebrated coterie of courageous presidents and New South governors/judges/journalists/civil rights activists/local litigators/progressive business leaders, it seems that some white politicians and black allies unheroically and undramatically started doing things differently—quietly, practically, biracially, and effectively. This heretofore unheralded action helped moderate Southern discourse, helped push segregationists to the periphery, and helped bring blacks into the routine of Southern politics and governance—in effect, these stealthy leaders helped normalize the South without the trauma of earlier days.

Obviously, our small, unscientific survey has its limitations; however, the findings definitely apply to this subset of respondents. We served in Washington during that time and have since studied that aspect of American history. We are convinced that these officials, who comprised a prominent, powerful presence in their districts, helped moderate governance, politics, and culture in the Southern region.

Second, we think that these respondents fairly typified a larger segment of the congressional body. A cursory glance at available data shows that there were many more white Southerners serving in Washington back then who represented significant black minorities and/or compiled substantial civil rights records. We expect that a sizeable contingent of regional leaders practiced such stealthy politics and reconstruction in their states and the U.S. Congress. Perhaps a more complete assessment of Southern representatives from that period is in order.

Third, we also believe that our proposition might apply beyond the congressional arena. It is reasonable to expect that many white officials in state, county, city, judicial, and special-district positions were stealthily oriented and situated within similar contextual settings. Interspersed throughout this manuscript are comments indicating that countless white leaders and black activists practiced our new brand of biracial politics in the region during that period of political change. Perhaps we also should replicate our study with more and different former officials.

Finally, we acknowledge that the reported incidents and commentary are open to criticism and debate; some will challenge our interpretations, both normatively and empirically. And rightly so. What we have reported here are the personal perspectives and subjective accounts of Southern white politicians about something that happened years ago. As we have noted before, the race game of Southern politics has a long and troubled history. Also, there are some things communicated in this survey that beg further inquiry among the black community of that time. Accordingly, in the following chapter, we will explore the perspectives of African American leaders and activists from the stealth era.

In summary, these former members of Congress have attested—through a combination of objective data and their subjective accounts—to our model of stealth leadership and politics, and these findings buttress our thesis of stealth reconstruction. Furthermore, we have suggested anecdotally throughout this project that the thesis may have much broader applicability among public officials in other offices and at various levels throughout the region during the 1970s, 1980s, and 1990s. Certainly, these ideas seem worthy of further discussion; we will assess our full findings and ramifications in the concluding chapters.

PART THREE

So What?

8

Biracial Roundtable
on Stealth Reconstruction

The premise of this project is that most people are unaware of how the heroic drama of the civil rights movement translated into meaningful change in the Southern political system over the ensuing years. Scholars, journalists, and political leaders have all failed to explain and deal satisfactorily with this continuing, contentious mystery of the past few decades.

Obviously, celebrated heroes and villains, courageous judges and journalists, prominent leaders, and even private citizens continued the struggle, albeit less dramatically, in the public arena. Furthermore, court litigation sporadically pushed the boundaries of equality in favorable forums; blacks registered to vote in unprecedented numbers; the rise of black public officials and party competition altered certain aspects of the political process; and societal developments slowly impacted the Southern way of life. But such factors do not tell the full story about how Southern politics moderated broadly and generally throughout this period.

We believe that we have supplied an additional and critical part of that story. As we have acknowledged throughout this book, stealth reconstruction is a controversial thesis. Our project thus far has articulated a new, unconventional proposition about Southern political change following the civil rights movement; we also have researched the practice of stealth leadership through a personalized case study and exploratory survey of white elected officials and their service from that era.

We now want to shift gears and close our examination with interactive discussion among other knowledgeable participants in that period of Southern politics. Therefore, in this chapter, we yield the podium to an eclectic group of ten key black and white officials, activists, staffers, and other operatives—all of whom practiced some aspect of what we consider quiet, practical, biracial politics in Alabama—for their current views and insights about our now told story of the 1970s, 1980s, and 1990s.

All of the following discussants, listed alphabetically, played varying yet important roles in local, state, regional, and national politics during the past several decades. All are still active in public life, but they agreed to talk openly about their previous activities and current perspectives. (For the benefit of readers unfamiliar with these individuals, House, Hubbert, Raby, and Wallace are white and Arrington, Dunn, Gray, Gray, Reed, and Zippert are black.)

RICHARD ARRINGTON JR. Dr. Arrington—a biology professor and college dean—became Birmingham's first African American mayor in 1979 and served in that position for the next twenty years. He built black organizational power through the Jefferson County Citizens Coalition in the 1970s, and he was a founder and leader of the powerful Alabama New South Coalition in the 1980s. Arrington generally enjoyed effective dealings with the white political and business leadership. While black-white skirmishing continued through his tenure, he helped Birmingham transition from a symbol of racist tyranny to a system of biracial governance.

JAMES A. "PAPPY" DUNN. Dunn has provided long and special public service, including five terms as Calhoun County Commissioner after a full career in local education. As coach and principal at the all-black Calhoun County Training School, "Pappy" Dunn established a solid reputation among both blacks and whites. Now in his nineties, he has served as president of the Alabama Association of County Commissioners, has been recognized as the *Anniston Star's* "Citizen of the Year," and has been honored by special resolution of the Alabama legislature. While he never marched in the front lines of the civil rights movement, Dunn was a stalwart example of biracial leadership during the 1970s, 1980s, and 1990s and into the new century.

FRED GRAY. Gray is a legendary figure with major legal impact on Alabama, Southern politics, and American democracy. He represented Mrs. Rosa Parks in integrating Montgomery city buses; he was the first civil rights lawyer for Dr. Martin Luther King Jr.; he litigated landmark redistricting through *Gomillion v. Lightfoot*; he successfully challenged Alabama Governors John Patterson and George Wallace and various state agencies on important rights issues; and he fought the United States government for justice for victims of the Tuskegee Syphilis Study. Additionally, he served a term in the Alabama legislature and has been the moving force in establishment of the Tuskegee Human and Civil Rights Multicultural Center. Soft-spoken but strong-willed, Gray has exercised singular influence on civil rights developments throughout the past half-century.

JEROME GRAY. As longtime field director for the Alabama Democratic Conference, Jerome Gray has been the quiet personification of racial change in the Heart of Dixie. He has coordinated all administrative, electoral, and legal activities for the ADC, known as "the black political caucus of Alabama" since the 1970s. Most recently, he campaigned for Barack Obama in Alabama. Gray is one of the most respected and effective players in Alabama civil rights history.

MIKE HOUSE. House, now one of Washington's leading governmental relations figures, was Howell Heflin's top assistant from Heflin's entrance into politics during the early 1970s to the mid 1980s. House ran Alabama Supreme Court Chief Justice Heflin's judicial operations and he served as U.S. Senator Heflin's chief of staff until going into the private sector in 1986. His background in campaigning and public service make him one of the most knowledgeable players in biracial relations of the stealth era.

PAUL HUBBERT. Dr. Hubbert has been the most powerful unelected leader in Alabama for the past several decades. As executive director of the Alabama Education Association, his influence extends comprehensively across the spectrum of politics and policy. Since overseeing, along with Joe Reed, the merger of the white and black teacher unions in the 1970s, he has been the central figure in Democratic Party activities and state governmental politics. Despite losing the gubernatorial general election in 1990, Hubbert is often called "the real governor" in Montgomery.

STEVE RABY. Raby, former chief of staff for U.S. Senator Howell Heflin, is a political and governmental consultant. He handled a variety of office, field, and political duties as a staff assistant (1983–96) for Heflin, including most of that time as chief of staff; he is now considered among the smartest and most effective operatives to work the Montgomery-Washington circuit. Raby is often mentioned as a potential candidate for public office.

JOE L. REED. As profiled in an earlier chapter, Dr. Reed was an important part of the heroic drama and the subsequent period of our interest. He continues his leadership even today as executive chairman of the Alabama Democratic Conference, vice chair of the Alabama State Democratic Executive Committee, and associate executive secretary of the Alabama Education Association. More pertinently, he has been a chief architect of what we have labeled stealth politics in Alabama.

GEORGE WALLACE JR. Both his father and mother occupied the governor's office, but George Wallace Jr. has forged his own career as a contemplative, low-key populist in Alabama politics. His resume includes two terms as state treasurer and two terms on the Alabama Public Service Commission. His future in state politics is an open question; but it is clear that this Democrat-turned-Republican bears both the lessons and burdens of a tumultuous era in Alabama and Southern history.

CAROL ZIPPERT. Dr. Zippert has operated as a multi-faceted force in Alabama's Black Belt since coming to the state in 1971. She was one of the founders of the Alabama New South Coalition; she served two terms on the Greene County School Board; she co-publishes the weekly *Greene County Democrat* (with husband John); but mainly she considers herself a community worker helping Black Belt communities achieve social transformation. A published poet, Dr. Zippert articulates a message of justice and peace.

Through a variety of interviews—conducted in person, by telephone, via email, and through written correspondence—we have "convened" these ten prominent individuals in a virtual roundtable discussion with some interactive capability. Of course the group never really sat down in the same room at the same time. Their remarks have been edited slightly and technically to approximate the imagined roundtable setting and topical questions; each participant was provided a copy of the virtual conversation for corrections, elaborations, and responses to the group discussion.

In this chapter, co-author and moderator Artemesia Stanberry will lead the virtual discussion of stealth leadership, politics, and reconstruction. She will ask these individuals (a) to assess the stealth thesis, (b) to recount some of their experiences in "stealth politics" during those years, and (c) to comment on the significance of "stealth reconstruction" as a new century dawns.

General Comments on the Stealth Thesis

MODERATOR STANBERRY: Our approach thus far has dealt with white elected officials—through our case study and survey—about their stealth leadership and politics. Now, we have assembled ten political veterans to evaluate the thesis of "stealth leadership, politics, and reconstruction" from their perspectives as non-elected partners in stealthy politicking. To put it as simply as possible, we hope that you all can help us assess, more validly, our notion that "quiet, practical, biracial" action challenged traditional Southern ways—i.e., white supremacy and segregation—and contributed to a more normalized, moderated system in this region. Let's begin by talking generally about the stealth thesis presented in this project.

Co-author and former public official Glen Browder set the tone for our project in the theoretical chapter by noting the nature of his stealthy service in the 1970s, 1980s, and 1990s. Browder acknowledged that his primary interest was pursuing American democracy and conventional concerns like political reform, fiscal responsibility and national security issues; and he diligently but less-publicly focused on race and racism. As he explained: "I worked very hard and quietly to secure enough black support to get elected in majority white areas; I sincerely tried to be fair, moderate, and progressive in my politics; and I didn't talk much publicly about any of this stuff."

Attorney Gray, your work with Mrs. Parks and Dr. King were, arguably, the opening skirmishes of the civil rights movement not only in Alabama but throughout the South. You were there at the beginning; you championed legal causes through the courts; you broke electoral barriers in the Alabama legislature; and you're still fighting for civil rights today. So let's start with you. What do you think about this thesis of "quiet, practical, biracial politics,"—or "stealth leadership, politics, and reconstruction"—during that era?

FRED GRAY: I think the thesis is valid. It happened. The civil rights movement began long before the 1950s and extended beyond the 1960s; and a lot of people don't realize that it took many forms—not just famous legal cases and dramatic protests against segregated buses, schools, and facilities. I served in the Alabama legislature in the early 1970s, and most white politicians and black leaders didn't even talk to each other back then. So those who could work together did some things quietly and practically, and sometimes in back rooms.

STANBERRY: Do you see this thesis as challenging or contradicting the civil rights movement?

FRED GRAY: No, not really. As I've written in an earlier book, we had our hands full back then with a white power structure that didn't want to do what was right and never went beyond what the courts ordered. I fought and won a lot of cases against white racism, and I'm still fighting against injustice. But a lot of good things happened, legislatively and otherwise, because black and white politicians got together quietly and worked some things out to make it better. The fact is that "stealth politics" happened; and these changes fit in with what the movement had been pushing in the early years.

STANBERRY: Commissioner Dunn, you've been around longer than anybody else, even longer than Fred Gray, and you've seen major change in your lifetime. You worked as a coach at an all-black high school long before the courts outlawed segregation and as a principal for years thereafter. Now you're an elected county commissioner. Was there anything like "quiet, practical, biracial progress" in those early days?

James Dunn: The entire situation and atmosphere was different in the days before the civil rights movement. Both blacks and whites around here accepted the way things were because that was all they had ever known. We never worked together because whites took advantage of blacks and blacks didn't have the confidence or resources to fight them. When I tried to talk with white leaders about the difference between how our school was treated and the white schools were funded, they'd say "We're just not going to get involved with that stuff." They had the power and the money and all we could do was put up with it until the federal government got involved and we started organizing as a group.

I have to give a lot of credit to younger leaders for mobilizing black people during and after the civil rights movement. That is what really got white politicians to pay attention and do more than they had ever done in the past. So, I guess biracial politics seemed to work best after black voters got organized and could really impact elections.

Stanberry: Dr. Reed, you were an educator yourself, and you were very openly and actively involved in the fight for fair treatment in the civil rights movement of the 1950s and 1960s. Did you have any "quiet, practical, biracial relations" with white politicians during the years following the movement, during the 1970s, 1980s, and 1990s?

Joe Reed: Make no mistake about it, blacks have always had to struggle for their rights in Alabama and this country. White politicians have fought us all the way. But there's more to this story.

Civil rights attorneys like Fred Gray fought a lot of legal wars for us, and it helped to have the Selma march, the freedom rides etc. But I also have to say that blacks have always needed white allies, and we've always had white collaborators. There is white folks' blood as well as black folks' blood on the ground in Alabama. As a matter of fact, it was whites on the U.S. Supreme Court and the judiciary who helped pave the way long before and during the civil rights movement. For example, I don't think anything can be written about Alabama black progress without first looking at Judge Frank M. Johnson Jr. who set the tone. Whether it was the Montgomery bus boycott, the freedom rides, or whether it is was the right to vote, he set the tone.

Also, especially in the days following the civil rights movement, we worked quietly with white friends in elective office. But you sure couldn't go to the top of the mountain and tell everything you knew and what you were doing with white politicians. There were some of them that we wanted to give awards to but we never could because it would have killed them if it got out about what they were doing for blacks.

That quiet accommodation—or "stealth politics" as you call it—was the only way we could accomplish anything politically during those times.

STANBERRY: Dr. Arrington, Birmingham was a special part of the civil rights movement. Because of the mistreatment of African American citizens— including Bull Connor's dogs, Dr. King's jailing, the church bombings—no other major American city earned such a racist reputation. Did "stealthy leaders" and biracial politics play any role in turning Birmingham around?

RICHARD ARRINGTON: Certainly. This quiet cooperation was an effective cornerstone of much of the heralded and hard-won racial transitions in Southern attitudes and politics. Without it, the courageous and well-recorded acts of the modern civil rights movement would have had a much more difficult course.

In fact, my own political participation was grounded in "stealth politics" as much as in the movement. For example, I probably would have never been elected to the Birmingham city council in 1971 and as mayor in 1979 without these joint black-white efforts.

Upon reflection and thinking of my own experiences, I can recall numerous important people—white and black working together—who quietly laid foundations for change in our area during the 1960s and 1970s. I doubt that they knew at the time just how productive and far-reaching their stealthy actions were for biracial progress in the South.

STANBERRY: Mr. Wallace, these comments must be very interesting to you. Your father's career took many tumultuous turns during the 1960s and 1970s; and he spent his last few years apologizing to African Americans and pushing biracial cooperation and progress. In addition, throughout your career during the 1980s and 1990s, you normally enjoyed good relations with black Alabamians. How did this happen?

GEORGE WALLACE JR.: I think the thesis of "stealth politics" accurately depicts what happened with a lot of people, including myself, during the period that we're talking about. The truth is that this dramatic social change brought with it the stark, practical realization that our future would rest on the spirit in which people worked to come together. We would need common ground, but more importantly we would need a sense of our common humanity.

STANBERRY: Dr. Hubbert, you "grew up" as an educator and political leader during those times. What's your response to what's been said here?

PAUL HUBBERT: I agree with all these gentlemen. Out-front leaders were leading the march, leading the parades, doing all of the things that you have to do to bring about social change in a dramatic sort of fashion. But there comes a time in any social movement that you have to regroup and pull together your gains and begin to institutionalize those gains, either in statute or common law. Especially after the Voting Rights Act, some blacks and whites realized that they had to begin to understand one another; and for the first time in this region, they worked together. These moderate whites were not firebrands or fire-eaters, but they managed to get elected and they were sensitive to black constituents, whom they had never represented before. These transitional leaders helped institutionalize the demands of foot soldiers in the civil rights movement.

STANBERRY: Dr. Zippert, I know you've got some different ideas about "stealth reconstruction." What's your take on this discussion so far?

CAROL ZIPPERT: In all honesty, I'm uncomfortable with the notion of "stealth reconstruction" because it gives white politicians credit for all the work that African Americans did during and after the civil rights movement. It's kind of like Hillary Clinton telling Barack Obama that President Johnson created voting rights legislation. We did work biracially back then, but it is somewhat offensive to blacks to hear whites talk about how they did this or they did that to change Southern politics.

STANBERRY: Are you disputing that some white leaders joined with black activists in quiet, practical, biracial action that achieved significant progress during the 1970s, 1980s, and 1990s?

CAROL ZIPPERT: No, not at all. It is a fact that a coalition of white leaders and black activists worked together for more progressive objectives. But calling it a "reconstruction" misrepresents what happened; it belittles strong black leadership, sacrifices, and accomplishments.

STANBERRY: So, how would you characterize what happened back then?

CAROL ZIPPERT: I agree that there was a biracial partnership. Blacks helped get some white progressives elected, but they really didn't change things enough to my satisfaction. I don't consider what they did once they got into office so effective and important that I would describe their service that positively. There's still so much to be done.

White-Black Politicking During the 1970s, 1980s, and 1990s

STANBERRY: All of you bring valuable personal experiences to our roundtable discussion, so let's talk about some of those situations. I'd like to focus our attention in this section on three topics: First, let's talk about some definitive experiences or aspects of white-black politicking during the

1970s, 1980s, and 1990s; second, I'd like to probe more specifically some of your dealings with Howell Heflin, Alabama's most prominent practitioner of biracial leadership throughout the stealth era; and, third, I'll conclude with a few pointed questions about stealth politics for selected discussants.

Let's start with James Dunn, whose career experience as an educator goes all the way back to the 1940s. Commissioner Dunn, did the white leaders do anything for your school and the black community after the Supreme Court rulings and the civil rights movement?

JAMES DUNN: Not in the early days. They'd talk about helping but they didn't do anything. Gradually, however, things changed. The county officials and local school board people would come out to my office, kind of quietly, and ask me to put in a good word for them with the parents of our students; and I would speak to about fifty or so of our people, telling them what this or that candidate said he wanted to do to help our community. I considered that was a positive thing to do. Then I suggested to them that they should talk directly with our people; and some of them began showing up at our meetings, and speaking in our schools. We took these things to mean that they were sincere and they got a lot of our votes. And sure enough, some leaders actually started helping us, treating blacks more like their other constituents. But, as I've already said, things didn't get a lot better until our young people got organized and black voters started participating in large numbers in elections.

STANBERRY: Dr. Reed. In a recent, extended visit in your office, you said that you and your organization played an instrumental role in getting commitments from white politicians and ensuring that campaign promises resulted in public service actions. What did you want from these politicians?

JOE REED: What we asked for was basic fairness and equity. We wanted access, we wanted them to employ black employees on the staff, and we didn't want them up there beating up black people.

STANBERRY: And what did you offer to politicians?

JOE REED: Most white politicians knew that we could get black folks to vote for and against them. We sent a lot of bad white politicians home.

STANBERRY: Dr. Hubbert and Dr. Reed, you both were involved politically, sometimes separately and sometimes together, back then. Exactly how did this stealthy biracial leadership develop during the early years of the post-movement era?

PAUL HUBBERT: Blacks began to organize in Alabama as a result of the court decisions and new laws. They created organizations that carried a lot of weight, and they caused a lot of whites, particularly candidates for office, to have to pay attention to black agendas.

That situation also caused supportive blacks and whites to understand the realities of politics. "Stealth politics" was right for those times because there was too much white resistance. It brought some people to the table because they wanted government to work and both sides had to be pragmatic. The blacks needed friendly whites to get elected; and the white people who got elected felt beholden to the black people who put them there.

One of the things I give credit to Joe Reed for is that he understood early that there were some times and places that you couldn't do much in the way of public endorsements because, again, it's a matter of counting votes. Sometimes you kept your endorsement quiet where it helped and you made it public where it helped.

As a result of these new relationships, the black community benefited in ways that they had not benefited before. They began to see improvements like deputy registrars, redistricting, healthcare, and better schools.

JOE REED: We fought every inch for civil rights changes, but I knew from the beginning that we had to play the cards that were dealt at that time. I knew that demands without pragmatism were not going to produce immediate results. Entrenched white society was not going to be bullied into giving up or sharing power.

But I also knew that there were white politicians who truly wanted to institute good government policies and to do right by their black constituencies. Their hands were often tied as well as ours.

Thus we were not going to be successful if every dollar they sent to Alabama State, every redistricting plan that favored blacks, and every black federal judge appointed to the bench made the front pages of the newspapers. No, that is not how moderate politicians at that time in that moment would be successful, as measured by getting reelected. Black and white activists had to put themselves in the shoes of a politician. They had to understand the limits of a politician seeking to move the South forward. They also had to put themselves in the mindset of many whites who felt threatened by the changing South.

I remember occasions when politicians with a favorable record towards issues we supported would be quietly applauded in the background. Senator Howell Heflin is an example. If I had spread the word that Heflin and others had supported issues advocated by the ADC, there would likely have been a backlash. They might have lost the election or not gotten re-elected.

Stanberry: How did you get along with white politicians during that period, Dr. Reed? What did they think about you or say to you?

Joe Reed: For those politicians who knew me, I think our relations were good. They knew me to be fair and knew that my word was good and that I wouldn't insult them.

For example, I once went to ask Governor George Wallace for $15 million for the construction of a building at Alabama State University. The project had been on hold for eight years due to lack of funds. So I approached Wallace and asked for help. He said, "You know Joe, even though you publicly disagree with me, you have never been nasty towards me. You criticize me a lot, but you were never nasty." And we got the money.

Stanberry: Can you give us another specific example of dealing quietly, practically, and biracially with a white official?

Joe Reed: Yes, I can. During the bitter years of the civil rights movement, Jimmy Clark had been chair of the Alabama Sovereignty Commission which spied on blacks in the 1960s. Later on, in the 1980s, when we successfully pushed for equitable representation, House Speaker Clark's legislative district was on the list of those to be carved up in court-ordered reapportionment.

Clark exercised great power in the white-dominated legislature, but black litigants—under my direction—had controlling influence with the U.S. Justice Department, which had to approve any redistricting effort.

So I went to him and said, "Tell me what you want." Clark's response was, "I don't want my home county cut up." I said, "OK, I will keep Barbour County whole." After we redrew the entire state to get our share of the seats, I went back to Clark and said, "Mr. Speaker, I gave you all of Barbour County and part of Henry County." And he said, "Well, Joe, that's a fine plan."

My point is that I didn't go there to try to kill him off. If I saved him, then I would save myself. This case just demonstrates that biracial politics during that period was simply trying to understand the other person's plight and working something out.

Stanberry: Dr. Hubbert, you and Dr. Reed worked closely together at the helm of the AEA during those years, making it difficult for you to separate yourself from the actions of the black organizations. I remember your run for governor in 1990, and there were political ads targeting you and Reed. Did your relationship with Reed help or harm you in your campaign?

Paul Hubbert: I publicly sought and the ADC publicly gave me their endorsement for governor in 1990. As I mentioned earlier, there had long been a racist mentality perpetuated by Southern segregationists. This sentiment carried over to my election where they basically labeled me as a liberal integrationist. I was not successful in winning the statewide office, so I guess I wasn't a very good "stealth politician."

Stanberry: Let's move on to ADC's longtime field director, Jerome Gray, who was involved in numerous specific actions reflecting stealthy politicking during that period. Mr. Gray, would you recite for our roundtable some of those negotiations and accomplishments in "quiet, practical, biracial politics?"

JEROME GRAY: Sure. As I have communicated to you in various documents, the following cases all reflected certain aspects of "stealth politics."

In the 1970s, ADC asked and got commitments from candidates Jimmy Carter, Howell Heflin, and Donald Stewart that if they got elected they would support the appointment of black federal judges in Alabama. The evidence shows that they cooperated and kept their word to the black community.

We negotiated with cooperative white state legislators to pass 1978 legislation opening the door for appointment of deputy registrars, who could then register black voters. This act was important for us because it opened up the dialogue between elected officials, appointed officials, and black citizens groups around the issue of voters assisting in the act of voter registration.

We worked with Senator Heflin in support of extension of the Voting Rights Act in 1982. Senator Heflin let us know that he might vote for some of the weakening amendments that might be put forth by the opponents, which were destined to fail. However, when the final important votes were cast, Heflin may have been the only deep South senator to vote for the extension of the Voting Rights Act.

We collaborated with black state representative Fred Horn and white state senator John Teague in 1983 to pass legislation virtually requiring the appointment of black deputy voter registrars in Alabama. Although the bill was essentially about bringing uniformity to the voter reidentification and purge process, we used this opportunity, through our stealth collaborators, to include a landmark provision in this bill that said that "boards of registrars shall appoint one or more deputy registrars in each precinct in the county for a four-year term, running concurrently with members of board of registrars."

We achieved considerable success during the 1980s and 1990s in getting many majority-white governmental entities throughout the state to voluntarily change historically discriminatory systems for electing local leadership.

Through quiet and practical negotiations, we succeeded in convincing a number of officials to cooperate in these changes. In fact, in many of the settlement agreements between black plaintiffs and white elected officials in countless redistricting lawsuits at the local level, one of the novel, stealthy outcomes involved various affirmative "racial" enhancements which were not required to settle the lawsuit or to fix the Voting Rights Act violations.

STANBERRY: Dr. Arrington, let's talk some more about Birmingham. What can you share with us about biracial relationships in the 1970s, 1980s, and 1990s?

RICHARD ARRINGTON: My experiences in this arena were greatly influenced by the privilege I had at Miles College working as part of President Lucius Pitts's administration between 1960–70. I worked at his side and as his messenger in his quiet diplomacy of building bridges of biracial communication in a bitterly divided Birmingham. Biracial meetings were a violation of city ordinances, and he made Miles the place in Birmingham where biracial meetings and other quiet and courageous acts were carried out. Pitts built bridges between important corporate leaders and black community leaders.

STANBERRY: You also mentioned earlier the special role of churches.

RICHARD ARRINGTON: Yes, when I think back on that period in Birmingham, I think immediately of the black churches as well as Miles College. The black church was one of the few places where courageous white politicians seeking black support could go to meet quietly with black civic leaders.

STANBERRY: Who were some of the black and white leaders who engaged in stealthy politicking in Birmingham back then?

RICHARD ARRINGTON: Of course, Lucius Pitts was my primary mentor during the Miles days; but there were other key power brokers between the black and white communities of Birmingham. Some of the black leaders that come to mind were businessman A. G. Gaston, physician Dr. James Montgomery, and attorneys Arthur Shores and David Hood. Among the whites were [*Birmingham News* executive] Vincent Townsend and David Vann, councilman and later mayor. Shores and Hood, leaders of the Jefferson County Progressive Democratic Council, handpicked me to become one of the "insiders" of that group. We consulted with Alabama Democratic Party Chairman Robert Vance about black-white political strategies for the party. I have to give special credit to David Vann, who was always there working for biracial cooperation, sometimes openly and dangerously and sometimes behind the scenes. Liberal corporate leaders channeled funds through Vann to me and other black council candidates for our campaigns. He taught me more about city government than anyone else I can think of.

STANBERRY: Dr. Zippert, you were a critical player in the founding of a new organization, the Alabama New South Coalition, that began to assert major influence in the 1980s and is very powerful in contemporary political affairs. Can you tell us how that group got started?

CAROL ZIPPERT: There were some of us throughout the state who wanted to do things differently from the past, so we started meeting and formed our own organization in the 1980s. We really were not for any single person or against any other organization; we simply had a philosophy of broad progressive change and biracial, bipartisan approaches to problems in our communities.

STANBERRY: What made that philosophy different from what other black organizations were doing?

CAROL ZIPPERT: In the first place, we were interested in progress for everybody, not just African Americans. We had both blacks and whites among our members and we endorsed some Republicans as well as Democrats. I always considered the late Senator Michael Figures (Mobile) and Senator Hank Sanders (Selma) our "righteous leaders," because they constantly preached to us that we had to be inclusive and fair in whatever we did. Senator Sanders, for example, always told us in the Black Belt that we needed to be sure to give whites a say-so when we finally got majority control in a particular area; he insisted on drawing county commission and school board district lines to give white citizens rightful access to their government. And I remember Mayor Richard Arrington from Birmingham—who was our first statewide president and whom some considered our "Moses"—speaking softly yet eloquently about human rights rather than simply black rights.

STANBERRY: Who were some of the white leaders who came to the ANSC for help?

CAROL ZIPPERT: I remember that most major state leaders, like Senator Howell Heflin, always came to our conferences, as did many other candidates and local politicians. But mainly, I remember Don Siegelman, who ran so many times for so many offices that he almost lived with us. He came to our meetings, he came to our churches, he came to everything. And he didn't just talk, he listened. He seemed sincere in wanting to represent all the people. We supported him faithfully for most of his career because we knew him and trusted him. Of course, we did not support him in his last race. As much as I loved Don as a bridge-builder, we felt like he had been taking African Americans for granted, so we endorsed Lucy Baxley for governor in 2006.

STANBERRY: What did you ask from these white leaders? And what did you offer to them?

CAROL ZIPPERT: I don't like to talk about these things as quid pro quo trading. Of course, we were always interested in fair appointments to positions like voter registrars and judgeships. We did not ask for special treatment, but we wanted them to open doors that had always been closed to blacks. We wanted qualified citizens to be considered regardless of color.

What did we offer? We always considered it a matter of trust. We extended our votes to white politicians who we felt we could trust to do what was right for everybody.

Howell Heflin's Service in Alabama and Washington Politics

STANBERRY: Howell Heflin served as Alabama Supreme Court Chief Justice, 1971–77, and as U.S. Senator, 1979–97. Since we have designated "the Judge" as our trailblazing model of stealth leadership for the period under study, we would like to talk further about his biracial politics in Alabama and Washington.

Mr. House, you helped Heflin win his early elections in Alabama and served as his top aide while he was chief justice of the Alabama Supreme Court, and you went with him as his chief of staff in Washington. How would you characterize his leadership?

MIKE HOUSE: Howell Heflin's leadership—whether "stealthy" or otherwise—has to be viewed within the framework of his basic philosophical and political character. One thing I always understood about the Judge is that he was a great believer in equal rights for all people. He knew how far he could push that agenda in Alabama and knew that quiet pragmatism was the most successful way to achieve lasting results.

STANBERRY: Can you give us an example of Heflin's "stealthy politics" in his early days as an Alabama jurist?

MIKE HOUSE: Yes. Something that was very important but that is rarely mentioned is his work to reform the Alabama Constitution through passage of the judicial article amendment in the 1970s. Heflin knew that this was not only needed and good for the state, but especially important to the black community in places like the Black Belt, where the local court system was weighted against them. Many blacks worked in the Citizens Conference on State Courts and the ensuing campaign for ratification. Heflin made it a point to include them. They understood the significance of this reform. He didn't say much about it, but he and I had many conversations about what it meant in those rural counties in particular. This reform represented structural and long-term racial progress, not simply politics-as-usual in Alabama.

STANBERRY: Mr. Raby, you served as Heflin's chief of staff for a decade in Washington. Can you cite some examples of Heflin's "quiet, practical, biracial leadership" in the U.S. Senate?

STEVE RABY: I remember several events in which the Judge, or our organization, would attempt to operate in "stealth" mode. As I've already mentioned, there were meetings with Reverend Jesse Jackson regarding legislative strategy on civil rights and voting rights bills and no photos were allowed. We established regular meetings with the Birmingham business community and Mayor Dick Arrington, with no public announcements or media coverage.

Also, without publicity, Senator Heflin amended the farm bill during consideration by the Senate Agriculture Committee to include Tuskegee University as part of the 1890 Land Grant system.

Senator Heflin had several personal conversations with Senator Kennedy after which Kennedy sponsored some amendments for us on controversial bills. I also remember Senator Heflin once asked Senator Bob Dole to stop giving him credit for the compromise on extension of the Voting Rights Act.

STANBERRY: How did Heflin keep the support of conservative Alabamians while promoting such biracial progress at the national level?

STEVE RABY: Senator Heflin recognized that there was a lot of opposition to liberal change among Alabamians as part of their Southern tradition or heritage. So he communicated often with these people. He assured them by words, actions, and deeds that he was an Alabamian who shared their conservative values, as those values relate to such things as God, prayer, patriotism, gun ownership, and a strong military. And his willingness to focus on legislative remedies for their economic interests distinguished him from the position a "liberal" would take. The Senator and the entire staff worked to demonstrate that he could advance their agenda without adverse action to the civil and basic economic rights of African Americans.

STANBERRY: How did that play out in specific situations?

STEVE RABY: The best example is our dealings with rural and agricultural groups that were traditionally conservative and might oppose efforts by the federal government on civil rights.

For example, the Alabama Farm Bureau (which became the Alabama Farmers Association) sometimes promoted the national Republican agenda and the elected leaders would talk to us about all sorts of national partisan issues such as abortion and Supreme Court nominations. But we worked so hard on critical agricultural issues that it was not easy for ALFA to label him as a liberal.

We also did the same thing on gun control. We had so many things going with the National Rifle Association—cosponsoring legislation, helping them get certain votes to the floor, and otherwise championing their cause—that, at crunch time, we could go to these groups to say that we moved to help on the issues important to them.

Then when some people in these groups would try to put us on the spot, the Judge would counter with a question of his own: "Do you want us to work to get the peanut quotas straight or do you want to talk about Robert Bork?" Or he'd ask, "You want us to look out for your right to keep your guns or to mess around with affirmative action?" In making ourselves accessible and invaluable to the membership on their base issues, it became more difficult for the leadership of some of these conservative organizations to convince their members to oppose us. The rank-and file would say "Leave Heflin alone, he's with us on what's really important."

STANBERRY: Dr. Reed, you sometimes cite Heflin as a good public official for all the people of Alabama. Tell us generally about your political relationship with him.

JOE REED: I always tried to respect Judge Heflin and his position and I never asked him to do anything that would hurt him politically. He did a good job, and he struck a good balance to help everyone. If you'll read his memoirs, you'll understand why I said he was the only senator from Alabama that blacks have ever had.

STANBERRY: Dr. Arrington?

RICHARD ARRINGTON: Joe Reed and I, along with some others (and with the backing of our political groups) quietly negotiated numerous racially sensitive political transactions—such as the first black federal judges—with Senator Heflin. He is one of the best examples of the promotion of racial tolerance and cooperation during that period.

STANBERRY: Several discussants have mentioned that the appointment of black judges was a priority for the African American community in Alabama. I am curious about the inside politicking on how these appointments came about?

JOE REED: Well, from my view, the efforts to appoint a black federal judge began in earnest with the late Senator John Sparkman. When he was running for the Senate seat, he contacted me and said he needed my help. We supported him and he went on to be elected. Later on, I approached him about the lack of black judges on the federal bench. I told him that blacks had supported him ever since he ran for office. I said, "Senator, you had to vote against us sometimes even when you didn't want to. You didn't vote for the voting rights bill. But the same people who you voted against, voted for you and helped you get elected." Sparkman agreed. And I said, "Well, you ought to leave us a legacy, and the legacy you can leave is the appointment of a black judge." He leaned back and said, "You know, you make your case well. I will see what I can do about that."

You see, it's the approach that is taken, I didn't go to his office demanding that he appoint a black judge. I went into his office asking him for a federal judge. Mr. Jim Pierce, a political scientist at Alabama State University, told me something a long time ago . . . that there are two ways to approach a Southern white man, one, you get another Southern white man to talk to him for you. The other way you do it is that you go to him and ask him and not tell him. That's not what I would do today, but that was the way it was back then.

The important development is that Senator Sparkman responded positively to our discreet initiative; and our other senator, Jim Allen, did the same at a later time, and we never publicized those conversations. Unfortunately, both of them left the Senate in 1978 before getting the nominations in order [Sparkman retired and Allen died in office]. But Heflin picked up on it. We worked closely with him from the beginning, and we got two black federal judges.

STANBERRY: Mr. House, you were there, in the "back rooms" when the matter of black federal judges was discussed in Judge Heflin's 1978 campaign for the open seat of retiring Senator John Sparkman. Give us your version of these dealings.

MIKE HOUSE: As for Joe Reed and Richard Arrington's characterizations, they are accurate. I remember the Alabama Democratic Conference meeting that Judge Heflin and I attended the night before the black endorsement in the 1978 campaign. We were the only white people in the room during that historic discussion with Alabama's African American political leadership. They talked about U.S. Senator John Sparkman's comments and Jim Allen's support for two black judges on the federal bench. They asked Heflin what he thought. He said that it was right and fair and that, if elected, he would honor the commitment. This is interesting because no one in the white community knew anything about the promise from Alabama's previous senators about possible nomination of black federal judges. After his election to the U.S. Senate, Heflin and Senator Donald Stewart [who won the vacant Allen seat] nominated two blacks for judge appointments—U. W. Clemon and Fred Gray.

Both nominees ran into trouble in the Senate judiciary committee, where Heflin worked the committee hard. He was successful with U. W. Clemon, but he saw that Fred Gray would not make it. Fred asked for a special hearing. Heflin got that, but afterwards told Gray he wouldn't make it and he should pull out, which he did.

STANBERRY: I imagine Senator Heflin received much criticism because of these nominations?

MIKE HOUSE: The nominations were very controversial in Alabama, and the Republicans were after both of them; but Heflin and Stewart stuck to their guns.

When Fred Gray withdrew his nomination, the black community worried that Heflin would bow to political pressure from the white community and not appoint another black, but he stood firm and nominated Myron Thompson, a black attorney from Dothan. Judge Thompson was confirmed and still serves today.

Judge Heflin took a lot of hits because of these nominations, but he knew it was the right thing for him to do and he honored his word to the black leaders and the black community. He was tough and worked very hard to get both these judges through the process.

STANBERRY: Apparently there also were some late-developing problems holding up the nominations of U. W. Clemon and Myron Thompson, and Senator Heflin had to intercede with the Republicans. Is that right?

STEVE RABY: Yes. During the Carter administration, Heflin and Donald Stewart worked hard, together, to get the president's support for black judges in Alabama. But, after Carter's election defeat, Judiciary Committee Chairman Strom Thurmond announced that there would be a moratorium on the approval of new judges until after the Reagan administration took over, which would have killed the two black nominations. Because of Heflin's relationship with Thurmond, he was able to get the schedule changed and those judges were approved.

STANBERRY: Shifting the conversation slightly, it seems to me that Southern politicians didn't like reporters or cameras around when it came to sensitive or contentious negotiations on racial politics. How important was it for Senator Heflin to make sure that such situations stayed out of the public purview?

STEVE RABY: Heflin wanted to avoid public conflict for fear that the rhetoric would become so extreme that any efforts to find a compromise would be eliminated. Once, Jesse Jackson came to Heflin's Senate office during the discussion of a high-profile piece of legislation, with media and photographers in tow. Jackson was keen on meeting with reporters but had not been involved with behind-the-scenes work on that legislation. Heflin was always respectful to Jackson and invited him to visit his office, but he was aware that media attention would not necessarily bring about passage of legislation. I remember Senator Heflin came out and said, "Reverend, do you want my picture or do you want my help?"

STANBERRY: That story reminds me of my days in the congressional office. I was often impressed by the diversity of congressional staffs in both the Washington and district offices. Glen Browder had a diverse staff, including a black press secretary. Congressman Ronnie Shows (Mississippi) had blacks in leadership positions, including as chief of staff and district director. Congresswoman Eva Clayton (North Carolina), who was an African American with a district nearly equally divided between blacks and whites, hired both groups in key positions. What was the situation in the Heflin office?

STEVE RABY: Senator Heflin was determined to have his Senate staff "look like Alabama," in terms of African American staff members. He made the commitment, before it was asked of him. For at least ten years of his service in the Senate, two of the top three staff positions were African Americans, the legislative director and the office manager.

MIKE HOUSE: As Steve mentioned, Senator Heflin set out from day one to have a staff that had the same number of blacks as the population and prided himself on always having approximately 25 percent blacks on the staff, including some in leadership positions. We used to laugh and say that Ted Kennedy talked about civil rights, but we had more blacks on our staff than he did. Heflin didn't advertise it, but he took great pride in this accomplishment.

A Few Pointed Questions for Selected Discussants

STANBERRY: Let's wrap this discussion up with a few, more pointed and perhaps touchy questions about "stealth politics."

I'll start with you Dr. Reed. As you can imagine, some of my African American colleagues have problems with the notion of "stealth reconstruction." They consider these efforts as unacceptable compromise, a sell-out, regardless of whether it's done by whites and/or blacks in partnership. So I want to throw a hardball your way. Would you describe your relationship with white officials—like George Wallace—as "Uncle Tomism"?

JOE REED: For those who label this relationship as me playing the role of an Uncle Tom, I would say, "You don't know what you're talking about!" and move on. This wasn't "Uncle Tomism" because I was open with it. Everyone knew what I was doing and I can go back and look at the results of these activities. Look at how we persuaded Wallace to sign a bill allowing deputy registrars to register black people at any time anywhere in Alabama. And look at how many legislative seats we have now. And look at all the good laws that are on the books.

STANBERRY: Attorney Gray, you've got a particularly interesting history in this discussion. You were nominated for one of those two federal judge-ships in Alabama, but opposition killed your confirmation in the Senate. So, did "stealth reconstruction" not work in this situation?

FRED GRAY: Actually, if ever there was an example of "stealth reconstruction," then this was it. That was how Alabama got two African American judges on the federal judiciary. We negotiated in good faith with the U.S. Senators, and it was a real breakthrough in Southern politics.

Of course, it did not work out very well for my nomination, because a bunch of politicians didn't like what I had done on civil rights. That was a great disappointment for me, but, fortunately, everything turned out okay in the long run. I was able to continue some important civil rights projects and I got to see my family more than if I had been a federal judge.

STANBERRY: Next, Dr. Hubbert. In our recent office visit, you talked about the positive impacts of "stealth politics"—such as more minority representatives and progressive policies in public education, social welfare, etc. But you also expressed some concern about the side-effects of Alabama's new black influence in electoral politics. What downside were you talking about?

PAUL HUBBERT: I think there were uncertain developments during those years that would be very clear and somewhat troubling later on. For example, reapportionment redrew districts in such a way to accommodate certain groups, certain populations, who otherwise couldn't elect their own representatives. That was a positive advancement in policies and it greatly impacted the party system in Alabama. But, in doing so, we sometimes marginalized big blocs of African American citizens, thereby entrenching conservative districts that could not be influenced by moderates among the Democrats and Republicans.

Joe and I never really sat down to talk about this and one of these days we need to. He probably single-handedly had more impact on reapportionment to secure equitable representation than any one else in the state. But my question to him is this: "Did you gain more from that for the black community or did you lose from that?" Symbolically, it was a gain. Pragmatically, it may have been a loss because you now have twenty-seven black House members out of 105 and eight black senators out of thirty-five and they are in districts where a black can get elected over and over and over because of the way the district lines are drawn. So the result is that there's probably today fewer than a third of the whites who have to pay much attention to what the black agenda may be. What the African American community thinks is irrelevant to this group. This situation is not very encouraging for biracial relations of a progressive nature in contemporary politics. And maybe we need to address that situation sometime in the near future.

STANBERRY: Dr. Zippert, it seems that, amid all this positive talk about peace and justice and biracial partnership, the two races are still fighting like always in some locales and situations. For example, black-white feuding still rages in certain areas of the state, and especially in parts of the Black Belt. What's going on there?

CAROL ZIPPERT: If you're talking about Greene County, we've tried biracial partnership and it didn't work. The problem was that local whites just wanted to get back into office on the backs of black voters. The whites had a complex of "internalized privilege" and the blacks suffered from "internalized oppression." It's just hard to have any biracial partnership with whites insisting on being in charge and blacks not stepping up to their responsibilities; there's no real progress in such an environment.

But we haven't given up. We are continuing our appeal to fair, biracial community governance. For example, we formed the Black Belt Community Foundation several years ago; and now we have Governor Bob Riley's new Black Belt Action Commission. Through these efforts, we hope to find biracial solutions to the special problems of this area.

STANBERRY: Mr. Raby, I'm curious about something. If you folks did all this black-white partnering back then, why do you think nobody—neither the white politicians nor the black activists—has ever written or talked publicly about the important role and contributions of "stealth politics" in Alabama and Southern political history?

STEVE RABY: I guess we were uncomfortable, and maybe a little ashamed that the political landscape required "stealth politics." While we took some actions that were bold and positive for the times in changing Alabama, we obviously, for political reasons, couldn't talk about it then. Later, as the political environment progressed, our biracialism didn't really seem like much to brag about. We hadn't been villains, but we weren't full heroes either.

It may not seem like much today, but we did do some things under difficult circumstances back then that helped make our state a better place for everybody. So I'm glad that we can now bring all this stuff out into the open and acknowledge this important, constructive part of Southern politics and history.

STANBERRY: Before moving on to conclusions, I want to ask George Wallace Jr. to explain what he meant earlier when he cited our "sense of common humanity."

GEORGE WALLACE JR.: I have always believed that one of the big reasons some Southerners dealt with the new order after such traumatic early years was because of our common relationship with the land. Given that the South was an agricultural region, many blacks and whites had worked the land together and they came to understand each other in a way that was missing in other parts of the country.

I also think that much of our ability to come together was the manifestation of our strong Christian ethic and devotion to Christ's teachings. Therefore, when the fighting ran its course, we were prepared to seek and find our common humanity.

There are some of the intellectual elite who scoff at such notions, but it is true nevertheless.

Overall Assessment of Stealth Reconstruction

STANBERRY: Now, we need to conclude our discussion about the heretofore untold story of "stealth leadership, politics, and reconstruction." As we proceed in the twenty-first century, what's your closing comment about "quiet, practical, biracial politics" during the 1970s, 1980s, and 1990s? We'll go alphabetically, starting with Mayor Arrington.

RICHARD ARRINGTON: As I have previously said, I find the characterization of "stealth reconstruction" to be provocative, informative, and realistic. I believe that it would have been very difficult for the civil rights movement to have been as effective without the black-white cooperation discussed in this thesis.

JAMES DUNN: Well, I can say without question that things are very different now. It's not a hundred percent perfect because whites tend to be the money folks and blacks seem to be the poor folks. But because some black and white leaders decided to do things differently and better years ago, the two races now can sit down at the same table and work for what's good for the community.

FRED GRAY: I think that we accomplished a lot of good things through such biracial negotiations back then. As has been reported in this project, there's sound evidence for the thesis of "stealth leadership, politics, and reconstruction." We know about some of this progress, and some we may never know about. If young people today were to ask for my advice, I'd tell them that sometimes you have to do things in a variety of ways, in a mixture of approaches, and not always in the public arena. I've concentrated on the legal system mainly, but they should look at the law, politics, education, and other activities as important for racial progress. And they should conduct themselves, publicly and privately, to make a difference in society.

JEROME GRAY: We were able to achieve important objectives through what you call "stealth politics." We got black federal judges in Alabama; we helped push laws through the state legislature and Washington aiding black voter registration; and we worked with majority white governmental entities throughout the state to voluntarily change historically-discriminatory systems for electing local leadership. These things would not have happened back then except through stealthy politicking.

MIKE HOUSE: Howell Heflin knew that the best way to achieve real results in Alabama was to push his agenda with quiet pragmatism. The respect in which he was held by his colleagues from all political stripes made a big difference; he could broker situations even liberal politicians couldn't handle. And the black community trusted him, which allowed him to do some things others couldn't do in the way of biracial progress.

PAUL HUBBERT: "Stealth politics" brought together, in common acceptance and practice, some things that had previously not been accepted in the South. Of course, civil rights protests and federal laws allowed people to be able to sit where they wanted to, to go to school where they wanted to, and to spend money and eat where they wanted to. But I think it was stealth leaders of later years that kind of made it okay among Southern whites. It took the civil rights movement and later stealthy politics to transition us from a totally segregated society to a society that accepted the notion that people ought to be treated equally.

STEVE RABY: What was achieved through "stealth politics"? Senator Heflin genuinely believed that there should be racial progress, and I think he was instrumental in many of the changes that occurred. He truly believed that African Americans needed to see that they had leaders who represented them and their interests. It was a very conscious effort on his part to position us and our operation to work with other leaders in this capacity, in trying to keep some issues in the forefront that all people can see as helping all Alabamians in their lives. His approach assured that we continued to make progress without calling attention to the positive but more controversial aspects of our work.

JOE REED: Throughout history, and especially in the days following the civil rights movement, we worked quietly and effectively with white friends. [ADC]'s history has been marked by consistent, widespread support for hundreds of white candidates who have been sensitive to the needs of blacks and poor people. Quiet, practical, biracial politics was an important part of this history. We couldn't talk publicly about those relationships, but that was the only way we could accomplish anything during those times. In short, our organized network of voting members, coupled with civic pressure and "stealth politics," have brought about significant social change since the civil rights movement.

GEORGE WALLACE JR.: I think that stealthy interactions of the type we've discussed helped bring together black folks with whites of good will and dedication of purpose to help improve their lives. I like to think that this combination of principle and politics reflected the best within Southerners of both races. The examples cited here were what our people needed in order to build bridges for the transformation that was occurring all around us. Alabama and our nation are better because of their service.

CAROL ZIPPERT: I'm still uneasy about calling the changes of that period a "reconstruction"; and I'm unsatisfied about the amount and extent of racial progress. But I cannot deny that biracial coalitions helped get progressive whites into office during that period and there were some positive developments. I don't know what the future holds, but we haven't given up. Young Alabamians and other Americans have got to figure out how to achieve real biracial progress beyond the unsavory aspects and connotations of "stealth politics."

Moderator's Summation

STANBERRY: It is now my assignment—as co-author and moderator—to ask: "What have we learned from this virtual roundtable discussion?"

The leaders participating in the discussion have shed much light on the pragmatic aspects of our thesis of stealth leadership, politics, and reconstruction. Through their eyes and voices we are able to witness quiet, practical, biracial attempts by politicians and activists to find real ways to make government more accessible and responsive to all people during the 1970s, 1980s, and 1990s.

Our conversation here has provided interesting follow-up to the experiences of Richmond Flowers and Carl Elliott immediately following the civil rights movement. They both openly courted, campaigned for, and took pride in their association with the black vote. They lost miserably, Lurleen Wallace won, and other progressive white would-be office-holders learned their lesson from this experience: the time was too soon to openly campaign on racial inclusion. One either operated on practicalized principle, or watched from the sidelines as others took the reigns of government. To quote again from Flowers on his miscalculation of the Alabama political situation:

> That was my biggest disappointment in politics. When I ran for governor, I was thoroughly confident. My polls had told me, with the black vote I was going to receive, I could win with a small percent of the whites. That's one time I was completely wrong. I took a calculated risk and lost. I thought I had it figured, but I didn't . . . I guess I should have kept talking about the Southern Way of Life.[1]

In performing such practical service, white officials had to placate their majority-white electorate by maintaining conservative traditional values, such as the right to bear arms, while also pursuing social justice for their black constituents. Many of the comments made by the roundtable participants replicated the sentiments and activities of Howell Heflin, Glen Browder, and the participants in the congressional survey.

Moreover, it is clear to me as a political scientist that black leaders and activists had to accept the realities of the situation while ever pressing for more progress than the white establishment would accede. For example, the common thread throughout that period is that black leaders practically targeted and achieved partial and incremental victories in the face of broad white political resistance. It was simply too soon to expect that a long-entrenched racial caste system and political and social attitudes would disappear overnight.

Speaking more personally—as a young African American and native Alabamian who did not experience the Old South or the civil rights movement—I find this candid discussion intriguing and insightful. I must admit that, like many contemporary black citizens, I harbor mixed, normative feelings about the biracial politics of that period. However, I also have to admit that this discussion has strengthened my belief that these leaders set a constructive course for the South during the 1970s, 1980s, and 1990s.

Particularly interesting is hearing bona fide veterans of the civil rights movement talk positively about stealth reconstruction. Some may believe that our thesis undermines the struggles of icons like Rosa Parks and Martin Luther King Jr.; to the contrary, this discussion supplements the civil rights movement. These remarks demonstrate that it took a comprehensive effort—including battles fought in the streets, in the courtrooms, in the political trenches, and in the corridors of public power—to bring white politicians and black activists together for progressive change in a unique period of regional and national history.

Consider the integrated and developmental narrative of our discussants.

It is important to note, at the outset, the remarks of Commissioner James "Pappy" Dunn, whose adult life spans a great portion of twentieth century Southern history. He said that prior to the civil rights movement, blacks and whites never worked together because whites took advantage of blacks and blacks did not have the resources to fight them. The strategic use of the black vote to support friendly officials and to throw unfriendly politicians out of office cannot be overestimated.

Dr. Paul Hubbert also stated that the post-civil rights era brought about a need for leaders of both races to institutionalize the gains of the civil rights movement. Only because some practical black leaders took a measured, cautious approach to responsive white politicians did the South begin its quiet transition from the movement to biracial politics and progress.

As Dr. Joe Reed said, blacks have always had to fight for any racial gains, and none of the political changes during this era came easily. But little would have happened without stealth politics. He credited black organization and civic demands—mainly through the Alabama Democratic Conference—for more progressive public policies; but he also said that blacks needed white allies in the political system. Obviously, blacks could not shout from the mountaintop about the work of relatively progressive white leaders, because white constituents likely would have thrown these politicians out of office.

According to Jerome Gray, such quiet, practical biracial efforts as designating blacks as deputy voter registrars, influencing key figures to create majority-minority districts, and furthering the appointment of black federal judges gave African Americans the confidence and resources to exercise their rights within the system. Furthermore, he said, biracial negotiations not only produced fairer public policies but also resulted in good-faith accommodations in local governance that went beyond the requirements of the law.

Moreover, we cannot overlook how Dr. Richard Arrington became the first black mayor of Birmingham. Arrington has reminded us that there were ordinances in place that made it illegal for blacks and whites to meet in Birmingham in the 1960s, so white leaders often were invited to black schools and churches for discreet conversations. By his own admission, his election to the city council and mayor's office could not have happened without quiet, biracial coalitions that set the tone for a new day in that city.

We should remember, too, the expansive and challenging approach articulated by Dr. Carrol Zippert. She, along with Hank Sanders, Arrington, and the late Michael Figures, formed the Alabama New South Coalition to emphasize broad human rights as well as the election of friendly white officials or even black politicians. As she admonished during this conversation, there are still many pockets of poverty and discrimination, so we should not ignore her continuing plea for full equality—political, economic, and social—along the lines preached by Fannie Lou Hamer.

Nor should we African Americans forget the personal responsiveness of some white Southern leaders. George Wallace Jr. referred, for example, to "our common humanity" in the South's willingness, finally, to accept change. Mike House talked about Judge Heflin's advancing equal rights with "quiet pragmatism" and "real progress"; and Steve Raby admitted that "it may not seem like much today, but we did do some things under difficult circumstances back then that helped make our state a better place for everybody." These remarks by white participants, taken in concert with those of our black discussants, present a full and rich elaboration of politics of that era.

No one put this discussion into more direct and moving perspective for me than did attorney Fred Gray, who was there in the beginning with Mrs. Parks and Dr. King and is still fighting the good fight for civil rights. Gray noted that, in the years during and immediately after the movement, most white politicians and black leaders didn't even talk to each other; and the white political structure would not go beyond what the courts ordered. Also, as our research has shown, the federal government wasn't pushing Southerners forward with any real deliberate speed. Gray said, without reservation or recrimination, that it took a lot of different elements—including cooperative political arrangements with white Southern politicians—to further the goals of racial justice. Not surprisingly, he urges young people today to continue the pursuit of civil rights through a variety of legal, political, educational, and other approaches.

So our virtual roundtable discussion tells us that, as the civil rights movement struggled in the 1970s, well-meaning people could either wait, seemingly forever, while the established white Southern power structure dithered with legal wranglings, or they could step up to the plate and do something differently on their own. Fortunately, even in the deepest and most segregated parts of the South, some like-minded blacks and whites were willing to take risks to bring about progress.

Malcolm X strongly admonished black people to join together, in blunt electoral action, to change an unresponsive political order. He said: "Whenever a group can vote in a bloc, and decide the outcome of elections and it fails to do this, then that group is politically sick."[2] He noted that immigrants once made Tammany Hall the most powerful force in American politics: New York City elected its first Irish Catholic mayor in 1880, and by the 1960s, America had its first Irish Catholic president. "America's black man, voting as a bloc," he predicted, "would wield an even more powerful force."[3] The Voting Rights Act helped to eliminate barriers hindering black voter registration in the South, and black leaders like the participants in this discussion helped move those voters in the direction envisioned by Malcolm X. They strategically used the bloc vote to negotiate changes for the black community in this part of the country.

The changes were not satisfactory to all involved, for there is still much room for progress in the South in specific and in the nation in general. But at a time when it was still popular to be against the federal government and "outside agitators" imposing their might on the South, the strategic use of the black vote and the earnest attempts by stealthy white officials and black activists to impact positive change in a new direction certainly had a lasting impact on the South.

Southern black and white leaders of that time figured out how to be strategic, effective, and relatively progressive. While some may be uncomfortable with the quiet, back-room dealing of politics, the words from the mouths of these diverse participants go a long way in demonstrating what happened in the South to help bring about lasting change.

Bringing this chapter to a close, therefore, is an easy assignment. Undoubtedly, our roundtable participants would disagree among themselves about specific aspects of race relations during that period. However, we conclude that this virtual discussion has generally affirmed our original hypothesis. These testimonials—from both black and white activists and operatives who conducted biracial politics back then—support the Browder case study and the congressional survey; and all three original research efforts in this project provide convincing argument and evidence for the stealth thesis. In summary, the Southern political system was reconstructed, to a significant degree and in supplementary manner, through the quiet leadership and biracial politics of practical politicians and activists during the 1970s, 1980s, and 1990s.

9

SUMMARY: THE PAST, THE PRESENT, AND A CHALLENGE FOR CONTEMPORARY LEADERS

We conclude with a general overview of the project, specific elaboration on the past, some speculative remarks about the present, and a pointed challenge for today's leaders.

Political Reality and Historical Significance

To begin, our case study, survey, and roundtable discussion suggest several conclusions about the new stealth thesis.

First, we stated in the introduction that it has been common for scholars of Southern history to fixate on the civil rights movement of the 1950s and 1960s, or to focus only on remarkable development in various "New Souths" since the movement. There has been a tendency to slight moderate politicians and real Southern politics of the past half-century as historical irrelevancies in the "dramatic" story of Southern change.

Secondly, our thesis proposed new, alternative ideas about recent Southern history, and our conceptual model delineated some important elements of changing politics during that time. We proposed that during the 1970s, 1980s, and 1990s, some leaders in the South (particularly white Democratic politicians and their black allies) practiced a new kind of quiet, practical, biracial leadership—or "stealth politics"—that helped change their region significantly. For a variety of personal and political reasons, they tried in their electoral campaigns and public service to address minority black interests without overly antagonizing the white majority. We did not claim to have found "the" single most important or best agent of change, but we insisted that our stealth alliances represented much more than flaccid, irrelevant, opportunism. We contended that stealth leaders functionally took up where the movement seemingly waned; they contributed to the evolving civil rights struggle and helped reconstruct Southern politics through the end of the century. We also proposed that their collective action merits inclusion among the more prominent explanations of Southern change.

Thirdly, our case study, survey, and roundtable discussion attempted to obtain evidence for the stealth thesis. We note with interest here that while most of our black and white project participants eagerly welcomed the opportunity to discuss this aspect of their careers, some were awkward, uncomfortable, and hesitant in talking about the stealth phenomenon. A few political veterans were sensitive about the idea that they had cut biracial deals for their own advantage during that difficult time in Southern political history. Others resented any insinuation that whites were claiming credit for civil rights gains or that blacks had compromised their commitment to racial justice. Academic friends cautioned about the substantive, methodological, and normative pitfalls of such inquiry. However, almost all those that we approached for this project agreed, upon reflection, that this is an important, heretofore unknown part of the story of Southern politics and history.

The leaders who participated in this study and follow-up discussion provided sound testimony for our *a priori* modeling of stealth politics. They either acknowledged outright their stealthy nature or provided indirect indication of quiet, practical, biracialism; and they fleshed out their stealthy pursuit of relatively moderate and progressive objectives with interesting remarks, insights, and anecdotes.

Co-author Glen Browder, for example, talked at length and in detail about his thinking and actions as "A New Kind of Leader" during his successful political career. He presented a clear picture of pursuing an openly civic agenda while practicing stealthy racial leadership and politics. The Browder Collection furnished documentary evidence for his contentions, and the public record corresponded to the basic proposition.

Browder's former congressional colleagues supplied survey support for the stealth thesis. While their perspectives were sometimes less structured and precise than our theoretical construct, these moderate white politicians from other Southern states met the objective, quantifiable standards of the stealth model, and they themselves reported practicing a politics of quiet, practical, biracial leadership. They also generally believed that their service helped change politics in their areas.

Perhaps the most convincing articulation of stealth reconstruction came not from white politicians but from a biracial group of activists and operatives of post-movement politics. Leading black and white veterans who had participated in the racial adjustments of that period acknowledged stealthy politics as both a reality and a requirement for the times. For the most part, these civil rights icons and practicing politicos endorsed the stealth thesis and added their own testimony to that of Browder and his congressional colleagues.

In sum, we found that these inside players collectively and substantially contributed to the moderation and normalization of regional politics by writing an unheroic but critical chapter—"Stealth Reconstruction"—in the long, arduous, evolving story of Southern systemic progress. This biracial alliance quite often succeeded—as our case study, survey, and roundtable discussion show—in facilitating black participation and producing successful candidates and moderate public officials. The stealth campaigns observed in this project utilized personal relationships, organizational endorsements, and get-out-the-vote efforts run mainly through black churches, civil rights groups, and their networks; these endeavors were supported financially by various white candidates, the party organizations, and their associated interest groups. Our survey and roundtable discussion showed varying perspectives and some important disagreements in the stealthy relationship; however, overall, the evidence presented here suggests that the biracial alliance encouraged more progressive public dialogue, policy initiatives, voting records, hiring practices, and constituency services.

Stealth leaders and activists did not accomplish enough change to satisfy most Southern blacks, nor did they please resistant Southern whites. Obviously, based on the roundtable discussion, stealthy race-gaming was never an easy ride for either side of the arrangement. However, whether judged through the leaders' personal, retrospective assessments or the public record of official history, the South changed reconstructively during their stealthy service. We conclude that the stealth leaders helped moderate the tone of regional public discourse, helped promote the normalization of Southern politics, and helped end racist vestiges of Old South governance. Thus we consider "stealth reconstruction" a real and significant part of Southern political history.

We believe, furthermore, that our research may and should impact the study and practice of Southern politics. The idea that quiet, practical, biracial relations might figure into Southern political life of that time is not a shocking revelation; what is striking is the fact that such a critical aspect of history has been virtually absent—perhaps due to normative, theoretical, and methodological reasons—from conventional scholarship and acceptable political discussion. Our project attests to this heretofore untold story of Southern political history. Henceforth, in our opinion, no account of regional development will be complete or valid without considering the contributive element of stealth politics. It is impossible to understand or explain what happened over the past half-century simply by celebrating the heroic drama, recounting selected narratives, and describing contemporary political patterns as direct derivatives of the movement. We also are convinced that future progress in this region, and nationally, depends upon some similarly inspired version of racial action. Whether in Montgomery or Washington or anywhere else in this nation, progressive leaders must practice a politics that skillfully and realistically builds on common democratic values without unduly aggravating past sins and grievances. We hope that the stealth project will encourage full exploration of this "new history" of Southern politics, and we would be pleased indeed if it facilitated constructive public discourse about the role of race in the "Great Experiment" of American democracy.

In addition to these general observations about our stealth thesis and research, we think it appropriate, in the remaining paragraphs of this book, to elaborate on the past, speculate about the present, and offer some challenges to contemporary scholars, journalists, and public officials.

Elaboration on the Past

(1) Besides generally supporting our thesis about the "untold story" of Southern politics and history, this project emphasized the diversity of constituency situations and leadership styles among Southern politicians of that time. We were not surprised that their districts varied in terms of the size of their black constituencies and that they had widely ranging civil rights support scores. What was interesting was their individualized approach to dealing with racial factors. About half acknowledged their stealthness; the other half quibbled with this terminology but likewise pursued biracial leadership in quiet, practical manner. A few practiced a fairly open style of biracial politics, without regard for electoral ramifications.

(2) Our research also generated a historical finding that we had not really considered but that made interesting logic. Apparently, stealth leadership and politics unfolded in three distinct stages of the "race game" in Southern politics. The early pattern of stealthy race-gaming was one in which stealthy politicians considered the white, conservative, mainstream constituency within the Democratic Party as their major concern; blacks were cooperative partners and Republicans were relatively unimportant. Later, stealth leaders increasingly had to deal with assertive blacks in the primary and formidable Republicans in the general election. Finally, as Southern politics moderated toward the end of the century, stealth leadership dissipated.

(3) Another interesting aspect of this historic transformation was that there often were two functionally distinct, semi-segregated electoral campaigns in Democratic Party politics: the formal, moderate, mainstream campaign directed at white voters, as usually depicted in news media and academic research; and an informal, relatively progressive, black campaign (low-profile, somewhat secretive, sometimes uncomfortable, oftentimes less-than-noble operations) designed to maximize black support/influence without alienating white society.

(4) As the stealth campaign extended into actual governance, successful biracial politicians embarked on less segregated but equally tricky public service. These leaders generally attempted more moderate courses with constructive modification of Southern political style; they articulated a populist philosophy of "representing everybody," "helping folks," and "traditional

values"—in keeping with their majority white constituency—which also allowed them to look out for the special needs and wishes of their black electorates.

(5) Our unconventional research into Southern politics of the 1970s, 1980s, and 1990s also led us to the discovery of an equally interesting development at the end of the twentieth century. "Stealth Reconstruction" has transitioned into a "New Racial Politics" of open, sophisticated, functional, but sometimes cynical race relations—a halfway house of neo-racial politics. In some ways, for many black and white Southerners, this new stage of regional public life is a real step forward; however, in other ways, especially from the perspective of progressive natives and incredulous outsiders, it is simply the same, old, racialized politics of a still peculiar and ever-reddening part of the country.

Speculation about the Present

(6) However the Southern drama unfolds in the future, we are confident that the heyday of stealth politics is over. The South was substantially reconstructed, in terms of institutional perversity and contortion, during the 1970s, 1980s, and 1990s; and a different brand of black-white relations—the neo-racial practice of open, sophisticated politics absent flagrant racism—seems to have taken hold in this century. More importantly, the South has been undergoing systemic political transformation—a rational regional alignment with national politics—as the white majority generally inclines toward the Republicans and the black minority aligns overwhelmingly with Democrats, in a logical normalization of politics similar to that of the rest of the nation. In this process of rational nationalization, both Southern politics and American democracy are being transformed systemically. Stealth leaders and black activists helped transform Southern politics in their day; but, as we will explain in the next few paragraphs, there would be little opportunity or demand for their service in the transforming system of the twenty-first century.

(7) In this new century, race still exercises important impact; most notably, there has been further proliferation of black elected officials and white movement toward the Republican Party. But Southern politics in the new

century also has changed in ways that have generally normalized and will increasingly mitigate the role of black voters, as a bloc, in the region. For a variety of reasons (such as more intense campaign practices and media attention), the stealth aspect of Southern politics no longer works as it did just a few years ago—particularly for Democrats. It is much more difficult for white politicians to conduct opportunistic dual campaigns, surreptitiously soliciting black support in the primary and then attracting white voters in the general election. Black activists increasingly flex their muscles in the Democratic primary, but they have not expanded their influence into the Republican Party, and they cannot automatically tilt the balance of power in general elections. Except in those areas with majority-minority concentrations, black influence is becoming more diffuse and sometimes less consequential in contemporary political life.

(8) Arguably, there's no great need for stealth politics as the Southern system operates more openly and moderately in relatively sophisticated manner. Partisans can debate the politics of the matter, but these developments seem to be a unique, functional, and sometimes healthy strategic adjustment for a South charting its course according to conventional cultural, economic, and political bases rather than historical perversities and contortions of race. Semi-stealth politics probably will persist in some manner; however, the official party organizations and mainstream media, assisted by professional campaign entities, increasingly will assume the functions of traditionally separate and different black operations.

(9) Future elections and policy-making in the South will occur on a case-by-case basis, in a two-party system, in a relatively transparent environment. Furthermore, the prospects are favorable for the Republicans in most of the region. Democrats will continue to be competitive in some races, in some areas, in some years; and blacks will have to figure out how to function constructively within the Democratic primary in some situations and how to develop influence in the general election otherwise.

(10) Twenty-first century Southern politics thus will take place within the usual interplay of racial, cultural, economic, and political factors in more open debate and more normalized, nationalized elections (although old-style Southern politics will occur sporadically in areas still burdened

with demographic and historical tension). Overall, the South likely will experience a more biracial and moderate leadership than in the past. Its participation in national politics will be more akin to practices in the rest of the country—but also likely is a less progressive politics than many had predicted, hoped for, or feared during the transformational era.

A Challenge for Contemporary Leaders

(11) It is clear that, between the civil rights movement and the election of President Barack Obama, the South and America have changed dramatically. However, if we have learned anything from this exercise, it is that, as much as Southern political practices have moderated, racial attitudes and biracial community have lagged behind. This region and the nation have a long way to go in the struggle for racial justice and democracy. African Americans are still not fairly represented descriptively or substantively; and clearly there is need for more meaningful participation in all forums of power and government.

(12) We also have learned that biracial leadership is both essential and very, very difficult. Actually, we ourselves have come to realize—even as close personal friends and professional colleagues—our own differing racial experiences and ideas about representation. However, we are convinced that the needs of black citizens will not be met by black officials alone, nor will the needs of white citizens be met by white officials alone. Unfortunately, within the current debate, the legitimate pursuit of greater black representation could reach its descriptive maximum with a racially segregating impact on society as a whole, a situation which probably would leave the minority far short of substantive representation and certainly without the full benefits of American democracy. There simply are geographical and statistical limits to the corrective strategy of race-defined districts; and we desperately need to seek open, alternative reconstruction of our elections and governance so that whites and blacks can represent diverse constituencies.

(13) Of course, such leadership is not possible everywhere. It appears that whether biracial leadership will work in an area depends on a complex combination of social, cultural, and political factors—especially the "racial

context" of that area and forum. We have found, furthermore, that racial dysfunction is no longer a simple case of whites misrepresenting blacks; some areas of African American dominance now witness ugly black politicking much akin to that of white racism in the Old South. The area's history, the racial mix of its citizenry, the number and race of competing candidates, the partisan environment, the electoral-representational arrangement, all these and other variables fit somehow into the calculation—and it's not always a neat and clean fit.

(14) Scholars and journalists should lead the way in expanding their focus beyond the civil rights movement. Included in that assignment is exploring anew the phenomenon of representation for discernable, constructive insights about biracial leadership and racial justice. They should follow up our project to ascertain the validity of our thesis; and they should attempt to determine whether our ideas have pertinence to other offices, levels, and areas. They should consider not only whites representing blacks, as in our case study, but blacks representing whites (and include Republicans in the mix). They should expand their re-thinking to other racial and cultural groups that are coming into play. Most importantly, scholars and journalists will have to sketch the practicalities as well as dramatic aspects of "big picture" Southern politics for future practitioners of our version of American democracy.

(15) For public officials and political leaders interested in pursuing "big picture visions" of progressive regional democracy in the twenty-first century, this discussion has serious ramifications. Some settings and contexts may decree that the representative will be one race or another; the politics of those areas may require dramatic strategies of black-white struggle. However, it seems from simple observation of the Southern political landscape that there are just as many areas and opportunities for meaningful, biracial progress as for the less inspiring practice of blatant race representation. Also, as our country becomes more diverse, we will have to think multiculturally rather than racially or even biracially, and we will have to be even more creative in dealing with the challenges of representation. If some Southern white politicians and black activists—despite their shared legacy of hard history and raw relationships—could

move their communities along a practical, moderate course during the 1970s, 1980s, and 1990s, then surely so can other leaders today.

Conclusion

To conclude, we think that our unconventional stealth thesis and original research add valuable context and information, heretofore privy to those intimately involved, about the drama of the civil rights movement and the subsequent, evolving transformation of Southern politics. Our stealthy biracial leaders—both white and black—assisted in the translation of raw racial confrontation into practical politics of campaigning and governing in the South; they therefore played important roles in America's ever-changing "Great Experiment."

In a way, our research simply confirms regionally what we've always known about the expansion of American democracy. Throughout our country's history, various societal subcultures have moved into the political mainstream through a combination of raw, dramatic pressure and the sensitive, circumspect, and sometimes unsavory machinations of practical politicians. Our findings evidence, in new fashion, the biracial relationships and unheroic dealings among officials and activists as they tried to address—with quiet, significant success—the difficult dilemma that had long bedeviled their fellow Southerners.

This is our story of "Stealth Reconstruction" in the South. We suspect that our controversial thesis and research characterize important transformational history in various communities and forums in the region; and we hope that this discussion provides valuable insights for future progress here and throughout the American nation.

∾

NOTES

Introduction

1   The reader will appreciate the impossibility of referencing every source for all aspects of this common vision for our project. For representative perspective and substance, consult the following sources: Taylor Branch's three-volume exploration of the civil rights movement, *Parting the Waters, Pillar of Fire*, and *At Canaan's Edge*; William H. Chafe, *Civilities and Civil Rights*; David L. Chappell, *Inside Agitators*; Charles W. Eagles, *The Civil Rights Movement in America*; David J. Garrow, *Bearing the Cross*; Clayborne Carson, *The Autobiography of Martin Luther King, Jr.*; John Lewis and Michael D'Orso, *Walking with the Wind*; Manning Marable, *Race, Reform and Rebellion*; Diane McWhorter, *Carry Me Home*; Rosa Parks, with Jim Haskins, *Rosa Parks: My Story*; Gene Roberts and Hank Klibanoff, *The Race Beat*; and J. Mills Thornton, III, *Dividing Lines*.

2   Stephan Lesher, *George Wallace*, 174.

3   Martin Luther King, Jr., *The Words of Martin Luther King, Jr.*, 95.

4   For recent, representative revisioning of Southern politics, see the following newspaper stories, listed chronologically: Shaila Dewan, "Southern Blacks Are Split On Clinton vs. Obama"; Patricia Cohen, "Interpreting Some Overlooked Stories From The South"; Phillip Rawls, "State House and Senate OK Slavery Apologies"; Tom Gordon, "From Black Belt Roots Grows New Racial View"; David J. Garrow, "The Klan Is Still Dead"; Shailagh Murray, "A Balancing Act In The Upper South"; Brian Lyman, "The Calculus Of Elections"; and an *Anniston Star* editorial, "Does Race Still Matter?" Also, for some interesting insights into contemporary life in the Deep South, see the ten-part *Anniston Star* series by John Fleming on "Economic and Social Justice in Alabama's Black Belt." Impatient readers can skip ahead to "Historical Overview: The South's Enduring Dilemma and Changing Politics" in Chapter 2.

5   Jason Sokol, *There Goes My Everything*, 9.

6   Charles W. Eagles, "Toward New Histories of the Civil Rights Era," 845–848.

7   Glenn Feldman, *Reading Southern History*, 11.

8   Richard K. Scher, "Unfinished Business: Writing the Civil Rights Movement," 88.

9   Lucius J. Barker, Mack Jones, and Katherine Tate, *African Americans and the American Political System*, 296–297.

10   For example, see Jim Vandehei and John F. Harris, "Obama's Racial Problems Transcend Wright"; Elizabeth Bumiller and John M. Broder, "McCain Regrets Vote Against King Holiday"; Ben Smith, "Racial Tensions Roil Democratic Race."

11   Ben Smith, "Racial Tensions Roil Democratic Race."

Chapter 1: A New Perspective on Southern Politics and History

1   Frederick M. Wirt provided rare theoretical discussion of these politicians and their leadership in *"We Ain't What We Was": Civil Rights in the New South*. He conceptualized developing roles and practices of "pragmatist" and "transformed" white leaders, as opposed to more traditional Southern politicians; and he called for "more study" of this aspect of regional change. See pp. 114–115, 225–231.

2   Definitions accessed at www.dictionary.com, a Random House Unabridged dictionary.

3   This term originated with C. Vann Woodward in "The Political Legacy of Reconstruction," 231–240.

4   Richard M. Valelly, *The Two Reconstructions*, 199–200.

5   Ibid., 213.

6   David J. Garrow, *Bearing the Cross*, 338–339.

7   Hanes Walton, Jr., *When the Marching Stopped*, 68.

8   Martin Luther King, Jr., "Where Do We Go From Here?"

9   Martin Luther King, Jr., *Where Do We Go From Here: Chaos or Community.*

10   King, Jr., "Where Do We Go From Here?" 171–173.

11   Ibid., 186–191.

12   King, Jr., *Where Do We Go From Here: Chaos or Community*, 152.

13   Ibid., 148.

14   Ibid., 157.

15   Chandler Davidson, *Biracial Politics*, 276.

16   Ibid., 273–274.

17   Ibid., 275.

18   Ibid., 274.

19   Eric Hoffer, *True Believer*, 130.

20   Ibid., 146.

21   Ibid., 146.

22   Ibid., 146–151.

23   Joe Reed, personal interview, August 3, 2007.

24   Richard Arrington, telephone and email communications, April, 2008.

25   Fred Gray, telephone communication, May 8, 2008.

26   Richard K. Cralle, *Works of John C. Calhoun*, 625–633.

27   For a concise but interesting account of the 1901 convention and constitutional history in Alabama, see Dana Beyerle, "How The Constitution Came To Be."

28   Gerald Johnson, email interview, April 30, 2008.

Chapter 2: Historical Overview

1 For useful discussion of the South's historical race problem, consult the bibliographical citations throughout this manuscript, particularly the work of Black and Black; Bullock; Cash; Davidson; Grofman; Keech; Key; Killian; Marable; Matthews and Prothro; Menifield and Shaffer; Scher; Sokol; Walton; and Woodward.

2 V. O. Key, Jr., *Southern Politics in State and Nation*, 4.

3 W. J. Cash, *The Mind of the South*, 131–132.

4 Key, Jr., *Southern Politics*, 361.

5 Donald R. Matthews and James W. Prothro, *Negroes and the New Southern Politics*, 334.

6 Earl Black and Merle Black, *Politics and Society in the South*, 127–133.

7 Richard K. Scher, *Politics in the New South*, 228–230.

8 Ibid., 230.

9 John Hayman, *Bitter Harvest*, 255.

10 Ibid., 255.

11 Ibid., 256–257.

12 Carl Elliott, Sr. and Michael D'Orso, *Cost of Courage*.

13 Ibid., 283–287.

14 William R. Keech, *Impact of Negro Voting*, 109.

15 For useful discussion of this systemic transformation, consult the bibliographical sources footnoted throughout this manuscript, particularly the work of Aistrup; Bartley and Graham; Bass and DeVries; Berard; Black and Black; Bullock and Rozell; Davidson and Grofman; Havard; Killian and Grigg; Lamis; Lublin; Menifield and Shaffer; Shafer and Johnston; Steed, Baker and Moreland; Streb; Swansbrough and Brodsky; and Woodard.

16 J. David Woodard, *New Southern Politics*, 169.

17 Earl Black and Merle Black, *Rise of Southern Republicans*, 244–245.

18 Robert P. Steed, Laurence W. Moreland, and Tod A. Baker, *Southern Parties and Elections*, 174–176.

19 Patrick R. Cotter, Stephen D. Shaffer, and David A. Breaux, "Issues, Ideology, and Political Opinions in the South," 200–202.

20 Pew Research Center, "The 2004 Political Landscape."

21 Black and Black, *Rise of Southern Republicans*, 3.

22 Charles S. Bullock and Mark J. Rozell, *New Politics of the Old South*, 1–2.

23 Ibid., 1–2.

24 Black and Black, *Rise of Southern Republicans*, 2.

25 Stanley P. Berard, *Southern Democrats in the U.S. House of Representatives*, 261.

26 John A. Clark, "Looking Back and Looking Forward," 293.

27 James E. Alt, "Impact of the Voting Rights Act," 372.

28 Peyton McCrary, Jerome A. Gray, Edward Still, and Huey L. Perry, "Alabama," 56.

29 Chandler Davidson and Bernard Grofman, *Quiet Revolution in the South*, 386. More

recently, J. Morgan Kousser argues that the federal judiciary has begun shirking its progressive responsibilities; see *Colorblind Injustice: Minority Voting Rights and the Undoing of the Second Reconstruction*.

30 Bullock and Rozell, *New Politics of the Old South*, 16.

31 Ibid., 16.

32 Ibid., 16.

33 David Lublin, *Republican South*, 25–26.

34 Bullock and Rozell, *New Politics of the Old South*, 19.

35 Black and Black, *Rise of Southern Republicans*, 183–184.

36 Alexander Lamis, *Southern Politics in the 1990s*, 8.

37 Ibid., 386–387.

38 Mary Herring, "Legislative Responsiveness to Black Constituents," 740–758.

39 Charles E. Menifield, Stephen D. Shaffer, and Barbara A. Patrick, "Politics in the New South," 198.

40 Ibid., 198.

41 Ibid., 184–185.

42 Ibid., 199.

43 John Lewis and Michael D'Orso, *Walking with the Wind*, 463–464.

44 Fred D. Gray, *Bus Ride to Justice*, 355–356.

45 J. L. Chestnut, Jr. and Julia Cass, *Black in Selma*, 418.

46 Lewis and D'Orso, *Walking with the Wind*, 464.

47 Gray, *Bus Ride to Justice*, 355–356.

48 Chestnut and Cass, *Black in 3*, 418.

49 John Fleming, "Selma's Salvation."

50 Ibid.

51 Ibid.

52 Frye Gaillard, *Cradle of Freedom*, xvi.

53 Ibid., xvi.

54 Accessed online at http://www.alabamademocraticconference.org/content/view/15/30.

55 Lewis Killian and Charles Grigg, *Racial Crisis in America*. Also consult Lewis Killian, *White Southerners*.

56 Matthew D. Lassiter, *The Silent Majority*.

57 Quoted in Patricia Cohen, "Interpreting Some Overlooked Stories from the South."

58 Sokol, *There Goes My Everything*, 4.

59 Ibid., 3.

60 Ibid., 18.

61 David Chappell, *Inside Agitators*, xv.

62 Ibid., xvi.

63 Clayborne Carson, Foreword to Chappell, *Inside Agitators*, xiv.

64 J. Mills Thornton, *Dividing Lines*, 500.

65 For a different perspective, see black activist Frederick Richardson's first-person account of Mobile politics in *The Genesis and Exodus of NOW*. Richardson wrote that local black leaders too eagerly cut small deals with the white power structure and squandered African American power in the aftermath of the civil rights movement.

66 Sokol, *There Goes My Everything*.

67 Cohen, "Interpreting Some Overlooked Stories from the South."

68 Carson, Foreword to *Inside Agitators*, by David Chappell.

69 Thornton, *Dividing Lines*.

70 Clark, "Looking Back and Looking Forward."

71 Cohen, "Interpreting Some Overlooked Stories from the South."

72 Joseph Crespino, *In Search of Another Country*.

73 Kevin M. Kruse, *White Flight*.

74 Lassiter, *The Silent Majority*.

75 Byron E. Shafer and Richard Johnston, *End of Southern Exceptionalism*, 173, 191.

76 Frederick M. Wirt, *"We Ain't What We Was,"* 29. Also consult *The Politics of Southern Equality*.

77 For a full analysis and commentary on this new system, see Glen Browder, *The South's New Racial Politics: Inside the Race Game of Southern History* (NewSouth Books, 2009). Also, see Mark Kelly, "Stealth Politics," *Thicket*, March–April, 2009. *Birmingham Weekly*, an alternative publication, ran a series on "Alabama's New Racial Order: The Future of Southern Politics," written by Browder, as its Fall 2008 cover story.

Chapter 3: Racial Representation in the South

1   Hanna F. Pitkin, *Concept of Representation*.

2   Lenneal J. Henderson, *Black Political Life in the United States*.

3   Ralph C. Gomes and Linda Faye Williams, *From Exclusion to Inclusion*.

4   Pitkin, *Concept of Representation*, 209.

5   Ibid., 11.

6   Ibid., 113–114.

7   Ibid., 240.

8   Henderson, *Black Political Life in the United States*, viii.

9   Mack Jones. "A Frame of Reference for Black Politics," 7.

10 Ibid., 7–8.

11 Ibid., 9.

12 Ibid., 9.

13 Ibid., 9.

14 Gomes and Williams, *From Exclusion to Inclusion*, 144.

15 Ibid., 155.

16 Ibid., 155.

17 Jones, "A Frame of Reference for Black Politics," 7–8.

18 Carol Swain, *Black Faces, Black Interests*, 212.
19 Ibid., 168.
20 Ibid., 168.
21 Ibid., 163.
22 Ibid., 164.
23 Ibid., 153.
24 Ibid., 168–169.
25 Nicol Rae, *Southern Democrats*, 69.
26 Ibid., 69.
27 Ibid., 70.
28 Ibid., 70.
29 Ibid., 75.
30 Ibid., 74.
31 Ibid., 70–71.
32 Ibid., 73.
33 Ibid., 73.
34 Ibid., 96.
35 James M. Glaser, *Race, Campaign Politics, and the Realignment in the South*, 73.
36 Ibid., 74.
37 James M. Glaser, *Hand of the Past in Contemporary Southern Politics*, 74.
38 Ibid., 74.
39 Kenny J. Whitby, *Color of Representation*, 112.
40 Ibid., 112.
41 Ibid., 87.
42 Ibid., 142.
43 David Lublin, *Paradox of Representation*, 97.
44 Ibid., 89–90.
45 Ibid., 97.
46 Ibid., 96.
47 Ibid., 133.
48 David T. Canon, *Race, Redistricting and Representation*, 200.
49 Ibid., 91.
50 Berard, *Southern Democrats*, 200.
51 Ibid., 201.
52 Ibid., 202.
53 Katherine Tate, *Black Faces in the Mirror*, 85.
54 Ibid., 159.
55 Ibid., 161–162.
56 Ibid., 161.

57 Ibid., 15.

58 Ibid., 155.

59 Ibid., 170.

60 Richard Fleisher, "Explaining the Change in Roll-Call Voting," 327–341.

61 Charles Cameron, David Epstein, and Sharyn O'Halloran, "Do Majority-Minority Districts Maximize Substantive Black Representation in Congress?" 794–812.

62 L. Marvin Overby and Kenneth Cosgrove, "Unintended Consequences?" 540–550.

63 Kenneth A. Wink and Allison L. Hayes, "Racial Redistricting and Ideological Polarization," 361–384.

64 Christian R. Grose, "Black-Majority Districts or Black Influence Districts?" 3–26.

65 Feldman, *Reading Southern History*, 11.

66 Gary Orfield, Foreword to *"We Ain't What We Was,"* by Frederick M. Wirt, xi.

67 Jacob Levenson, *Divining Dixie*, 20–27.

68 Ibid.

69 Joseph P. McCormick and Charles E. Jones, "Conceptualization of Deracialization," 73.

70 Harold W. Stanley, "Runoff Primaries and Black Political Influence," 261.

71 Eagles, "Toward New Histories," 845–848.

72 Ibid., 844.

73 Feldman, *Reading Southern History*, 11.

74 Richard K. Scher, "Unfinished Business: Writing the Civil Rights Movement," 88.

75 Ibid, 83–84.

76 Ibid, 88.

77 Barker, Jones, and Tate, *African Americans and the American Political System*, 296–297.

Chapter 4: The Alabama Setting for Stealth Politics

1 Journalist Geni Certain's biographical research—"Professor-Politician: An Examination of the Public Career of Glen Browder"—was accepted as an M.A. Thesis in History at Jacksonville State University in August, 2008; and NewSouth Books will publish its Certain-Browder version of *Professor-Politician* in 2010.

2 William Warren Rogers, Robert David Ward, Leah Rawls Atkins, and Wayne Flynt, *Alabama: The History of a Deep South State*, 566.

3 Jeff Frederick, *Stand Up For Alabama*, 406.

4 Goat Hill is the locally used nickname for Alabama's capitol in Montgomery, so-called because the building sits on a hill where goats once grazed.

5 Charles E. Menifield, Stephen D. Shaffer, and Brandi J. Brassell, "An Overview of African American Representation," 176, 178. This is a useful companion piece for our analysis of "stealth politics" because it delves into the relationship between African American and white politicians in Southern politics of the 1970s, 1980s, and 1990s. Many of the issues, challenges, and practices detailed among black elected officials provide mirrored comparison for the Browder case study and survey of former

members of Congress in the various Southern states.

6   For interesting review of Alabama political history in this period, see Wayne Flynt, *Alabama in the Twentieth Century*; also consult his chapters on "A Time To Hate: Racial Confrontation 1955–1970" and "A Time to Heal: Struggling To Find a New Vision 1970–1990" in Rogers, Ward, Atkins, and Flynt, *Alabama: The History of a Deep South State*. For a more analytical/statistical accounting, particularly during the post-Wallace years, see Matthew Streb's chapter on "Alabama: Exploiting Racial Fears" in his book *The New Electoral Politics of Race*.

7   Frank Sikora, *Until Justice Rolls Down*, 48.

8   For a colorful profile of Baxley's racial/populist politics, see Sikora's book, *Until Justice Rolls Down*; for biographical information, consult "Bill Baxley," Alabama Department of Archives and History: http://www.archives.state.al.us.

9   For representative material on Siegelman's biracial adventures, especially during his 1998 gubernatorial victory, see Matthew Streb's chapter on Alabama in *The New Electoral Politics of Race*. Also consult "Don Siegelman," Alabama Department of Archives and History: http://www.archives.state.al.us.

10 Paul M. Pruitt, Jr., "Howell Thomas Heflin," 4.

11 John Hayman with Clara Ruth Hayman, *Judge in the Senate*, 278.

12 Ibid, 452; quote is from Tom Gordon, "Heflin: Political Center Is Strength."

13 Ibid., 269.

14 Ibid., 260.

15 Ibid., 271.

16 Ibid., 452.

17 H. Brandt Ayers and Thomas H. Naylor, *You Can't Eat Magnolias*.

18 Toynbee quotation is from Ayers's opening essay in *You Can't Eat Magnolias*, 3–24.

19 This biographical discussion draws substantively from Browder's book, *The Future of American Democracy*, and a forthcoming biography by Geni Certain, *Professor-Politician*; the authors are grateful for permission to use this material. Additionally, the reader can consult the Browder Collection for more information.

20 Lewis M. Killian, *White Southerners*.

21 Hanes Walton, *Black Politics*.

22 William C. Havard, *Changing Politics of the South*.

23 Jack Bass and Walter DeVries, *Transformation of Southern Politics*.

24 Numan V. Bartley and Hugh Davis Graham, *Southern Politics and the Second Reconstruction*.

25 Ibid., 134, 200.

26 Jess Brown, email interview, April 28, 2008.

Chapter 5: A Case Study in Stealthy Campaigning

1   See "Silverberg Memorandum to Glen Browder, 1989" in the Browder Collection (Box 257, Browder's Desk Files/Notes/Materials).

2   Jim Yardley, "Racism Was Hidden Issue."

3   Ibid.

4   Ibid.

5   Christopher Smith, "Rice Workers All But Write Off Black Vote."

6   Ibid.

7   Ibid.

8   Justin Fox and Tom Gordon, "Black Empowerment With White Dollars."

9   Michael Brumas and Tom Gordon, "GOP Applies Bush Tactic To 3rd District Race."

10 Ted Bryant, "Solid Black Vote Is Disappearing."

11 Phillip Rawls, "Black Political Groups Feel Voters' Growing Independence."

12 Ibid.

13 Fox and Gordon, "Black Empowerment With White Dollars."

14 Patricia Dedrick, "Grayson Pleads Guilty,"; David Holden, "Grayson Gets Eight Month Sentence."

15 Fox and Gordon, "Black Empowerment With White Dollars."

16 Associated Press, "ADC Head Says Fake Ballots Surfacing."

17 Associated Press, "Alabama AG to Review Complaint About Fake Sample Ballots"; Jim Cox, "Fake Endorsement Ballot Furor Continues."

18 Amanda Casciaro, "Mud Thick in Preuit, Barton Primary Battle"; Todd South, "Senate District 11 Democratic Race Gets Rowdy."

19 Fox and Gordon, "Black Empowerment With White Dollars."

20 The Browder files include a few examples: the Alabama Democratic Conference (Macon County), the Alabama Democratic Conference (Calhoun County), the Alabama Democratic Conference (Talladega County), the Alabama New South Coalition (Talladega County), Talladega County Citizens Coalition (Talladega County), the New South Ecclesiastical Association (Talladega County), the Calhoun County Coalition (Calhoun County), and the Concerned Citizens for Equal Justice (Auburn).

21 Fox and Gordon, "Black Empowerment With White Dollars."

22 Justin Fox, "GOP Chief Asks Probe Of Shelby Donations."

23 Jess Brown, email communication, May 6, 2008.

Chapter 6: A Case Study in Stealthy Public Service

1   Betty Cork, "State Needs New Leadership, Browder Says."

2   Montgomery Advertiser, "Back to the Classroom."

3   Congressional Record, September 26, 1996.

4   Marti Thomas Doneghy, email interview, December 20, 2007.

5   Gadsden Times, "Browder Right Man To Make Polls Logical."

6   Huntsville Times, "State Help At The Polls." For other accounts of the poll-worker training initiative, see Scottsboro Daily Sentinel, "Browder Says Judge's Order 'Long Overdue'"; Associated Press, "Browder's Office Told To Pick Poll Workers"; Hamilton Journal-Record, "Court Order May Have Significant Impact on Alabama Elections."

7   See "Denkins Memorandum to Browder, April 12, 2007" in the Browder Collection

(Box 257, Browder's Desk Files/Notes/Materials).

8   *Randolph Leader*, August 17, 1994.

9   John W. Stevenson, "Prayers Call for Unity, Healing."

10 Ibid.

11 Rose Livingston, "Prayers and Hard Work in Wedowee." For other coverage of this event, see Anne Sciater, "Wedowee Students, Parents Pray Together"; Deborah Solomon, "Wedowee Tries To Heal a Racial Rift"; Thomas Spencer, "A Town Pauses for 'Healing,' Then Goes To Work on School."

12 "Denkins Memorandum to Browder, April 12, 2007" in the Browder Collection (Box 257, Browder's Desk Files/Notes/Materials).

13 Associated Press, "Black Leaders Criticize Response to Church Fires."

14 Penny Bender, "Official Reports of Church Fires Low"; see also Thomas Hargrove, "Patrick: Fire Probe Heating Up."

15 Alabama Advisory Committee to the United States Commission on Civil Rights: Transcript of a Community Forum held July 2, 1996.

16 National Church Arson Task Force, *First Year Report for the President,* 1997.

17 George Wallace, Jr., email interview, December 3, 2007.

18 Charles J. Dean, "The Rise and Stall of Politico Joe Reed: Battles Lost Begin to Mount for Black Alabama Legend."

19 Ford statement distributed by the Browder Campaign, March 1989.

20 Associated Press, "Rep. Alvin Holmes Named Dean of Alabama House."

21 John Lewis, letter to Dr. Joe Reed, May 15, 1996.

22 Jess Brown, email interview, May 7, 2008.

23 Jim Folsom, Jr., personal interview, June 20, 2007.

24 George Wallace, Jr., email interview, November 30, 2007.

25 Kelvin Cunningham, email interview, December 18, 2007.

26 Marti Thomas Doneghy, email interview, December 20, 2007.

27 Artur Davis, email interview, December 12, 2007.

28 John Lewis, letter to Dr. Joe Reed, May 15, 1996.

29 Joe Reed, personal interview, August 3, 2007.

Chapter 7: The Broader Scope of Stealth Leadership

1   For example, in addition to Pitkin, Henderson, and Jones, see Heinz Eulau and John Wahlke, *The Politics of Representation*; Richard F. Fenno Jr., *Home Style: House Members in Their Districts*; and David Mayhew, *Congress: The Electoral Connection.*

2   Richard F. Fenno Jr., *Congress at the Grassroots.*

3   Consult, for example, the work of Bartley and Graham; Bass and DeVries; Black and Black; Bullock and Rozell; Davidson and Grofman; Lamis; Lublin; Menifield and Shaffer; Prysby; Scher; Steed, Moreland, and Baker; and Swansbrough and Brodsky.

4   See Berard; Canon; Glaser; Lublin; Rae; Swain; Tate; and Whitby.

5   Such as Swain; Rae; and Glaser.

Chapter 8: Biracial Roundtable on Stealth Reconstruction

1   Hayman, *Bitter Harvest*, 256–257.
2   Malcolm X, *Autobiography of Malcolm X*, 314.
3   Ibid.

References and Bibliography

Aistrup, Joseph A. *The Southern Strategy Revisited: Republican Top-Down Advancement in the South.* Lexington: University Press of Kentucky, 1996.

Albritton, Robert B., George Amedee, Kennan Grenell, and Don-Terry Veal. "Deracialization and the New Black Politics." *Race, Politics, and Governance in the United States.* Ed. Perry. 1996, 179–192.

Alt, James E. "The Impact of the Voting Rights Act on Black and White Voter Registration in the South." *Quiet Revolution in the South.* Eds. Davidson and Grofman. 1994, 351–377.

Analytic Guidebook for The Browder Collection. Jacksonville: Jacksonville State University, 2007.

Anniston Star, "Does Race Still Matter?" September 6, 2006.

Appelbome, Peter. *Dixie Rising: How the South Is Shaping American Values, Politics, and Culture.* New York: Times Books, 1996.

Arrington, Richard, Jr. *There's Hope for the World: The Memoir of Birmingham, Alabama's First African American Mayor.* Tuscaloosa: University Press of Alabama, 2008.

Associated Press, "ADC Head Says Fake Ballots Surfacing." June 3, 1994.

Associated Press, "Alabama AG To Review Complaint About Fake Sample Ballots." June 20, 2006.

Associated Press, "Black Leaders Criticize Response To Church Fires." March 3, 1996.

Associated Press, "Browder's Office Told To Pick Poll Workers." September 13, 1988.

Associated Press, "Rep. Alvin Holmes Named Dean of Alabama House." January 23, 2007.

Ayers, H. Brandt, and Thomas H. Naylor, eds. *You Can't Eat Magnolias.* New York: McGraw-Hill, 1972.

Baker, Tod A., Robert P. Steed, and Laurence W. Moreland, eds. *Religion and Politics in the South: Mass and Elite Perspectives.* New York: Praeger, 1983.

Baldwin, Elisa. *A Guide to the Papers of John L. LeFlore, 1926–1976.* Mobile: University of South Alabama Archives, 1996.

Baldwin, James. *The Fire Next Time*. New York: Dial Press, 1963.

Barker, Lucius J., Mack Jones, and Katherine Tate. *African Americans and the American Political System*. Englewood Cliffs: Prentice Hall, 1998.

Barnard, William D., *Dixiecrats and Democrats: Alabama Politics, 1942–50*. University: University of Alabama Press, 1974.

Bartley, Numan V., and Hugh Davis Graham. *Southern Politics and the Second Reconstruction*. Baltimore: Johns Hopkins University Press, 1975.

Bass, Jack. *Unlikely Heroes*. New York: Simon and Schuster, 1981.

Bass, Jack, and Walter DeVries. *The Transformation of Southern Politics: Social Change and Political Consequence Since 1945*. New York: Basic Books, 1976.

Bass, Jack, and Marilyn W. Thompson. *Strom: The Complicated Personal and Political Life of Strom Thurmond*. New York: Public Affairs, 2005.

Bayerle, Dana. "How the Constitution Came To Be." *Tuscaloosa News*, November 18, 2001.

Bender, Penny. "Official Reports of Church Fires Low." *Montgomery Advertiser*, April 17, 1996.

Berard, Stanley P. *Southern Democrats in the U.S. House of Representatives*. Norman: University of Oklahoma Press, 2001.

———. "Congress and the South." *Writing Southern Politics*. Eds. Steed and Moreland. 2006, 241–268.

Black, Earl. *Southern Governors and Civil Rights*. Cambridge: Harvard University Press, 1976.

Black, Earl, and Merle Black. *Politics and Society in the South*. Cambridge: Harvard University Press, 1989.

———. *The Rise of Southern Republicans*. Cambridge: Belknap Press, 2002.

———. *Divided America: The Ferocious Power Struggle in American Politics*. New York: Simon & Schuster, 2007.

Black, Merle. "Racial Composition of Congressional Districts and Support for Federal Rights in the American South." *Social Science Quarterly* 59 (October 1978): 435–450.

Branch, Taylor. *Parting the Waters: America in the King Years*. New York: Simon & Schuster, 1988.

———. *Pillar of Fire: America in the King Years*. New York: Simon & Schuster, 1998.

———. *At Canaan's Edge: America in the King Years, 1965–68*. New York: Simon & Schuster, 2006.

Brinkley, Douglas G. *Rosa Parks: A Life*. New York: Penguin, 2005.

Brooks, Gary W. "Black Political Mobilization and White Legislator Behavior." *Contemporary Southern Political Attitudes and Behavior*. Eds. Moreland, Baker, and Steed. 1982, 221–228.

Browder Collection. Jacksonville State University. Jacksonville, AL.

Browder, Glen. *The South's New Racial Politics: Inside the Race Game of Southern*

History. Montgomery: NewSouth Books, 2009.

Brown, David, and Clive Webb. *Race in the American South: From Slavery to Civil Rights.* Gainesville: University Press of Florida, 2007.

Brumas, Michael, and Tom Gordon. "GOP Applies Bush Tactic To 3rd District Race." *Birmingham News,* February 17, 1989.

Brundage, W. Fitzhugh. *The Southern Past: A Clash of Race and Memory.* Cambridge: Belknap Press, 2008.

Bryant, Ted. "Solid Black Vote Is Disappearing." *Birmingham Post-Herald,* May 24, 1994.

Bullock, Charles S., III. "Congressional Voting and the Mobilization of a Black Electorate in the South." *Journal of Politics* 43 (1981): 662–682.

———. "The Impact of Changing the Racial Composition of Congressional Districts on Legislators' Roll Call Behavior." *American Politics Research* 23 (1995): 141–158.

Bullock, Charles S., III, and Mark J. Rozell. *The New Politics of the Old South: An Introduction to Southern Politics.* Lanham: Rowman and Littlefield Publishers, 2007.

Bumiller, Elizabeth, and John M. Broder. "McCain Regrets Vote Against King Holiday." *International Herald Tribune,* April 4, 2008.

Cameron, Charles, David Epstein, and Sharyn O'Halloran. "Do Majority-Minority Districts Maximize Substantive Black Representation in Congress?" *American Political Science Review* 90 (1996): 794–812.

Campbell, Angus, Phillip E. Converse, Warren E. Miller, and Donald E. Stokes. *The American Voter.* New York: Wiley, 1960.

Canon, David T. *Race, Redistricting, and Representation: The Unintended Consequences of Black Majority Districts.* Chicago: University of Chicago Press, 1999.

Carr, Johnnie Rebecca, and Randall Williams. *Johnnie: The Life of Johnnie Rebecca Carr, With Her Friends Rosa Parks, E. D Nixon, Martin Luther King, Jr., and Others in the Montgomery Civil Rights Struggle.* Montgomery: Black Belt Press, 1997.

Carson, Clayborne, ed. *The Autobiography of Martin Luther King, Jr.* New York: Warner Books, 1998.

Carson, Clayborne. Foreward to *Inside Agitators: White Southerners in the Civil Rights Movement,* by David L. Chappell. Baltimore: Johns Hopkins University Press, 1994.

Carson, Clayborne, and Kris Shepard. *A Call to Conscience: The Landmark Speeches of Dr. Martin Luther King, Jr.* New York: International Properties Management, 2001.

Carter, Dan T. *The Politics of Rage: George Wallace, the Origins of the New Conservatism, and the Transformation of American Politics.* Baton Rouge: Louisiana State University Press, 1996.

Casciaro, Amanda. "Mud Thick In Preuit, Barton Primary Battle." *Talladega Daily Home,* June 3, 2006.

Cash, W. J. *The Mind of the South*. New York: Alfred A. Knopf, 1941.

Chafe, William H. *Civilities and Civil Rights: Greensboro, North Carolina, and the Black Struggle for Freedom*. New York: Oxford University Press, 1980.

Chappell, David L. *Inside Agitators: White Southerners in the Civil Rights Movement*. Baltimore: Johns Hopkins University Press, 1994.

Chestnut, J. L., Jr., and Julia Cass. *Black in Selma: The Uncommon Life of J. L. Chestnut, Jr*. New York: Farrar, Straus and Giroux, 1990.

Clark, E. Culpepper. *The Schoolhouse Door: Segregation's Last Stand at the University of Alabama*. New York: Oxford University Press, 1993.

Clark, John A. "Looking Back and Looking Forward: A Research Agenda for Southern Politics." *Writing Southern Politics*. Eds. Steed and Moreland. 2006, 291–302.

Clark, John A., and Charles L. Prysby, eds. *Southern Political Party Activists: Patterns of Conflict and Change, 1991–2001*. Lexington: University Press of Kentucky, 2004.

Clay, William L. *Just Permanent Interests: Black Americans in Congress, 1870–1992*. New York: Amistad Press, 1993.

Clubok, Alfred B., John M. De Grove, and Charles D. Farris. "The Manipulated Negro Vote: Some Pre-Conditions and Consequences." *Journal of Politics 26* (1964): 112–129.

Clyburn, James, and Jennifer Revels. *Uncommon Courage: The Story of Briggs V. Elliott, South Carolina's Unsung Civil Rights Battle*. Spartanburg: Palmetto Conservation Foundation, 2004.

Cobb, James C. *Redefining Southern Culture: Mind and Identity in the Modern South* Athens: University of Georgia Press, 1999.

———. *Away Down South: A History of Southern Identity*. New York: Oxford University Press, 2005.

Cohen, Patricia. "Interpreting Some Overlooked Stories From The South." *New York Times*, May, 1, 2007.

Combs, Michael W., John R. Hibbing, and Susan Welch. "Black Constituents and Congressional Roll Call Votes." *Western Political Quarterly 37* (1984): 424–434.

Cork, Betty. "State Needs New Leadership." *Montgomery Advertiser*, May 9, 1996.

Corrigan, Matthew T. *Race, Religion, and Economic Change in the Republican South: A Study of a Southern City*. Gainesville: University Press of Florida, 2007.

Cotter, Patrick R., and James Glen Stovall. *After Wallace: The 1986 Contest for Governor and Political Change in Alabama*. Tuscaloosa: University of Alabama Press, 2009.

Cotter, Patrick R., James Glen Stovall, and Samuel H. Fisher, III. *Disconnected: Public Opinion and Politics in Alabama*. Northport: Vision Press, 1994.

Cotter, Patrick R., Stephen D. Shaffer, and David A. Breaux. "Issues, Ideology, and Political Opinions in the South." *Writing Southern Politics*. Eds. Steed and Moreland. 2006, 168–218.

Cox, Jim. "Fake Endorsement Ballot Furor Continues." *Clarke County Democrat*, June 15, 2006.

Cralle, Richard K. *The Works of John C. Calhoun*. New York: Russell & Russell, 1968.

Crespino, Joseph. *In Search of Another Country: Mississippi and the Conservative Counterrevolution*. Princeton: Princeton University Press, 2007.

Davidson, Chandler. *Biracial Politics: Conflict and Coalition in the Metropolitan South*. Baton Rouge: Louisiana State University Press, 1972.

Davidson, Chandler, and Bernard Grofman, eds. *Quiet Revolution in the South: The Impact of the Voting Rights Act, 1965–1990*. Princeton: Princeton University Press, 1994.

Dean, Charles J. "The Rise and Stall of Politico Joe Reed: Battles Lost Begin to Mount For Black Alabama Legend." *Birmingham News*, June 22, 2008.

Dedrick, Patricia. "Grayson Pleads Guilty." *Huntsville Times*, April 30, 1993.

Dewan, Shaila. "Southern Blacks Are Split On Clinton vs. Obama." *New York Times*, January 18, 2008.

Dunbar, Anthony, ed. *American Crisis, Southern Solutions: From Where We Stand, Promise and Peril*. Montgomery: NewSouth Books, 2008.

Durr, Virginia Foster, and Hollinger F. Barnard. *Outside the Magic Circle: The Autobiography of Virginia Foster Durr*. University: University of Alabama Press, 1985.

Eagles, Charles W., ed. *Is There a Southern Political Tradition?* Jackson: University of Mississippi Press, 1996.

———. *Outside Agitator: Jon Daniels and the Civil Rights Movement in Alabama*. Tuscaloosa: University of Alabama Press, 2000.

———. "Toward New Histories of the Civil Rights Era." *Journal of Southern History*. 66 (November 2000): 815–848.

———, ed. *The Civil Rights Movement in America: Essays*. Jackson: University Press of Mississippi, 2006.

Eddins, Don. *AEA: Head of the Class in Alabama Politics*. Montgomery: Alabama Education Association, 1997.

Elliott, Carl, Sr., and Michael D'Orso. *The Cost of Courage: The Journey of An American Congressman*. New York: Doubleday, 1992.

Endersby, James W., and Charles E. Menifield. "Representation, Ethnicity, and Congress: Black and Hispanic Representatives and Constituencies." *Black and Multiracial Politics in America*. Eds. Alex-Assensoh and Hanks. 2000, 257–272.

Engstrom, Richard L. "Race and Southern Politics: The Special Case of Congressional Districting." *Writing Southern Politics*. Eds. Steed and Moreland. 2006, 91–118.

Eskew, Glenn T. *But for Birmingham: The Local and National Movements in the Civil Rights Struggle*. Chapel Hill: University of North Carolina Press, 1997.

Eulau, Heinz, and John Wahlke. *The Politics of Representation*. Beverly Hills: Sage Publications, 1978.

Feagin, Joe R., and Harlan Hahn. "The Second Reconstruction: Black Political Strength in the South." *Social Science Quarterly* 51 (1970): 42–56.

Feldman, Glenn, ed. *Reading Southern History: Essays on Interpreters and Interpretations*. Tuscaloosa: University of Alabama Press, 2001.

————. *The Disfranchisement Myth: Poor Whites and Suffrage Restriction in Alabama*. Athens: University of Georgia Press, 2004.

Fenno, Richard F., Jr. *Home Style: House Members in Their Districts*. Boston: Little, Brown, 1978.

————. *Congress at the Grassroots: Representational Change in the South, 1970–1998*. Chapel Hill: University of North Carolina Press, 2000.

Fleisher, Richard. "Explaining the Change in Roll-Call Voting Behavior of Southern Democrats." *Journal of Politics* 55 (1993): 327–341.

Fleming, John. "Economic and Social Justice in Alabama's Black Belt." *Anniston Star*. Ten-part series, 2006.

Fleming, John. "Selma's Salvation." *Anniston Star*, September 3, 2006.

Flynt, Wayne. *Dixie's Forgotten People: The South's Poor Whites*. Bloomington: University of Indiana Press, 1980.

————. *Poor but Proud: Alabama's Poor Whites*. Tuscaloosa: University of Alabama Press, 1989.

————. *Alabama in the Twentieth Century (The Modern South)*. Tuscaloosa: University of Alabama Press, 2006.

Fox, Justin. "GOP Chief Asks Probe Of Shelby Donations." *Birmingham News*, October 2, 1992.

Fox, Justin, and Tom Gordon. "Black Empowerment With White Dollars." *Birmingham News*, October 4, 1992.

Franklin, Jimmie Lewis. *Back to Birmingham: Richard Arrington, Jr. and His Times*. Tuscaloosa: University of Alabama Press, 1989.

Franklin, John Hope. *Mirror to America: The Autobiography of John Hope Franklin*. New York: Farrar, Straus, and Giroux, 2005.

Frederick, Jeff. *Stand Up For Alabama: Governor George Wallace*. Tuscaloosa: University of Alabama Press, 2007.

Frederickson, Kari A. *Dixiecrat Revolt and the End of the Solid South, 1932–1968*. Chapel Hill: University of North Carolina Press, 2001.

Gaddie, Ronald Keith, and Donna R. Hoffman. "Critical Events in Contemporary Southern Politics: Dynamic Growth and Partisan Percolations." *Eye of the Storm*. Eds. Kuzenski, Moreland, and Steed. 2001, 17–38.

Gadsden Times, "Browder Right Man To Make Polls Logical," September 19, 1988.

Gaillard, Frye. *Cradle of Freedom: Alabama and the Movement That Changed America.* Tuscaloosa: University of Alabama Press, 2004.

Garrow, David J. *Bearing the Cross: Martin Luther King, Jr., and the Southern Christian Leadership Conference.* New York: Morrow, 1986.

Garrow, David J. "The Klan Is Still Dead." *Los Angeles Times,* February 27, 2007.

———. *The Walking City: The Montgomery Bus Boycott, 1955–1956.* Brooklyn: Carlson, 1989.

Gillespie, Andra, ed. *Whose Black Politics? Cases in Post-Racial Black Leadership.* New York: Routledge, 2009.

Glaser, James M. *Race, Campaign Politics, and the Realignment in the South.* New Haven: Yale University Press, 1996.

———. *The Hand of the Past in Contemporary Southern Politics.* New Haven: Yale University Press, 2005.

Gomes, Ralph C., and Linda Faye Williams. "Coalition Politics: Past, Present and Future." *From Exclusion to Inclusion.* Eds. Gomes and Williams. 1995, 129–160.

Gomes, Ralph C., and Linda Faye Williams. "The Future: What Is To Be Done?" *From Exclusion to Inclusion.* Eds. Gomes and Williams. 1995, 187–196.

———, eds. *From Exclusion to Inclusion: The Long Struggle for African American Political Power.* New York: Praeger, 1995.

Gonzales, James Joullian. *Memoirs of Mobile's Southside: Riding Alabama's Tide of White Supremacy.* Greenwood Village: Academy Books, 2007.

Gordon, Tom. "From Black Belt Roots Grows New Racial View." *Birmingham News,* April 24, 2007.

Gordon, Tom. "Heflin: Political Center Is Strength." *Birmingham News,* December 28, 1996.

Gossom, Thom, Jr. *Walk-on: My Reluctant Journey to Integration: A Memoir.* Ann Arbor: State Street Press, 2008.

Graetz, Robert S. *A White Preacher's Message on Race and Reconciliation: Based on His Experiences Beginning with the Montgomery Bus Boycott.* Montgomery: NewSouth Books, 2005.

Grafton, Carl, and Anne Permaloff. *Big Mules and Branchheads: James E. Folsom and Political Power in Alabama.* Athens: University of Georgia Press, 1985.

———. *Political Power in Alabama: The More Things Change.* Athens: University of Georgia Press, 1996.

Gray, Fred D. *Bus Ride to Justice: Changing the System by the System.* Montgomery: NewSouth Books, 2002.

Gray, Jerome. *Winning Fair Representation in At Large Elections: Cumulative Voting and Limited Voting in Alabama Local Elections.* Pamphlet printed by Southern Regional Council and The Center for Voting and Democracy, 1999.

Greenhaw, Wayne. *Watch Out for George Wallace.* Englewood Cliffs: Prentice Hall, 1976.

————. *Elephants in the Cotton Fields: Ronald Reagan and the New Republican South*. New York: Macmillan Publishing, 1982.

————. *Alabama On My Mind: Politics, People, History, and Ghost Stories*. Montgomery: Sycamore Press, 1987.

Grofman, Bernard, ed. *Race and Redistricting in the 1990s*. New York: Agathon Press, 1998.

Grofman, Bernard, and Chandler Davidson. *Controversies in Minority Voting: The Voting Rights Act in Perspective*. Washington, DC: Brookings Institution, 1992.

Grofman, Bernard, Lisa Handley, and Richard G. Niemi. *Minority Representation and the Quest for Voting Equality*. Cambridge: Cambridge University Press, 1992.

Grofman, Bernard, Robert Griffin, and Amihai Glazer. "The Effect of Black Population on Electing Democrats and Liberals to the House of Representatives." *Legislative Studies Quarterly* 17 (1992): 365–379.

Grofman, Bernard, and Lisa Handley. "Minority Population Proportion and Black and Hispanic Congressional Success in the 1970s and 1980s." *American Politics Quarterly* 17 (1989): 436–445.

Grose, Christian R. "Disentangling Constituency and Legislator Effects in Legislative Representation: Black Legislators or Black Districts." *Social Science Quarterly* 86 (2005): 427–443.

————. "Black-Majority Districts or Black Influence Districts? Evaluating the Representation of African Americans in the Wake of *Georgia v. Ashcroft*." *Voting Rights Reauthorization of 2006*. Eds. Henderson and Edly. 2007, 3–26.

Grose, Christian R., Maruice Mangum, and Christopher Martin. "Race, Political Empowerment, and Constituency Service: Descriptive Representation and the Hiring of American-American Congressional Staff." *Polity* 90 (October 2007), 449–478.

Guide to the Howell Thomas Heflin Collection. Tuscaloosa: University of Alabama School of Law, 2001.

Guinier, Lani. *The Tyranny of the Majority: Fundamental Fairness and Representative Democracy*. New York: Free Press, 1994.

Hackney, Sheldon. *Magnolias without Moonlight: The American South from Regional Confederacy to National Integration*. New Brunswick: Transaction, 2005.

Hadley, Charles D. "The Transformation of the Role of Black Ministers and Black Political Organizations in Louisiana Politics." *Blacks in Southern Politics*. Eds. Moreland, Steed, and Baker. 1987, 133–148.

Hadley, Charles D., and Lewis Bowman, eds. *Southern State Party Organizations and Activists*. New York: Praeger, 1995.

————, eds. *Party Activists in Southern Politics: Mirrors and Makers of Change*. Knoxville: University of Tennessee Press, 1998.

Hamilton, Charles V. "Deracialization: Examination of a Political Strategy." *First World 1* (1977): 3–5.

Hamilton Journal-Record, "Court Order May Have Significant Impact on Alabama

Elections," October 20, 1988.

Hamilton, Virginia Van der Veer. *Hugo Black: The Alabama Years*. Tuscaloosa: University of Alabama Press, 1972.

———. *Lister Hill: Statesman from the South*. Chapel Hill: University of North Carolina Press, 1987.

Hargrove, Thomas. "Patrick: Fire Probe Heating Up." *Birmingham Post-Herald*, April 17, 1996.

Harvey, Gordon E. *A Question of Justice: New South Governors and Education, 1968–1976*. Tuscaloosa: University of Alabama Press, 2002.

Harvey, Gordon E., Richard D. Starnes, and Glenn Feldman. *History and Hope in the Heart of Dixie: Scholarship, Activism, and Wayne Flynt in the Modern South*. Tuscaloosa: University of Alabama Press, 2006.

Havard, William C. *The Changing Politics of the South*. Baton Rouge: Louisiana State University Press, 1972.

Hayman, John. *Bitter Harvest: Richmond Flowers and the Civil Rights Revolution*. Montgomery: Black Belt Press, 1996.

Hayman, John, with Clara Ruth Hayman. *A Judge in the Senate: Howell Heflin's Career of Politics and Principle*. Montgomery: NewSouth Books, 2001.

Henderson, Ana, and Christopher Edly, Jr., eds. *Voting Rights Reauthorization of 2006: Perspectives on Democracy, Participation, and Power*. Berkeley: Berkeley Public Policy Press, 2007.

Henderson, Lenneal J., ed. *Black Political Life in the United States: A Fist as the Pendulum*. San Francisco: Chandler Publishing Co., 1972.

Herring, Mary. "Legislative Responsiveness to Black Constituents in Three Deep South States." *Journal of Politics* 52 (August 2001): 740–758.

Hill, Kevin. "Does the Creation of Majority Black Districts Aid Republicans?" *Journal of Politics* 57 (May 1995): 384–401.

Hoffer, Eric. *The True Believer: Thoughts on the Nature of Mass Movements*. New York: Harper, 1951.

Holden, David. "Grayson Gets Eight Month Sentence." *Huntsville Times*, June 11, 1993.

Howard, Gene. *Patterson for Alabama: The Life and Career of John Patterson*. Tuscaloosa: University Press of Alabama, 2008.

Huntsville Times, "State Help At The Polls." September 15, 1988.

Ingram, Bob. *That's The Way I Saw It*. Montgomery: B&E Press, 1986.

———. *That's The Way I Saw It II*. Montgomery: B&E Press, 1987.

Jackson, Harvey H. *Inside Alabama: A Personal History of My State*. Tuscaloosa: Fire Ant Books, 2004.

Jeffries, Hasan. *Bloody Lowndes: Civil Rights and Black Power in Alabama's Black Belt*. New York: NYU Press, 2009.

Jones, Bill. *The Wallace Story*. Northport: American Southern Pub. Co, 1966.

Jones, Mack. "A Frame of Reference for Black Politics." *Black Political Life in the*

United States. Ed. Henderson. 1972, 7–20.

Kapeluck, Branwell Dubose, Laurence W. Moreland, and Robert P. Steed, eds. *A Paler Shade of Red: The 2008 Presidential Election In the South.* Fayetteville: University of Arkansas Press, 2009.

Keech, William R. *The Impact of Negro Voting: The Role of the Vote in the Quest for Equality.* Westport: Greenwood Press, 1968.

Kelly, Mark. "Stealth Politics." *Thicket* (March-April 2009): 34–35.

Kemp, Mark. *Dixie Lullaby: A Story of Music, Race, and New Beginnings in a New South.* New York: Free Press, 2004.

Kennedy, Robert, Jr. *Judge Frank Johnson: A Biography.* New York: Putnam, 1976.

Key, V. O., Jr. *Southern Politics in State and Nation.* New York: Alfred A. Knopf, 1949.

Killian, Lewis M. *Black and White: Reflections of a White Southern Sociologist.* Dix Hills: General Hall, 1994.

———. *The Impossible Revolution? Black Power and the American Dream.* New York: Random House, 1968.

———. *White Southerners.* New York: Random House, 1970. Also Amherst, MA: University of Massachusetts Press, 1986.

Killian, Lewis M., and Charles Grigg. *Racial Crisis in America: Leadership in Conflict.* Englewood Cliffs: Prentice-Hall, 1964.

Kimbrell, Fuller. *From the Farm House to the State House: The Life and Times of Fuller Kimbrell.* Tuscaloosa: Word Way Press, 2001.

King, Martin Luther, Jr. *Stride Toward Freedom: The Montgomery Story.* New York: Harper & Row, 1958.

———. "Where Do We Go From Here?" *A Call to Conscience.* Carson and Shepard, 2001, 165–200.

———. *Where Do We Go From Here: Chaos or Community.* New York: Harper and Row, 1967.

———. *The Words of Martin Luther King, Jr.: Selected by Coretta Scott King.* New York: Newmarket, 1984.

Kousser, J. Morgan. *Colorblind Injustice: Minority Voting Rights and the Undoing of the Second Reconstruction.* Chapel Hill: University of North Carolina Press, 1999.

Kruse, Kevin M. *White Flight: Atlanta and the Making of Modern Conservatism.* Princeton: Princeton University Press, 2005.

Kuzenski, John C., Laurence W. Moreland, and Robert P. Steed, eds. *Eye of the Storm: The South and Congress in an Era of Change.* Westport: Praeger, 2001.

Kuzenski, John C., Laurence W. Moreland, and Robert P. Steed. "Introduction: The South and Congress." *Eye of the Storm.* Eds. Kuzenski, Moreland, and Steed. 2001, 1–16.

Kuzenski, John C., Charles S. Bullock, III, and Ronald Keith Gaddie, eds. *David*

Duke and the Politics of Race in the South. Baton Rouge: Louisiana State University Press, 2009.

Lamis, Alexander P. *Southern Politics in the 1990s*. Baton Rouge: Louisiana State University, 1999.

Lassiter, Matthew D. *The Silent Majority: Suburban Politics in the Sunbelt South*. Princeton: Princeton University Press, 2005.

Lawson, Steven F., and Charles Payne. *Debating the Civil Rights Movement*. Lanham: Rowman and Littlefield, 2006.

Lesher, Stephan. *George Wallace: American Populist*. Reading: Addison-Wesley Publishing Company, 1994.

LeVeaux-Sharpe, Christine. "Congressional Responsiveness to Redistricting-Induced Constituency Change." *Eye of the Storm*. Eds. Kuzenski, Moreland, and Steed. 2001, 81–96.

Levenson, Jacob. "Divining Dixie: Is It Another Country? Or a Place To Stow National Problems?" *Columbia Journalism Review* (March/April 2004): 20–27.

Lewis, John, and Michael D'Orso. *Walking with the Wind: A Memoir of the Movement*. New York: Simon & Schuster, 1998.

Liu, Baodong. "Deracialization and Urban Racial Context." *Urban Affairs Review* 38 (2003): 572–591.

Liu, Baodong and James M. Vanderleeuw. *Race Rules: Electoral Politics in New Orleans, 1965–2006*. Lanham: Lexington, 2007.

Livingston, Rose. "Prayers and Hard Work in Wedowee." *Birmingham News*, August 22, 1994.

Lublin, David. *The Paradox of Representation: Racial Gerrymandering and Minority Interests in Congress*. Princeton: Princeton University Press, 1997.

———. *The Republican South: Democratization and Partisan Change*. Princeton: Princeton University Press, 2004; New Edition 2007.

Lyman, Brian. "The Calculus Of Elections." *Anniston Star*, October 15, 2006.

Manis, Andrew M. *A Fire You Can't Put Out*. Tuscaloosa: University of Alabama Press, 1999.

Mansbridge, Jane J. *Beyond Adversary Democracy*. New York: Basic Books, 1980.

Marable, Manning. *Race, Reform and Rebellion: The Second Reconstruction in Black America, 1945–1982*. Jackson: University Press of Mississippi, 1984.

———. *Black American Politics: From the Washington Marches to Jesse Jackson*. London: Verso, 1985.

———. *Black Leadership*. New York: Columbia University Press, 1995.

———. *Race, Reform, and Rebellion: The Second Reconstruction and Beyond in Black America, 1945–2006*, Third Edition. Jackson: University Press of Mississippi, 2007.

Martin, David L. *Alabama's State and Local Governments*. Tuscaloosa: University of Alabama Press, 1994.

Matthews, Donald R., and James Warren Prothro. *Negroes and the New Southern*

Politics. New York: Harcourt, Brace & World, 1966.

Mayhew, David. *Congress: The Electoral Connection.* New Haven: Yale University, 1974.

McCormick, Joseph P., and Charles E. Jones. "The Conceptualization of Deracialization: Thinking Through the Dilemma." *Dilemmas of Black Politics.* Ed. Persons. 1993, 66–84.

McCrary, Peyton, Jerome A. Gray, Edward Still, and Huey L. Perry. "Alabama." *Quiet Revolution in the South,* Eds. Davidson and Grofman. 1994, 38–66.

McWhorter, Diane. *Carry Me Home: Birmingham, Alabama; The Climactic Battle of the Civil Rights Revolution.* New York: Simon & Schuster, 2001.

Menifield, Charles E., ed. *Representation of Minority Groups in the U.S.: Implications for the Twenty-First Century.* Lanham: Austin & Winfield, 2001.

Menifield, Charles E., and Stephen D. Shaffer, eds. *Politics in the New South: Representation of African Americans in Southern State Legislatures.* Albany: State University of New York Press, 2005.

Menifield, Charles E., Stephen D. Shaffer, and Barbara A. Patrick. "Politics in the New South: Looking Ahead." *Politics in the New South.* Eds. Menifield and Shaffer. 2005, 179–200.

Menifield, Charles E., Stephen D. Shaffer, and Brandi J. Brassell. "An Overview of African American Representation in Other Southern States." *Politics in the New South.* Eds. Menifield and Shaffer. 2005, 157–178.

Miller, Steven P. *Billy Graham and the Rise of the Republican South.* Philadelphia: University of Pennsylvania Press, 2009.

Mitchell, Dennis. *Mississippi Liberal: A Biography of Frank E. Smith.* Jackson: University Press of Mississippi, 2001.

Montgomery Advertiser, "Back to the Classroom." December 10, 1996.

Moreland, Laurence W., Tod A. Baker, and Robert P. Steed, eds. *Contemporary Southern Political Attitudes and Behavior: Studies and Essays.* New York: Praeger, 1982.

Moreland, Laurence W., Robert P. Steed, and Tod A Baker, eds. *Blacks in Southern Politics.* New York: Praeger, 1987.

Murray, Shailagh. "A Balancing Act in the Upper South." *Washington Post,* October 9, 2006.

Myrdal, Gunnar. *An American Dilemma: The Negro Problem and Modern Democracy.* New York: Harper and Brothers, 1944.

National Church Arson Task Force. *First Year Report for the President.* June 15, 1997.

Noble, Phil. *Beyond the Burning Bus: The Civil Rights Revolution in a Southern Town.* Montgomery: NewSouth Books, 2003.

Nunnelley, William A. *Bull Connor.* Tuscaloosa: University of Alabama Press, 1991.

Ogletree, Charles. *All Deliberate Speed: Reflections on the First Half-Century of Brown v. Board of Education*. New York: W. W. Norton, 2005.

Orfield, Gary. Foreward to *"We Ain't What We Was": Civil Rights in the New South*, by Frederick M. Wirt. Durham: Duke University Press, 1997.

Overby, L. Marvin, and Kenneth Cosgrove. "Unintended Consequences? Racial Redistricting and the Representation of Minority Interests." *Journal of Politics* 58 (1996): 540–550.

Parker, Frank R. *Black Votes Count: Political Empowerment in Mississippi After 1965*. Chapel Hill: University of North Carolina Press, 1990.

Parks, Rosa, with Jim Haskins. *Rosa Parks: My Story*. New York: Dial Books, 1992.

Parsons, Sara M. *From Southern Wrongs to Civil Rights: The Memoir of a White Civil Rights Activist*. Tuscaloosa, AL: University of Alabama Press, 2000.

Perry, Huey L. "Deracialization as an Analytical Construct in American Urban Politics." *Urban Affairs Quarterly* 27 (1991): 181–191.

———. "An Analysis of Major Themes in the Concept of Deracialization." *Race, Politics, and Governance in the United States*. Ed. Perry. 1996, 1–11.

———. "The Value of Deracialization as an Analytic Construct in American Politics." *Race, Politics, and Governance in the United States*. Ed. Perry. 1996, 193–196.

———, ed. *Race, Politics and Governance in the United States*. Gainesville: University Press of Florida, 1996.

Persons, Georgia A., ed. *Dilemmas of Black Politics: Issues of Leadership and Strategy*. New York: Harpercollins College Division, 1993.

Pew Research Center. "The 2004 Political Landscape." http://people-press.org.

Pitkin, Hanna F. *The Concept of Representation*. Berkeley: University of California Press, 1967.

———. *Representation*. New York; Atherton Press, 1969.

Pruitt, Paul M., Jr. "Howell Thomas Heflin." *The Howell Thomas Heflin Collection*. University of Alabama School of Law, Tuscaloosa, AL, 2001.

Prysby, Charles. "Southern Political Party Development Since World War II." *Writing Southern Politics*. Eds. Steed and Moreland. 2006, 11–40.

———. "Southern Congressional Elections in the 1990s: The Dynamics of Change." *American Review of Politics* 21 (2000): 155–178.

Rae, Nicol C. *Southern Democrats*. New York: Oxford University Press, 1994.

Rawls, Philip. "Black Political Groups Feel Voters' Growing Independence." Associated Press, June 27, 2002.

Rawls, Philip. "State House and Senate OK Slavery Apologies." Associated Press, April 25, 2007.

Reed, John Shelton. *Surveying the South: Studies in Regional Sociology*. Columbia: University of Missouri Press, 1993.

Reeves, Keith. *Voting Hopes or Fears? White Voters, Black Candidates, and Racial Politics in America*. New York: Oxford University Press, 1997.

Richardson, Frederick. *The Genesis and Exodus of NOW*. Boynton Beach: Futura

Printing, 1996.

Roberts, Gene, and Hank Klibanoff. *The Race Beat: The Press, the Civil Rights Struggle, and the Awakening of a Nation*. New York: Knopf, 2006.

Rogers, William Warren, Robert David Ward, Leah Rawls Atkins, and Wayne Flynt. *Alabama: The History of a Deep South State*. Tuscaloosa: University of Alabama Press, 1994.

Romano, Renee Christine, and Leigh Raiford, eds. *The Civil Rights Movement in American Memory*. Athens: University of Georgia Press, 2006.

Sabato, Larry J., and Glenn R. Simpson. "Street Money: Minority Votes for Sale or Rent?" *Dirty Little Secrets: The Persistence of Corruption in American Politics*. Eds. Sabato and Simpson. 1996, 187–206.

———. *Dirty Little Secrets*. New York: Times Books, 1996.

Scher, Richard K. *Politics in the New South: Republicanism, Race, and Leadership in the Twentieth Century*. Armonk: Sharpe, 1997.

———. "Unfinished Business: Writing the Civil Rights Movement." *Writing Southern Politics*. Eds. Steed and Moreland. 2006, 65–90.

Scher, Richard K., Jon L. Mills, and John J. Hotaling. "Voting Rights in the South after Shaw and Miller." *Southern Parties and Elections*. Eds. Steed, Moreland, and Baker. 1997, 9–36.

Sciater, Anne. "Wedowee Students, Parents Pray Together." *Montgomery Advertiser*, August 22, 1994.

Scottsboro Daily Sentinel, "Browder Says Judge's Order 'Long Overdue.'" September 11, 1988.

Shafer, Byron E., and Richard Johnston. *The End of Southern Exceptionalism: Class, Race, and Partisan Change in the Postwar South*. Cambridge: Harvard University Press, 2006.

Sikora, Frank. *Until Justice Rolls Down: The Birmingham Church Bombing Case*. Tuscaloosa: University of Alabama Press, 1991.

———. *The Judge: The Life and Opinions of Alabama's Frank M. Johnson, Jr.* Montgomery: NewSouth Books, 2007.

Sims, George E. *The Little Man's Big Friend: James E. Folsom in Alabama Politics, 1946–1958*. Tuscaloosa: University of Alabama Press, 1985.

Smith, Ben. "Racial Tensions Roil Democratic Race." *The Politico*, January 11, 2008. http://dyn.politico.com.

Smith, Christopher. "Rice Workers All But Write off Black Vote." *Anniston Star*, April 1, 1989.

Smith, Frank Ellis. *Congressman from Mississippi*. New York: Pantheon Books, 1964.

Sokol, Jason. *There Goes My Everything: White Southerners in the Age of Civil Rights, 1945–1975*. New York: Knopf, 2006.

Solomon, Deborah. "Wedowee Tries To Heal A Racial Rift." *Birmingham Post-Herald*, August 22, 1994.

South, Todd. "Senate District 11 Democratic Race Gets Rowdy." *Anniston Star*, June 25, 2006.

Spencer, Thomas. "A Town Pauses For 'Healing,' Then Goes To Work On School." *Anniston Star*, August 22, 1994.

Stanley, Harold W. "Runoff Primaries and Black Political Influence." In *Blacks in Southern Politics*. Eds. Laurence W. Moreland, Robert P. Steed, and Tod A. Baker. 1987, 259–276.

Stanton, Elvin. *Faith and Works: The Politics, Business, and Philanthropy of Alabama's Jimmy Faulkner.* Montgomery: NewSouth Books, 2002.

Steed, Robert P., Lawrence Moreland, and Tod A. Baker, eds. *Party Politics in the South.* New York: Praeger, 1980.

———. *The Disappearing South?* Tuscaloosa: University of Alabama Press, 1990.

———. *Southern Parties and Elections: Studies in Regional Political Change.* Tuscaloosa: University of Alabama Press, 1997.

———. "Introduction: Politics and Race in the South." *Blacks in Southern Politics.* Eds. Moreland, Steed, and Baker. 1987, 1–8.

———. "Searching for the Mind of the South in the Second Reconstruction." *The Disappearing South?* 1990, 125–140.

Steed, Robert P., John A. Clark, Lewis Bowman, and Charles D. Hadley. *Party Organization and Activism in the American South.* Tuscaloosa: University of Alabama Press, 1998.

Steed, Robert P., and Laurence W. Moreland, eds. *The 2000 Presidential Election in the South: Partisan and Southern Party Systems in the 21st Century.* New York: Praeger, 2002.

———, eds. *Writing Southern Politics: Contemporary Interpretations and Future Directions.* Lexington: University Press of Kentucky, 2006.

Stern, Mark. "Assessing the Impact of the 1965 Voting Rights Act: A Microanalysis of Four States." *Contemporary Southern Political Attitudes and Behavior.* Eds. Moreland, Baker, and Steed. 1982, 254–267.

Stevenson, John W. "Prayers Call For Unity, Healing." *Randolph Leader*, August 24, 1994.

Stewart, William Histaspas. *The Alabama State Constitution: A Reference Guide*, Vol. 20. Westport: Greenwood Publishing Group, 1994.

Stovall, James Glen, Patrick R. Cotter, and Samuel H. Fisher, III. *Alabama Political Almanac.* Various editions.

Streb, Matthew J. *The New Electoral Politics of Race.* Tuscaloosa: University of Alabama Press, 2002.

Sugrue, Thomas J. *Sweet Land of Liberty: The Forgotten Struggle for Civil Rights in the North.* New York: Random House, 2008.

Suitts, Steve. *Hugo Black of Alabama: How His Roots and Early Career Shaped the Great Champion of the Constitution.* Montgomery: NewSouth Books, 2005.

Swain, Carol M. *Black Faces, Black Interests: The Representation of African Americans in Congress*. Cambridge: Harvard University Press, 1993.

Swansbrough, Robert H., and David M. Brodsky, eds. *The South's New Politics: Realignment and Dealignment*. Columbia: University of South Carolina Press, 1988.

Tate, Katherine. *Black Faces in the Mirror: African Americans and Their Representatives in the U.S. Congress*. Princeton: Princeton University Press, 2003.

Thernstrom, Abigail. *Whose Votes Count? Affirmative Action and Minority Voting Rights*. Cambridge: Harvard University Press, 1987.

Thomas, James D., and William H. Stewart. *Alabama Government and Politics*. Lincoln: University of Nebraska Press, 1988.

Thomson, H. Bailey. *A Century of Controversy: Constitutional Reform in Alabama*. Tuscaloosa: University of Alabama Press, 2002.

Thornton, J. Mills, III. *Dividing Lines: Municipal Politics and the Struggle for Civil Rights in Montgomery, Birmingham, and Selma*. Tuscaloosa: University of Alabama Press, 2002.

Trest, Warren. *Nobody But the People: The Life and Times of Alabama's Youngest Governor*. Montgomery: NewSouth Books, 2008.

Valelly, Richard M. *The Two Reconstructions: The Struggle for Black Enfranchisement*. Chicago: University of Chicago Press, 2004.

Vandehei, Jim, and John F. Harris. "Obama's Racial Problems Transcend Wright." *The Politico*, March 18, 2008. http://dyn.politico.com.

Wahlke, John, Heinz Eulau, William Buchanan, and Leroy Ferguson. *The Legislative System: Explorations in Legislative Behavior*. New York: Wiley, 1962.

Walters, Ronald W. *Freedom Is Not Enough: Black Voters, Black Candidates, and American Presidential Politics*. Lanham: Rowman & Littlefield, 2005.

Walters, Ronald W., and Robert C. Smith. *African American Leadership*. Albany: State University of New York Press, 1999.

Walton, Hanes. *Black Politics: A Theoretical and Structural Analysis*. Philadelphia: Lippincott, 1972.

———. *Invisible Politics: Black Political Behavior*. Albany: State University of New York Press, 1985.

———. *When the Marching Stopped: The Politics of Civil Rights Regulatory Agencies*. Albany: State University of New York Press, 1988.

———. *The Native Son Presidential Candidate: The Carter Vote in Georgia*. New York: Praeger, 1992.

Walton, Hanes, and Robert C. Smith. *American Politics and the African American Quest*. Reading: Addison-Wesley, 2005.

Washington, James M., ed. *A Testament of Hope: The Essential Writings and Speeches of Martin Luther King, Jr*. New York: HarperCollins, 1986.

Webb, Samuel L., and Margaret E. Armbrester. *Alabama Governors: A Political History of the State*. Tuscaloosa: University of Alabama Press, 2001.

Whitby, Kenny J. *The Color of Representation: Congressional Behavior and Black*

Interests. Ann Arbor: University of Michigan Press, 1997.

Whitby, Kenny J., and Franklin D. Gilliam, Jr. "A Longitudinal Analysis of Competing Explanations for the Transformation of Southern Congressional Politics." *Journal of Politics* 53 (1991): 504–518.

Wiggins, Sarah W. *From Civil War to Civil Rights, Alabama 1860–1960.* Tuscaloosa: University of Alabama Press, 1987.

Williams, Donnie, and Wayne Greenhaw. *The Thunder of Angels: The Montgomery Bus Boycott and the People Who Broke the Back of Jim Crow.* Chicago: Chicago Review Press, 2005.

Williams, Horace Randall, and Ben Beard. *This Day in Civil Rights History.* Montgomery: NewSouth Books, 2009.

Williams, Juan. *Eyes on the Prize: America's Civil Rights Years, 1954–1965.* New York: Penguin Books, 1987.

Willingham, Alex, ed. *Beyond the Color Line? Race, Representation and Community in the New Century.* New York: Brennan Center for Justice at NYU School of Law, 2002.

Wilson, Charles Reagan, and William Ferris, eds. *Encyclopedia of Southern Culture.* Chapel Hill: University of North Carolina Press, 1989.

Wink, Kenneth A., and Allison L. Hayes. "Racial Redistricting and Ideological Polarization in Southern U.S. House Delegations." *Politics and Policy* 29 (2001): 361–384.

Wirt, Frederick M. *The Politics of Southern Equality: Law and Social Change in a Mississippi County.* Chicago: Aldine, 1970.

———. *"We Ain't What We Was": Civil Rights in the New South.* Durham: Duke University Press, 1997.

Woodard, J. David. *The New Southern Politics.* Boulder: Lynne Rienner, 2006.

Woodward, C. Vann. *The Strange Career of Jim Crow.* New York: Oxford University Press, 1955.

———. "The Political Legacy of Reconstruction." *Journal of Negro Education* 26 (1957): 231–240.

———. *The Burden of Southern History.* Baton Rouge: Louisiana State University Press, 1968.

X, Malcolm. *Autobiography of Malcolm X.* New York: Ballentine Books, 1992.

Yarbrough, Tinsley. *Judge Frank Johnson and Human Rights in Alabama.* University: University of Alabama Press, 1981.

Yardley, Jim. "Racism Was Hidden Issue." *Anniston Star*, March 13, 1989.

Zellner, Bob. *The Wrong Side of Murder Creek: A White Southerner in the Freedom Movement.* Montgomery: NewSouth Books, 2008.

INDEX

About the Authors

DR. GLEN BROWDER is Professor Emeritus of American Democracy at Jacksonville State University in Alabama; he served as U.S. Congressman, Alabama's Secretary of State, and Alabama State Legislator. He is the author of *The South's New Racial Politics,* published by NewSouth Books. DR. ARTEMESIA STANBERRY is Assistant Professor of Political Science at North Carolina Central University; she also worked for several members of Congress.